Beating the Breaks

Beating the Breaks

Major League Ballplayers Who Overcame Disabilities

Rick Swaine

McFarland & Company, Inc., Publishers
Jefferson, North Carolina, and London

Photographs courtesy of National Baseball Hall of Fame Library, Cooperstown, New York.

LIBRARY OF CONGRESS CATALOGUING-IN-PUBLICATION DATA

Swaine, Rick, 1950–
    Beating the breaks : major league ballplayers who overcame disabilities / Rick Swaine.
       p.   cm.
    Includes bibliographical references and index.

    ISBN 0-7864-1828-1 (softcover : 50# alkaline paper)

    1. Baseball players with disabilities—United States—Biography.   I. Title.
GV865.A1S93   2004
                                        2004012372

British Library cataloguing data are available

©2004 Rick Swaine. All rights reserved

No part of this book may be reproduced or transmitted in any form or by any means, electronic or mechanical, including photocopying or recording, or by any information storage and retrieval system, without permission in writing from the publisher.

Cover image: Pete Gray's batting form (National Baseball Hall of Fame Library, Cooperstown, New York)

Manufactured in the United States of America

McFarland & Company, Inc., Publishers
  Box 611, Jefferson, North Carolina 28640
  www.mcfarlandpub.com

To the memory of my father,
Russ Swaine,
a prominent high school athlete
in the Boston area
before he was disabled during World War II.

He was confined to a wheelchair but
through his coaching and his encouragement
inspired my enduring love
for the game of baseball.

Contents

Author's Note	1
Introduction	3

One: Missing Limbs or Extremities
    Jim Abbott   9
    Hugh "One Arm" Daily   19
    Pete Gray   24
    Monty Stratton   34
    Bert Shepard   40

Two: Severely Damaged Limbs
    Lou Brissie   48
    Whitey Kurowski   54
    Eddie Kazak   60
    Charley Gelbert   62
    Bo Jackson   68
    Dave Dravecky   75

Three: Maimed or Disfigured Extremities
    Mordecai "Three Finger" Brown   82
    Charley "Red" Ruffing   89
    Hal Peck   96
    Carlos May   97
    Gil Coan   104
    Jim Mecir   106

Four: Impaired Organ Function or Chronic Illness

William "Dummy" Hoy	112
George "Specs" Toporcer	123
Chick Hafey	128
Ron Santo	132
Russ Christopher	140
Joe Hoerner	144
John Hiller	147
Danny Thompson	150
Walt Bond	156

Five: Neurological and Psychological Disorders

Grover Cleveland Alexander	159
Tony Lazzeri	168
Jimmy Piersall	170
Jim Eisenreich	184

Six: Other Disabilities   192

Bibliography   221
Index   227

Author's Note

The ongoing battle for equal access and basic respect for individuals with disabilities is a serious political and moral issue. Although much progress has been made — and more is needed — the basic aim has been constant. The language or jargon is, however, subject to constant change — sometimes for the sake of precision or clarity, sometimes not.

At some point, certain phrases and terms in this text will be considered obsolete or politically incorrect. Not long ago, for instance, the term *handicapped* was routinely accepted in reference to disabled individuals, but today the word is no longer considered appropriate for that usage.

It is to be hoped that readers will understand if the terminology used in this volume differs somewhat from their expectations.

Introduction

Professional baseball players are always looking for an advantage — something that will give them the slightest edge on the field — anything that can make the difference between winning and losing.

In pursuit of the elusive "edge," players endlessly study their opponents to spot weaknesses to be exploited or strengths to be avoided. Untold hours are devoted to honing their bodies to be in top competitive condition. Millions are spent on performance enhancing gear and equipment. Sports psychology is becoming a science, with some players employing personal psychological trainers, as well as the more traditional physical trainers.

It's no secret, in fact, that players have been known to employ "edge gaining" devices or techniques that are not strictly ethical or legal. Pitchers have intentionally roughed up or applied foreign substances to the ball. Batters have been known to cork their bats to generate more power. Although the debate about the number of offenses rages on, there's little doubt that some players have ignored baseball's rules, the law, and their personal well-being by using controlled substances such as steroids and amphetamines to improve performance.

How far players will go in their quests to obtain an advantage gives perspective to the achievements of those players who've been able to perform at the major league level with built-in disadvantages.

The uncompromising world of professional sports has never been kind to individuals with disabilities, especially at the highest levels. Sports are generally designed for healthy, fully functional bodies. At the ultra competitive professional level, there are no allowances for disabilities — no attempt to eliminate or mitigate disadvantages. Professional golfer Casey Martin, for example, recently went all the way to the Supreme Court for the right to use a golf cart on the Professional Golfer's Association (PGA) Tour. Martin suffers from a congenital degenerative circulatory disorder which makes it extremely painful and physically dangerous for him to walk long distances. Yet, the PGA's position was that riding a cart between shots would give Martin an "advantage" over other golfers.

Organized baseball has been no different from the rest of the sports world in this regard. Ironically, the major leagues have permitted the use of golf carts to haul fully ambulatory relief pitchers to the mound, but there would undoubtedly be a tremendous uproar if one was requested for a hurler with a bum leg.

Baseball has decreed that players must be almost identically equipped when it comes to athletic gear. There are regulations concerning the size, shape, and composition of gloves, bats, and even uniforms. Yet, there are no regulations regarding natural physical equipment. No requirement that a player be equipped with two arms and two legs, ten fingers and ten toes, or a sound mind and body. Nor are there provisions to compensate for a lack of natural faculties. It wouldn't be surprising if baseball's rulemakers developed a rule to disqualify modern-day reliever Antonio Alfonseca, who has six fingers on each hand.

In fact, the basic physical construction of the baseball field itself could be considered an affront to the equal access provisions of the Americans with Disabilities Act (ADA) since the design functionally prohibits a class of players from performing certain jobs solely due to a physical attribute that they have no control over. Of course, we're talking about lefties who simply aren't able to play several positions because the layout of the diamond makes it impossible for them to perform efficiently there. Who knows how many fancy fielding southpaw shortstops have been doomed to careers as journeyman outfielders because someone decided to set the bases up counterclockwise back in the 1800s?

Not that there haven't been some minor concessions. In the 1950s, Dale Long of the Pittsburgh Pirates was permitted to catch a few innings with a first baseman's mitt to compensate for his left-handedness (there was no left-handed catcher's mitt available). Current major leaguer John Olerud, who underwent an operation for a brain aneurysm in college, was granted a special waiver to wear a protective helmet on defense. Incidentally, there's absolutely no truth to the rumor that Jose Canseco unsuccessfully demanded equal protection for his remarkably sturdy noggin. It would've been interesting to observe baseball's reaction if Los Angeles Dodgers hurler Kazuhisa Ishii had resumed his career wearing a hockey mask after almost being killed by a vicious line drive to the face.

Despite organized baseball's reluctance to "level the playing field" for disadvantaged players, a remarkable number of men have overcome serious obstacles to perform at the major league level — disabilities that would qualify them for special consideration in the outside world, but don't get them any special treatment between the foul lines.

Beating the Breaks is a collection of profiles of men who have overcome disabilities to play professional baseball. The featured players range from all-time greats to one-game big leaguers. Their disabilities run the gamut from missing or incomplete limbs to chronic illness to psychiatric or neurological disorders.

Few baseball fans are conscious of the number of players who have serious disabilities and have succeeded in professional baseball. Nor is there a realization of the full extent of the challenges they faced. Much of this unawareness is due to the attitudes of the affected players themselves, who've been conditioned to publicly downplay weaknesses or lack of ability and naturally tend to minimize disabilities as well. Players with disabilities tend to consider their affliction as just one of those chinks in the armor that everyone has in some form or another — something to be offset by other abilities. To them, their disability is like another player's lack of speed, inexperience, or weak throwing arm.

Jim Abbott clearly articulated this perspective when he said, "Everyone has limitations. It's just that mine are different from most people's. So I learned to do things differently." This outlook undoubtedly served these men well in dealing with their conditions and probably made them better ballplayers.

Almost 30 players with various disabilities are profiled in this book. Each profile includes biographical data and statistical information, as well as a description of each player's disability and an account of his success in dealing with the limitations imposed.

There's no intention to identify the most profoundly disabled players or those who have performed with the most debilitating condition. Hundreds of baseball players perform every day hindered by common occupational maladies such as sore arms, blown-out knees, and bad backs. It would be impossible to try to determine which players are the "most impaired." After all, who's to say that it was more difficult for Bo Jackson to perform with an artificial hip than for Mickey Mantle to star on a pair of gimpy legs; or that it was a greater accomplishment for southpaw Jim Abbott to pitch with a deformed right arm than for Tommy John to win 164 games with a surgically reconstructed throwing arm; or that Jimmy Piersall was more emotionally disturbed back in 1952 than early 20th-century ace Rube Waddell who reportedly chased fire engines, wrestled alligators, and married frequently.

Instead, the intent is to provide insight into the careers and lives of those players with the more apparent, unusual, or striking disabilities. The emphasis is on situations where the player not only had to overcome the physical limitations of his disability, but also had to overcome the doubts and prejudices of the baseball world just to get a chance.

In this regard, some basic criteria had to be established to arrive at a representative group. First, conditions that were caused by baseball injuries or ailments were excluded. This is not to minimize the seriousness of on-field injuries, but they are occupational hazards and are generally far too similar and numerous to distinguish from each other. Likewise, conditions that were not permanent or of long duration were excluded. So many players have been able to carry on for short periods under extremely difficult circumstances until they recovered that it would be impossible to consider them all. Several notable players who overcame disabilities that were baseball-related or of relatively short duration are mentioned in the last chapter, however.

With the list narrowed down considerably, the primary criterion for selection from the remaining players with disabilities was an admittedly subjective evaluation of the degree of difficulty involved in performing with the disability, weighed against the level of success achieved.

For instance, Red Ruffing enjoyed a lengthy Hall of Fame pitching career, while Bert Shepard threw less than six innings in the major leagues. The two don't compare unless an assumption is factored in that it was less difficult for Ruffing to pitch with several missing toes than for Shepard to pitch with a missing foot. The same process would apply the career-achievement-versus-severity-of-disability ratio to the all-star performance of Whitey Kurowski, whose right arm was seriously maimed, against the single, wartime season career of one-armed Pete Gray.

Another factor is if the afflicted player was a "trailblazer," the first to break down the barriers and perform with a certain disability. For instance, hundreds of ballplayers have played with glasses since 1920, but George Toporcer was the first player to make his living hitting 90-mile-per-hour fastballs through corrective lenses. He was the Jackie Robinson of myopic non-pitchers.

The historical importance or the stature of the player is another criterion. William "Dummy" Hoy, for example, is profiled in full rather than Ed Dundon, an obscure deaf contemporary who proceeded Hoy by a few years.

In addition, the player must have performed in the major leagues with the condition, although an exception has been made by the inclusion of pitcher Monty Stratton. Stratton never made it back to the major leagues after losing a leg, but he's profiled both because the magnitude of his accomplishments as a minor leaguer and because of the widespread notoriety his story gained when it was chronicled in a major Hollywood production.

Of course, the medical treatment available and the prevailing social attitudes of the time are other considerations. Epilepsy, for instance, is not the serious impairment that it was in the 1920s.

Please note that these chapters do not include players who had to surmount institutionalized or social classifications such being the "wrong" race, creed, or religion. Though those barriers may well have been the most difficult to overcome, they don't fall under the category of disabilities. Performers who had to overcome size barriers are also not included in the main chapters for the same reason. Although alcoholism can now be considered a disability under certain conditions, it has just recently been considered in that light and is also not included in this volume.

The individual profiles are grouped as follows:

The first group is composed of those players who were the most obviously disabled, players who performed with missing or partial limbs either due to a birth defect or amputation. Several of these players had only brief careers at baseball's highest level, but the difficulty of their achievements demands that they be included.

The second group is made up of players who performed in the major leagues despite permanently maimed or disfigured limbs.

The third group includes players who were missing digits or suffered other impairments to their hands or feet.

The fourth group is made up of players who suffered from internal or organic ailments that made may have been invisible to observers but were every bit as difficult to deal with under the daily grind of major league baseball.

The fifth group consists of players who suffered from behavioral problems caused by neurological or psychological disorders. In some ways these men may have had the most difficult kind of disability to deal with. Although there are no visible physical manifestations, these types of disorders are readily apparent to others because of the behavioral symptoms associated with the condition.

The final chapter is a catchall that includes an assortment of players who also overcame disabilities at some point in their careers. Generally these players are not included in the above groups because their conditions are not as dramatic or serious or they were excluded by the criteria. They are, however, performers who merit a mention for their accomplishments. Some may actually belong in an above group, but downplayed their affliction. In fact, there are undoubtedly other players who could be mentioned in these pages but managed to completely mask or disguise their conditions.

ONE

Missing Limbs or Extremities

JIM ABBOTT

Left-handed pitcher Jim Abbott is the most celebrated athlete with a major disability in modern times. Born with a deformed right arm, Abbott was already a national hero before signing a professional contract with the California Angels in 1989. As a sophomore pitcher for the University of Michigan in 1987, he was named the best amateur athlete and the top amateur baseball player in the nation and became the first U.S. pitcher to beat the Cuban "amateur" team in Cuba in 25 years. As a junior he garnered a Gold Medal as a member of the 1988 U.S. Olympic Baseball Team, crowning his amateur career by beating Japan in the final game in Seoul, Korea. In his first season in professional baseball, he won a spot in the starting rotation of the pennant-contending Angels without an inning of minor league seasoning and became established as a topflight major league pitcher.

Abbott's right arm ends about where his wrist should be. He doesn't have a right hand, just a loose flap of skin at the end of his underdeveloped arm. Otherwise, the strapping 6'3" two-hundred pounder's body could serve as a model for the ideal baseball player.

Jim, who retired in 1999, pitched with a righthander's fielder's glove perched pocket-down over the end of his stubbed right arm. At the conclusion of his delivery, he would deftly slip his left hand into the glove and be ready to field the ball. After catching the ball, he would cradle the glove against his chest in the crook of his right arm and extract the ball with his good left hand, ready to make another throw. Observers invariably marveled at how smoothly and efficiently he could catch and throw the ball with one hand.

Jim Abbott's parents were still teenagers when he was born in Flint, Michigan, on September 19, 1967. Having a child at such as young age was difficult enough, especially a child with a disability, but Mike and Kathy Abbott resolved to make their son's life as normal as possible. Just getting by was a struggle for the new family. Mike Abbott sold cars and packed meat and Kathy studied at home while raising Jim. Eventually both parents finished college and went on to successful careers, Mike in management and Kathy as a teacher and later an attorney. Jim's parents always encouraged him to try things and helped him acquire confidence. "We decided that if Jim wanted to (play sports) then to let him try," said Mike Abbott in a 1998 *USA Today* interview. "I helped out with some things. But in the end it was all Jim. It had to be."

Jim started showing an interest in sports at an early age. Trying to nudge him toward a sport that didn't depend on the use of hands, his parents bought him a soccer ball. But Jim didn't really like soccer. After all, every other kid in the neighborhood was playing baseball so that's what he wanted to do. Ironically, it was Jim's younger brother, Chad, who became a soccer player.

So Jim began developing the remarkable hand-eye coordination that would allow him to do with one hand what others did with two. He spent hours throwing a rubber ball against a brick wall and catching it on the rebound. His father helped him develop the glove-hand switch which allowed him to throw and catch the ball with the same hand. Over the years he continued this drill, moving closer and closer to the wall and making the glove transition faster and faster.

When Jim began school, he was fitted with a mechanical hand made of fiberglass and metal. But he hated the prosthesis, which he called a "hook," because it frightened some of his classmates and made him self-conscious. Eventually his parents stopped making him wear it.

At the age of eleven, Jim joined a Little League team and threw a no-hitter in the first game he pitched. Despite his early success, most people figured that the competition would soon pass him by. In fact, at every step, from Little League on, he kept hearing that his playing days would probably end at that level. But at each new level, Jim proved his doubters wrong. When he entered high school at Flint Central, his new coach doubted that Jim would be able to defend his position adequately. But Jim actually fielded well enough to play first base and the outfield when he wasn't pitching. Even his hitting was exceptional. Jim batted from the left side, wrapping his left hand around the bat and the stub of his right arm. He was able to generate remarkable power, blasting 7 homers and batting an excellent .427 as a senior. On the mound that year he won 10 games and lost 3

Chapter 1—Missing Limbs or Extremities

Jim Abbott delivers a fastball

with an incredibly low 0.76 earned run average and more than two strikeouts per inning pitched.

Jim was also the backup quarterback for Flint Central until the end of his senior year when he started the last three games, passing for 600 yards and six touchdowns. In addition, he was the team's punter, averaging 37.5 yards per kick as a senior. His first national exposure came when his high school football accomplishments were featured on NBC's *The NFL Today* pregame show.

Abbott was drafted by the Toronto Blue Jays out of high school in the 36th and last round of the 1985 draft, but turned down their $50,000 bonus offer to attend the nearby University of Michigan. Despite the major league offer and his high school achievements, Jim really wasn't heavily recruited by colleges with top baseball programs. There were still some reservations about his disability and Jim, himself, admitted to having some initial doubts about his ability to play college baseball. But they were quickly dispelled. As a freshman he was named the Most Courageous Athlete for 1986 by the Philadelphia Sportswriters Association after posting a record of six wins against two losses. The season was not without some embarrassment, however. After his first college game, Jim was mortified and suffered an unmerciful razzing from his teammates when the press held the team bus up for an hour to interview him.

Over the next two seasons, Jim continued to develop as a pitcher and began to think seriously about a career in professional baseball. In 1987 he pitched the Wolverines to first place in the Big Ten Eastern Division standings and then the conference championship. For the season he won 11 games against 3 losses. He then earned a spot on the United States national amateur baseball team, Team USA, and on the warm-up tour threw his complete game three hit victory against the vaunted Cuban national team in front of 50,000 spectators. In the Pan American Games, he not only carried the flag for the U.S. delegation, but also won two games without giving up an earned run as Team USA captured a silver medal. For the year his efforts earned him the Sullivan Award where he was chosen over hurdler Greg Foster and basketball star David Robinson as the outstanding amateur athlete in the country. He then beat out future major league stars Jack McDowell, Robin Ventura, and Ken Griffey for the coveted Golden Spikes Award, given to the top amateur baseball player.

Abbott had another fine season at Michigan in 1988, becoming the first baseball player to ever be named Big Ten Conference Player of the Year. He then pitched the United States Olympic Team to victory over Japan with a 5 to 3 complete game effort, which he still considers his biggest thrill in sports.

After his Olympic triumph, Abbott decided to forgo his last year of college eligibility to enter the professional ranks. He'd been selected by the California Angels with the eighth pick in the first round of the 1988 amateur draft and negotiated a $207,000 bonus. As happened whenever Jim moved up to another level in sports, skeptics came out of the woodwork to question whether a one-armed player could perform at the higher

Chapter 1—Missing Limbs or Extremities

level. The familiar old questions about his ability to defend his position resurfaced.

On bunts and slow rollers Jim often wouldn't have time to field the ball with his glove and make the transfer. So he usually discarded the glove and fielded the ball barehanded. In high school, an opposing coach once ordered the first eight batters to bunt. After the first one reached base, Jim shut down the bunting game by retiring the next seven in a row. Of course, he had to pass the same test in college, and the big leaguers would also give it a try. But once again, Jim Abbott answered with his great coordination and quick reflexes.

The 1989 edition of the Angels that Abbott joined as a rookie was a talented team — legitimate pennant contenders. They'd finished second to Kansas City in 1988 and were led by a young pitching staff which featured Mike Witt, Chuck Finley, Kirk McCaskill, and Willie Fraser as starters. The rotation had been further bolstered in the off-season by the acquisition of veteran ace Bert Blyleven who already had more than 250 major league victories under his belt. It certainly didn't seem likely that a raw, 21-year-old rookie could crack the rotation.

Since the establishment of the amateur draft in 1965 through 1988 only fifteen players had made their professional debut in the major leagues. Only a few, such as Dave Winfield, Burt Hooton, and Bob Horner, enjoyed successful careers, while most seemed to quickly return to oblivion. Everyone assumed Abbott would be farmed out to gain needed experience, but he made the team out of spring training and edged into the starting rotation. Actually, injuries to other members of the rotation, as much as his own performance, allowed Jim to make the opening day roster, but as expected there was a good deal of second guessing. Since he hadn't been that effective in exhibition games, there were those who felt that Abbott's retention was more about public relations than fielding the best baseball team.

It is true that Jim was a media sensation. His first appearance was in a "B" game that had to be moved from a practice field to the main stadium to accommodate the throng of fans and media representatives. At the postgame press conference, Abbott patiently discussed his pitching-fielding motion. "I've been doing this since I was five years old. Now it's as natural as tying my shoes," he said to reporters, who were then left to contemplate the mystery of exactly how one ties his shoes with one hand.

As with the beginning of every new phase in his career, his first regular season start was a major event. The media, including four television crews from Japan, converged on Anaheim Stadium in full force for the grand debut. Jim lasted less than five innings and racked up his first major league loss, but left to a standing ovation from the huge crowd. *Baseball America* ranked his debut second only to Jackie Robinson's breaking of the color barrier for historical significance. After another defeat, Jim beat the Baltimore Orioles in his third start and settled down to pitch good baseball the rest of the way. He ended the season with 12 wins against the same number of losses. The dozen victories were the most major league wins by a pitcher in his first professional season since long-forgotten Ernie Wingard won 13 in 1924 for the old St. Louis Browns before fading into obscurity.

The Angels finished the 1989 season in third place, and Abbott was voted the club's Rookie of the Year. He was also named the Most Inspirational Player by the Anaheim chapter of the Baseball Writer's Association of America.

Abbott's deft handling of the constant public pressure may have been his most impressive accomplishment, however. Handsome and articulate, he was interviewed countless times by the major networks and publications. He turned down repeated book offers and received tons of mail — including a personal telegram from Nolan Ryan before his first start. Hall of Famers Ernie Banks and Bobby Doerr asked for his autograph, and 363-game-winner Warren Spahn called him his hero. Jim studied communications in college and was better prepared than most 21-year-old rookies to handle the crush. His amazing maturity and cooperation with the press and the public won him a legion of loyal supporters and he naturally became an inspirational role model for kids with all kinds of disabilities.

Questions about his ability still remained, however. Jim had trouble holding runners on base and his fielding was weak. He was the second easiest pitcher in the league to steal against and he had a rather low fielding percentage. By his own admission, he missed many plays that he should have made.

Jim experienced a disappointing 1990 sophomore season, posting a 10–14 won-lost record. He got off to a terrible start in 1991, suffering four straight losses to begin the season after an unimpressive spring performance. Calls for his demotion to the minors lit up the phone lines to the local call-in sports talk shows, but the club stuck by him and he managed to turn the corner.

In fact, he ended up enjoying a breakthrough campaign in 1991. Although the Angels faded after the All-Star Game, Abbott won eleven games after the mid-season break and finished the season with an 18–11 won-lost mark and a stingy 2.89 earned run average. In the voting for the American League Cy Young Award, the most prestigious pitching honor in the league, he placed third as Roger Clemens of the Red Sox captured the trophy for the third time. Jim's 1991 record is even more impressive when the lack of run support provided by the Angels hitters is taken into account. According to a concept for rating pitcher performance developed by noted baseball statistician and author Bill James, Abbott led the American League in "tough losses" with eight.

Another highlight of Abbott's excellent 1991 campaign was a 375-foot triple he hit into the gap in a spring training contest against the San Francisco Giants. Since the Angels were in the American League, where the designated hitter is used, Abbott didn't get to bat during the regular season. The triple was his first hit in a major league uniform and Jim drove his teammates crazy talking about it.

In December 1991 Jim married Dana Douty who had grown up in the Anaheim area. What should have been a very satisfying off-season for young Jim Abbott was marred by antagonistic salary negotiations, but he eventually signed a one year contract for $1.85 million, which made him the highest paid fourth year pitcher in baseball history at that time.

The 1992 season was another memorable one for Jim, but for all the wrong reasons. The Angels won only 72 games and finished fifth in the seven-team American League Western Division. Despite pitching well all year, Abbott posted a dismal 7–15 won-lost record. But his sparkling 2.77 earned run average was a more accurate indicator of the quality of his efforts. Throughout his career Jim routinely suffered from poor run support, but in 1992 the Angels backed him with the lowest run-support figure in the American League since the adoption of the designated-hitter rule in 1973.

To top it off, in December 1992 he was swapped to the New York Yankees for three minor league prospects when the Angels couldn't sign him to a long-term agreement. The *Los Angeles Times's* Mike Downey found some irony in the Abbott trade. He wrote, "The one thing Jim Abbott wanted was to be treated like any other player. And so he was. Traded away, even though he was one of [Angels Owner] Gene Autry's most valuable players and undoubtedly the most popular.... Dependable as anyone. Expendable as anyone."

The Yankees were hungry for a pennant going into the 1993 season. They hadn't participated in a postseason game in more than a decade. But they'd signed Wade Boggs and Jimmy Key as free agents and acquired Paul O'Neill and Abbott in trades. With a roster that already included the likes of Don Mattingly, Bernie Williams, and Danny Tartabull, they looked like a solid contender. Abbott and agent Scott Boras, who'd rejected a four year, $4 million per year offer from the Angels in October, immediately ran into problems negotiating a 1993 contract with the Yankees. They ended up in arbitration, where the Yankees' $2.35 million offer won out over Abbott's $3.5 million request. The Yankees' negative arguments confused and upset the young hurler. "Why did they trade for me if that's what they think?" he wondered. It was an early sign that the sensitive pitcher might have a tough time in the Bronx.

Nevertheless, Jim tried to embrace the city and the team, but his entire term in New York was frustrating, and his performance was mediocre. In the two seasons he spent with the Yankees he lost more games than he won and had an earned run average well over 4.00 each year.

One of the few bright spots was a September 4, 1993, no-hit victory over the powerful Cleveland Indians in the midst of a tight pennant race. The no-hitter catapulted Abbott back into the national spotlight and once again focused on the unique accomplishments of a baseball player performing, and performing exceptionally well, with one hand.

But Jim was unimpressive in his next start. On September 13, a little more than a week after his no-hit gem, Yankees owner George Steinbrenner publicly blasted him for not doing the job. He even went so far as to question Abbott's courage. Steinbrenner's foolish outburst, with his team only a game and a half out of first place, seemed to take the heart out of the club. They limped home to a second place finish, seven games behind Toronto. Abbott's record was 11 wins against 14 losses.

Jim's second season in New York started out as turbulently as the first. Before spring training even started, "The Boss" had the audacity to blame Abbott's mediocre 1993 performance on his charity work and frequent visits with disabled children. "Jim Abbott's got to give 100 percent of his attention to baseball!" Steinbrenner demanded. Abbott, who'd been selected for the prestigious "Free Spirit Award" for 1993 for his work with children, was stunned and actually found himself having to defend his charitable work. Another confrontation occurred when the Yankees invented a new glove for Jim with a flap that was supposed to hide his grip on the ball from the opposing first base coach's sight. The theory was that Abbott was tipping his pitches because he wasn't able to pitch out of his glove like other pitchers. Jim warmed up with the new glove before his second start of the season, but didn't feel comfortable with the new device and refused to use it in a game.

The 1994 season ended in mid August when the players went out on strike. Abbott's final tally for the abbreviated season was nine wins versus eight losses. On December 23 the Yankees decided not to tender an offer for the 1995 season, and he became a free agent. There was little doubt that Jim intended to leave the Yankees whether they wanted to keep him or not. He was expected to sign with the Angels, who'd just named Marcel Lachemann, a big Abbott supporter and Jim's favorite pitching coach, as their manager. But the Chicago White Sox came up with a better offer.

Abbott pitched respectably in Chicago, but the Sox traded him to the Angels when they dropped out of the Central Division race early. The Angels, who were in the thick of the Western Division race, welcomed Jim back with open arms. He won five games and lost four for California, but the team came up a game short in its quest for the division title. For both teams combined his won-lost record was 11–8, and he posted a 3.70 earned run average, a substantial improvement over his performance in New York.

Before the 1996 season, Jim signed a new three-year deal with the Angels and reported to spring training set for a big season. But the wheels fell off almost immediately. For the year he posted a woeful 2–18 won-lost record, accompanied by a horrendous 7.48 earned run average. Even a mid-season trip to Vancouver, the first minor league action of his career, didn't help. In the spring of 1997 things didn't get any better and the Angels released him, eating the final years of his $7.8 million contract.

Out of baseball at the age of 29, Jim went home to spend time with his wife and new baby daughter and devote more time to his many charitable activities.

Jim, however, couldn't get rid of the nagging feeling that there was something unfinished — and he missed the game. After sitting out the entire 1998 season, he asked the White Sox for a chance to attempt a comeback. The impossible dream started as a struggle with the Class A Hickory Crawdads and included stints with Winston-Salem, Birmingham, and Triple A Calgary before culminating in a late season call-up to Chicago. With the White Sox, he won all five of his starts and in the off-season he received the Tony Conigliaro Award, which is given annually to the player who best overcomes obstacles and continues to thrive through adversity.

The miracle comeback was not to continue, however. The White Sox weren't confident Jim's resurgence was for real and didn't re-sign him for the 1999 season. Unfortunately, the Sox were right. Abbott signed with the Milwaukee Brewers, but was released in July after posting a 2–8 won-lost mark and a 6.91 earned run average. Jim did provide some heroics, though. Since Milwaukee was in the National League, where the designated hitter isn't used, Jim got a chance to bat and on June 15, 1999, he lined out the first base hit by a one-handed batter in more than 50 years.

Immediately after his release by Milwaukee, Jim announced his retirement from baseball. Now living in California, he's still very involved in disabled children's causes and continues to make appearances for various charitable organizations.

What happened to Jim Abbott's promising career? How could a

pitcher who was considered to have the best stuff of any lefthander in the league in 1993 be through six years later at 31 years of age? The most popular explanation is that the opposition was able to read his pitches because he couldn't shield the ball with his glove. Likewise, baserunners were also able to take advantage of him because he couldn't conceal his pick-off move to first base. Other experts insisted that he was bunted out of the league.

Jim, however, refused to blame his disability. He maintained that the problem was that his fastball started to lose velocity fairly early in his career and it was too big an adjustment to go from power to finesse. In his earlier years, Abbott's fastball consistently approached 95 mph, but by the end of his career he was topping out around 85 to 90 mph.

For his major league career, Jim Abbott won 87 games and lost 108 with an ordinary 4.25 lifetime earned run average. Yet, he had as much of an impact as any player who played the game, giving renewed hope to thousands with disabilities. He once estimated that he had at least one scheduled meeting with a disabled child during every road series of his career.

"My experiences, added up, make me feel like I've had a Hall of Fame Career," Jim said when announcing his retirement from the game.

JAMES ANTHONY ABBOTT
B. September 19, 1967

YEAR	TEAM	LEAGUE	G	IP	SO	BB	W	L	ERA	CG	SHO
1989	CALIFORNIA	AL	29	181	115	74	12	12	3.92	4	2
1990	CALIFORNIA	AL	33	212	105	72	10	14	4.51	4	1
1991	CALIFORNIA	AL	34	243	158	73	18	11	2.89	5	1
1992	CALIFORNIA	AL	29	211	130	68	7	15	2.77	7	0
1993	NEW YORK	AL	32	214	95	73	11	14	4.37	4	1
1994	NEW YORK	AL	24	160	90	64	9	8	4.55	2	0
1995	CHIC-CAL	AL	30	197	86	64	11	8	3.70	4	1
1996	CALIFORNIA	AL	27	142	58	78	2	18	7.48	1	0
	Vancouver	Pac Coast	4	29	20	20	0	2	3.41	1	0
1997		(Voluntarily Retired)									
1998	Hickory	S Atlantic	1	4	2	2	0	0	2.25	0	0
	Winston-Salem	Carolina	4	22	13	7	2	1	5.40	0	0
	Birmingham	Southern	8	43	35	21	2	3	5.40	0	0
	Calgary	Pac Coast	5	31	20	9	2	2	2.61	1	0
	CHICAGO	AL	5	31	14	12	5	0	4.55	0	0
1999	MILWAUKEE	NL	20	82	37	42	2	8	6.91	0	0
MAJOR LEAGUE TOTALS			263	1674	888	620	87	108	4.25	31	6

HUGH "ONE ARM" DAILY

Jim Abbott was not the first man to pitch in the major leagues with only one complete arm. He wasn't even the first "one-armed" pitcher to hurl a no-hitter in the big time. The first to accomplish the feat was Hugh Ignatius Daily, who threw a no-hit shutout in 1883 — more than a century before Abbott's gem.

Unlike Abbott, Daily was born with two good arms. While still a youth, he lost his left hand at the wrist in an accident. Nevertheless, he pitched in what was then considered the major leagues from 1882 to 1887 and was one of the top pitchers of his time. In addition to the no-hitter, he was the first major league pitcher to be credited with back to back one-hitters and he also established records for most strikeouts in a season and in a single game. His single season strikeout record was broken by Toad Ramsey in 1885 and Matt Kilroy in 1886, but hasn't been topped since. His single game strikeout record still stands, although it was tied by Roger Clemens in 1986 and Kerry Wood in 1998.

Hugh was known throughout his career as "One Arm" Daily, an exaggeration of his condition and a reflection of the era's general insensitivity toward the disabled. He dealt with his disability by fashioning a leather sleeve with a square pad on the end. The crude prosthesis fit over the stump of his left arm and was attached at the elbow. He practiced with it until he was able to efficiently trap the ball against the pad with his right hand. At the plate he used a whittled-down bat and learned to make contact by pushing his bat sharply at the ball.

Details of the accident which took his left hand are somewhat murky, as is much of Daily's personal life. His hand was amputated after an accident that occurred while he was working as a carpenter's assistant at the Front Street Theater in Baltimore. One version of the incident has a friend, who was visiting backstage, playfully pointing a supposedly unloaded musket, which was being used as a stage prop, at young Hugh. As Daily pushed the muzzle aside, the gun discharged two blank cartridges into his left hand, shattering the thumb joint. An older account of Hugh's early life attributes the accident to burns received while working with chemicals used to simulate fire on the theater set.

Daily's age at the time of the accident is also unclear. In fact, Daily's age throughout his baseball career is questionable. He was born and raised in Baltimore, and most references list his birth date as 1857. But an article in the 1991 *SABR Baseball Research Journal* states that he was born July 17, 1849, which would have made him a 33-year-old rookie in 1882. The same article gives his age at the time of the accident as 12 years, but according to another source, the accident occurred when he was 17 years old and was already established as an outstanding schoolboy pitcher. To compound the confusion, Daily's given name at birth was Harry Criss, and his adopted name is often misspelled "Daly" or "Dailey" in baseball literature. The reason he changed his name is unexplained, as is the unfortunate choice of Ignatius as a middle name.

In appearance, Daily is diversely described as a stocky red-faced man and a tall, mutton-chopped stringbean. The *Baseball Encyclopedia* lists him at 6'2" and 180 pounds, which would have almost made him a giant by 1880s standards. References are consistent, however, in indicating that Daily possessed great strength as well as a volatile temper and surly disposition.

Daily's career as a paid professional baseball player began in the mid-1870s with local teams in the Baltimore area. As his fame grew, he reportedly turned down several offers to pitch in faster company in order to stay close to home. In 1880 Baltimore fielded an entry in the newly created National Association and Daily joined up. The new league lasted a year, but Daily didn't. Already building a reputation for feistiness and umpire baiting, he was thrown off the team after shocking local fans with a particularly offensive temper tantrum.

The 1881 season found Daley pitching for the New York Metropolitans. The Metropolitans were formed by the legendary Jim "Truthful James" Mutrie, who was in the initial stages of creating a great baseball team, as well as a reputation for honesty and integrity. With the Metropolitans, Daily pitched (and won) the first baseball game ever played in New York City by acknowledged professionals. Technically the Metropolitans, who played in the newly constructed Polo Grounds, were not a major league team. They would not join the National League until 1883. But they played and beat almost every top team in the nation, including Cap Anson's Chicago White Stockings, who captured the National League championship that year. Daily was the Metropolitans' ace hurler, winning 38 contests despite missing a month due to illness.

Daily's major league career officially got underway the next year when he signed with Buffalo in the National League. With Buffalo he shared pitching duties with the great Pud Galvin, who would eventually be credited with 361 major league victories wins in a 14-year career. In addition to Galvin, future Hall of Famers Dan Brouthers and Jim "Orator" O'Rourke also toiled for Buffalo. Daily won 15 games against 14 losses and finished all 29 games he started.

Moving to Cleveland for the 1883 season, Daily won 23 games while losing 19. Included in his victories was his no-hit, 1 to 0 victory over

Philadelphia. Despite pitching in the rain that day, he walked only three batters, a notable accomplishment given that he led the National League in walks that year.

Hugh jumped to the new Union Association in 1884, lured by a revolutionary plan in which players shared in the team's revenue. He began the season with the Chicago "Onions" (a derivation of Unions) and was the team's only pitcher. On July 7 he fanned 20 Boston batters, walked none, and gave up only one hit. Three days later, against Boston again, he pitched another one-hitter and struck out 10 batters. Thus he became the first major league pitcher to throw consecutive one-hitters, a feat that's only been duplicated a few times since. In addition he pitched two other one-hitters that season, which some sources also claim were back-to-back.

Despite these heroics, the season did not end on a high note for Hugh Daily. The Chicago Onions became the Pittsburgh Stogies after 46 games and disbanded later in the year. After the franchise folded, Daily caught on with the Washington club, but he was cut after a short trial. Hugh sat out the last month of the season, but still won 28 games against the same number of losses for the year, struck out 483 batters in an incredible 500 innings, and completed 56 of 58 games started. Just as remarkable as his pitching stats, however, was his .214 one-handed batting average, which wasn't much lower than the league's .231 combined average.

The Union Association went out of business after the 1884 season, and Daily found himself blacklisted by the surviving major leagues. He reportedly paid a $500 fine to regain his eligibility, but couldn't regain his effectiveness. He bounced around for the next two seasons with St. Louis and Washington before drifting down to the minor leagues. He pitched well enough in the Northwestern League to earn a comeback shot with the American Association's Cleveland Spiders in 1887. Daily's last stand produced a disappointing 4–12 won-lost mark, despite a fine 3.67 earned run average, which was well below the league average. He was released by the last place club early in the season, but in his last game he established yet another first by pitching the first legal Sunday game in Cleveland history.

For his six-year career in the major leagues, Hugh Daily posted a modest 73–87 won-lost record, recorded a solid 2.93 earned run average, and completed more than 96 percent of his starts. His career was highlighted by his 20-strikeout one-hitter in 1884 and his 483 strikeouts for the season the same year. Unfortunately, both accomplishments have been somewhat clouded by circumstances.

Daily's single-game strikeout record was not recognized for almost one hundred years. He was originally only credited with 19 strikeouts, which merely tied the existing record. One batter he struck out managed to reach base safely when the catcher mishandled the third strike, and it wasn't recorded as a strikeout at the time. In fact, Hugh's claim to the record wasn't widely recognized until Roger Clemens tied it by fanning 20 Seattle Mariners in 1986. Cub rookie Kerry Wood also tied the record in 1998 with a one-hit, no-walk shutout, exactly the same stat line as Daily when he fanned 20.

Certainly there were some extenuating circumstances behind Daily's amazing 1884 strikeout total, which still stands as the third highest total of all time. After all, his next best effort was 171 strikeouts in 378 innings the previous year, and for his career he only fanned 846 in 1415 innings. For one thing the competition in the new Union Association was not top caliber. Only about 30 players jumped from the other major leagues to join the Union Association, although there were another 30 or so men who debuted in the Union Association and later went on to play in other major league circuits. In addition, a major rule change was implemented in 1884 that allowed pitchers to throw overhand. Under the new rule 11 pitchers recorded more than 300 strikeouts that season, but how much it helped Hugh is questionable since he reportedly threw sidearm throughout his career. Interestingly, Daily was called for a balk for throwing overhand during his 1883 no-hitter so he was probably an expert at straddling the fine line that defined a legal delivery at the time. Another significant rule modification that may actually have helped him more than allowing the overhand delivery was a change that raised to seven the number of balls allowed before a batter walked.

During Daily's career the pitching distance was 50 feet and pitchers were allowed to move freely around the "pitcher's box" during their delivery. Many took several steps to get more speed on their pitches. Daily, however, pitched from a stationary stance. On the mound he rolled the ball on his stump with his right hand before delivering the pitch. His repertoire consisted of a good fastball and drop, and his set delivery allowed him to hold runners well. But without the benefit of two hands or a glove he was a poor fielder.

Various profiles of Hugh Daily use adjectives like surly, mean, contentious, and uncommunicative to describe his personality. He was definitely a tempestuous presence on the mound, notorious for baiting hitters and berating teammates as well as badgering umpires. In fact, he was said to be popular with the fans for his "gamecock battling against umpires and rival players." An anecdote generally attributed to well known sportswriter Hugh Fullerton illustrates Daily's combative demeanor. Toiling through a difficult game one long afternoon, Hugh's stump was growing increasingly sensitive from too many hard return throws by catcher

Tom Dolan. "Arch 'em, Tom, arch 'em," Daily begged repeatedly, but Dolan kept firing them back to the box. Finally Hugh called for a conference on the mound and promptly decked the uncooperative backstop with his leather clad stump. "Now will you arch 'em?" he asked, standing over the prone receiver.

In his profile of "One-Arm" Daily in the 1999 edition of *The National Pastime,* author Frank Vaccaro theorizes that Daily's behavior may have resulted from frustration indirectly caused by his disability. Under the rules of his day, substitutions were only allowed when a player was injured. Therefore, Daily could only be relieved by another player who was already in the lineup and he would have had to assume a regular defensive position. Since using a one-handed player without a glove in the field would have obviously placed his team at a severe disadvantage, Daily was often forced to continue pitching when he was tired or didn't have his stuff. Under such circumstances it's easy to see how a pitcher could occasionally lose his composure.

The arrival of Jim Abbott on the major league scene renewed interest in Hugh Daily and prompted many comparisons between the two since they were similarly equipped from a physical standpoint. Abbott certainly enjoyed an advantage from being able to use a modern glove that enabled him to catch the ball one-handed. Abbott also benefited from modern rules which permit substitution at any time. While Daily was often forced to endure a statistical as well as emotional pounding, it wasn't necessary to keep Abbott on the mound when he didn't have his best stuff. In addition, Abbott spent most of his career in the American League, where the designated-hitter rule kept him from having to swing the bat.

Conversely, the ball wasn't as hard and as lively in Daily's day. Even though the pitcher was closer to the batter, the ball didn't come rocketing back through the box with anything approaching the velocity that today's pitchers have to contend with. Also, fielding standards were not the same when Daily played. If used at all, gloves functioned more to protect the hand against injury rather than assist in the catch. Therefore Daily's defensive deficiencies may have been considered less problematic in the 1880s than Abbott's were a hundred years later.

However, the greatest edge Abbott had over Daily might have been temperament. Abbott, aided by better education and more positive attitudes toward disabilities, was the consummate professional. Daily, on the other hand, was seemingly overcome by frustration, a situation that was no doubt compounded by the prevailing insensitivity of the times. Abbott suffered as a child when other children cruelly called him "Crab," but Daily was called "One-Arm" for his entire career. Also, Abbott was hindered from birth, while Daily had to go through a torturous adjustment period after being disabled later in life.

When Daily was released by the Washington Nationals during the 1886 season the *Washington Post* editorialized, "It will probably be gratifying to the friends of the Nationals to know that Hugh Daily pitched his last game for the Washington team yesterday." However, when Daily's Cleveland comeback was aborted a year later *The Sporting News* wrote, "One-armed Daily is still a great pitcher…never loses his head at critical stages…always smiling, always cool, and self possessed." Maybe he had finally come to terms with his disability.

Although there are reports that Daily pitched semipro ball in Pennsylvania for several years after leaving organized baseball, for all practical purposes he dropped out of sight after the 1887 season, leaving no record of his death or his life after baseball.

HUGH IGNATIUS "ONE ARM" DAILY
(born Harry Criss)
B. 1857 Deceased

YEAR	TEAM	LEAGUE	G	IP	SO	BB	W	L	ERA	CG	SHO
1881	New York	Independ.	37	*	*	*	24	12	*	*	*
1882	BUFFALO	NL	29	256	116	70	15	14	2.99	29	0
1883	CLEVELAND	NL	45	379	171	99	23	19	2.42	40	4
1884	CHIC-PITT-WAS	PU	58	501	483	72	28	28	2.44	56	4
1885	ST. LOUIS	NL	11	91	31	44	3	8	3.94	10	1
1886	WASHINGTON	NL	6	49	15	40	0	6	7.35	6	0
	Milw-St Paul	Northwest	17	*	*	*	9	8	*	*	*
1887	CLEVELAND	AA	16	140	30	44	4	12	3.67	16	0
MAJOR LEAGUE TOTALS			165	1415	846	369	73	87	2.93	157	9

PETE GRAY

Jim Abbott once said, "I never told myself that I wanted to be the next Pete Gray. I always said I wanted to be the next Nolan Ryan." This comment wasn't intended to be a slap at one-armed former outfielder Pete Gray's modest career. What Abbott meant was that he wanted to be thought of as a ballplayer — not a "one-armed ballplayer."

Which is exactly what Pete Gray wanted. Unfortunately he is remembered today, perhaps unfairly, as a one-armed outfielder who made the big leagues because of the wartime talent shortage and because the spectacle of a one-armed player would bring fans to the ballpark.

Gray only played one season in the major leagues. In 1944 he'd enjoyed a spectacular season for the Southern Association Memphis Chicks, winning the Most Valuable Player Award and drawing the interest of several big league organizations. The St. Louis Browns, coming off a pennant-winning season, purchased his contract for $20,000, the most money ever paid for a Southern Association player at the time.

In the big leagues with the Browns in 1945 Gray was not able to duplicate his minor league success, but he outperformed many two-armed major leaguers. For the season he played in 77 games and registered a .218 batting mark. He didn't hit any home runs, but did blast a triple and stole 5 bases. On May 19 and 20 he fulfilled a lifelong dream by playing in Yankee Stadium before a contingent of fans from his hometown who'd come just to see the "One-Armed Wonder," as he'd been dubbed by the press. Pete didn't disappoint them. He got two hits the first day, a Saturday. Then in the Sunday doubleheader he got three hits in the first game and another hit in second contest, while making a number of sparkling fielding plays.

Gray lost his right arm at the age of six when he slipped off the running board of a truck while hitching a ride with an itinerant produce salesman, and caught his arm in the spokes of the wheel. The traveling man went to the trouble of taking the badly injured youngster home and abandoning him on the doorstep to wait for his parents to come home from work. Fortunately, a neighbor noticed the bloodied boy sitting on the porch and took him to the hospital. The mangled arm had to be amputated above the elbow.

Young Pete was already playing ball with the neighborhood kids when he lost his arm, but afterward he decided that he wanted to be a baseball player more than anything. First, the natural righthander had to learn to throw left-handed. Then he learned to bat with one hand by tossing rocks in the air and hitting them with a broomstick by the hour. At first the other kids didn't think he could play and no one wanted him on their team, but before long he became one of the better young players in the area.

Initially, fielding was the hardest part of the game for Pete. He removed the padding from his glove and wore it on the tips of his fingers with his little finger sticking out so he could hang onto the ball better with one hand. He eventually developed a technique for getting rid of the ball which involved sticking the glove under the armpit of his stub after making the catch and grabbing the ball as it rolled out across his chest. On grounders

Pete Gray's batting form

he would flip the ball in the air and catch it after dropping his glove. Another hurdle that Pete had to overcome was that he did not have the balance that a two-armed person naturally possesses. He compensated by running closer to the ground to establish a lower center of gravity. This running style made it easier for him to slide head-first into the base, a crowd pleasing but somewhat dangerous practice.

Pete Gray was 6 feet tall and weighed a lean 160 pounds. His overdeveloped left forearm measured 11 inches, only an inch less that his biceps. His arm and wrist were so strong that he wielded a 36-ounce bat, heavier than most two-armed hitters used in that era. Batting from the left side of the plate, he held the bat slightly behind his head, gripping it about three inches up the handle. When the pitch came, he whipped the bat through the strike zone with a short crisp stroke, usually hitting to the opposite field.

Pete was born on March 6, 1915, in the Hanover section of Nanticoke, Pennsylvania. Nanticoke is located in northeastern Pennsylvania's Wyoming Valley, one of the largest coal mining areas in the country when Pete was growing up. His parents were Lithuanian immigrants who'd fled Russian oppression to come to the United States a few years before Pete was born. He was the youngest of five children and his given name at birth was Peter J. Wyshner, Jr.

By the age of 16, Pete was starring for semipro teams around Wilkes-

Chapter 1—Missing Limbs or Extremities

Barre and Scranton and was committed to becoming a professional baseball player despite his disability. But he couldn't attract the interest of the Wilkes-Barre Barons or the Scranton Miners, the area's two minor league clubs. He even changed his name to Gray about this time, figuring scouts would be more able to remember the simpler name. He hitchhiked to Hot Springs, Arkansas, where Ran Doanes, who ran a tryout camp there, tried to get him hooked up with a professional team, but none were interested in a one-armed player. He also went to training camps in Florida several years, but no one would give him a look because of his disability. Once he even managed to get a referral to the Philadelphia Athletics and spoke to owner-manager Connie Mack. But even kindly old Connie wouldn't give him a chance to prove himself.

In 1938 Pete finally got his first taste of professional baseball with the Three Rivers team in the Quebec Provincial League. He'd been signed, sight-unseen, on the recommendation of a former teammate. The Three Rivers' brass was more than a little surprised when a one-armed player showed up, but decided they didn't have anything to lose by giving him a chance.

The news that Three Rivers had signed a one-armed guy got around and there was a big crowd on hand for Gray's debut. Despite the pleas of the crowd, he sat on the bench until he was sent up to pinch-hit in the ninth inning with two out, two runners on, and his team behind 1 to 0. He promptly laced a hit to right field that drove in both runners, and the fans showered him with money to show their appreciation. He ended up with about $500 for the day's work. Although Gray played well for Three Rivers, the Quebec Provincial League was probably farther away from the big leagues than the fast-paced semipro leagues he'd been playing in back home.

In 1939, at the age of 24, Pete finally got his big break. While in New York with some buddies for the World's Fair, he conned Max Rosner, the owner of a topflight semipro team in Brooklyn, into a tryout. At first, Rosner had tried to brush him off, but Pete handed him a $10 bill and told him to keep it if he still wasn't interested after a tryout. Rosner admired Gray's spunk and was even more impressed with his performance on the field. He also recognized Pete's potential as a gate attraction and signed him up to play for both his Bushwick club and his brother's Bay Parkway team.

The Bushwicks and the Bay Parkways were made up primarily of former professional players and a few promising youngsters. It was Pete's first national exposure and he made the best of it. A 1940 issue of *Newsweek* magazine featured a picture of him in a Bay Parkway uniform with a short article that stated, "Pete Gray ... now plays center field for the Bay Parkways ... not because of his box office value as a curiosity but because he is really an asset." It's interesting that in Pete's first brush with fame, it was deemed necessary to explain that he wasn't simply being used as a drawing card — that he really could play ball. He was already having to fight the assumption that he was only playing because he was a physical curiosity.

Gray continued on the semipro circuit for the next few seasons. He played with the Bay Parkways, also played in the Scranton–Wilkes-Barre area, and made occasional excursions to Canada to play for Three Rivers. When Three Rivers landed a Class C franchise in 1942 Pete was immediately summoned to join the club. He batted a sensational .381 and even blasted a 417-foot home run, but he missed most of the season with a broken collarbone.

Before the 1943 campaign, the Three Rivers franchise sold Gray's contract to the Toronto Maple Leafs, a Triple A team in the International League — only one rung below the major leagues. But Pete had a run-in with Toronto manager Burleigh Grimes, the former Hall of Fame pitcher, and was quickly released. But Pete was not to be denied. He caught on with the Double A Memphis Chicks and proceeded to become the biggest gate attraction in the history of the Southern Association. Pete went all out on every play, making spectacular catches on balls other outfielders wouldn't even go for and running the bases with abandon. His hell-bent style made him a big crowd favorite. He hit a solid .289 in 1943 as the Chicks' regular center fielder and gained national attention by being voted the Most Courageous Athlete of the Year by the Association of Philadelphia Sportswriters.

Back with Memphis in 1944, Pete burst into stardom. He hit .333, swiped a league-record 68 bases, and led the league's outfielders with a .996 fielding average. Pete was acclaimed the league's Most Valuable Player and became so famous that the War Department made movies of him in action and showed them in veterans' hospitals all over the world. Although several major league clubs were interested in acquiring Gray for the 1945 season, the Browns had a working agreement with Memphis and had the inside track.

The 1945 baseball season probably established an all-time low for caliber of play in the major leagues. The campaign in Europe, which appeared to be nearly over in early 1944, took a turn for the worst in the fall of the year, and military manpower needs increased. In addition there was intense pressure on the armed services to explain why young men fit enough to play professional sports were considered unfit for military duty. The director of War Mobilization and Reconstruction, James F. Byrnes, ordered a reevaluation of all professional athletes who were classified 4-F or had received medical discharges. Byrnes further directed that 4-F athletes found unfit for combat should be put to work in war factories or in the military, performing less demanding duties. This policy was reversed in May of 1945 after the surrender of Germany, but many veteran major leaguers who'd previously been rejected for military service spent the 1945 season playing baseball for Uncle Sam on armed service teams across the world.

To fill big league rosters, old-timers like Jimmie Foxx and Babe Herman were brought out of retirement. In addition, below-draft-age teenagers like Art Houtteman, Billy Pierce, and Granny Hamner, who would later become major league stars, were pressed into service. The Brooklyn Dodgers had a 17-year-old infielder named Tommy Brown who was already in his second season in the big time. The 1945 St. Louis Browns, however, seemed to be in better shape than most of the other big league teams. They'd won the 1944 American League pennant and were returning with the nucleus of the team intact. They were favored by many to repeat as American League pennant winners.

The Browns more than recouped Gray's purchase price just from the publicity they received in the spring of 1945. For his part, Pete said all the right things and impressed writers with his intensity and devotion to the game. *The Sporting News* diligently tracked his progress and everyone, a baseball fan or not, was curious to see if this one-armed man could succeed.

Although the public and the press worshiped him, Gray's relationship with the other Browns players was not so blissful. His new teammates failed to welcome him with open arms. Many of them felt that he was only with the team as a public relations gimmick and his presence would hurt their chances to repeat as pennant winners.

Unfortunately, Pete's somewhat prickly personality didn't make things any better. In later years, former teammates would characterize him as an ornery, hardheaded loner who thought the world was against him and always felt that he was being exploited. They said Pete was extremely sensitive about his disability and deeply resented it if he thought someone felt sorry for him.

Pete had a decent spring and was in the Browns 1945 opening day lineup, playing left field and hitting in the second slot in the batting order. He got a hit in that game, but went hitless in his next thirteen at-bats and quickly found himself on the bench. His batting average was down around .180 when he was reinserted into the lineup for the big April series in New York.

But Pete's success against the Yankees seemed to turn things around for him. The Browns, who had gotten off to a bad start, had worked their way back into contention, and Gray began contributing on a regular basis. After one game against Philadelphia where he got two hits and stole three bases, Connie Mack apologized to him for not taking him more seriously when he sought a tryout with the Athletics five years earlier.

And the fans were coming out in droves to see Gray perform. By the beginning of June, the Browns had attracted about 150,000 more fans than they'd drawn at the same point the previous season. At every ballpark, men who'd lost limbs in the war were waiting to meet him. Pete was naturally introverted and had never been comfortable speaking in front of people, but he diligently visited groups of amputees and Veterans Administration hospitals around the country to raise the spirits of the sick and wounded servicemen. But the novelty wore off and Pete's playing time also diminished as the 1945 season went on. By mid-July he'd raised his average to a respectable .260, but frequently found himself warming the bench. The sportswriters for the *St. Louis Post-Dispatch* mounted an unsuccessful campaign to get him more regular duty, but he played little down the stretch and his average dwindled. His last major league appearance came on V-J day, September 30, 1945, the famous game in which returning veteran Hank Greenberg's grand-slam homer won the pennant for the Detroit Tigers.

Several St. Louis players felt that Gray cost them the pennant in 1945, which is probably untrue and unfair. They claimed that Pete's disability made him a poor defensive outfielder and that he didn't hit enough to justify a spot in the lineup. Runners were said to take liberties on him because of the valuable time lost transferring the ball to his throwing hand. At the plate, he couldn't generate the power to drive the ball between the outfielders, and they played him very close, often nabbing liners that would normally fall for singles. Likewise, corner infielders also crowded in on him, taking away the drag bunt.

Despite these limitations, which were probably exaggerated, Pete had other talents that could compensate for any deficiencies. He was known to have a fine throwing arm and tremendous range in the outfield, which offset his ball-handling difficulties. Offensively, he generally made contact at bat, ran the bases with lightning speed, and was a good bunter. At the very least, he added another dimension to the slow-footed St. Louis attack. His five steals in part-time play was the second highest total on the team and represented 20 percent of the team's stolen base total for the entire season.

Another complaint was that Pete cut into the playing time of more capable veteran outfielders. The Browns 1945 outfield corps, however, was not exactly Hall of Fame material. The top offensive producers were veteran Gene Moore, who paced the group with a mediocre .260 batting average, and weak fielding Milt Byrnes, who led in homers with a mere eight four-baggers. The man who lost the most playing time to Gray and most bitterly resented his presence was 37-year-old Mike Kreevich, the club's regular center fielder in 1944. But in 1945, Kreevich's .237 average when he was shipped to the Washington Senators was only slightly higher than Gray's final mark. In 81 games as the Browns center fielder, Kreevich averaged 2.84 putouts per game, while Gray averaged 2.66 for the season despite playing more than half of his games in left field. This indicates that Pete's range was at least as good, if not better, than that of Kreevich. The club's other outfielders were rookie Babe Martin, who's .200 batting average in 185 at-bats was lower that Gray's .218 in 234 plate appearances, and Chet Laabs, a veteran slugger with a .239 batting average who was only available on a part-time basis because he was working in a war-industry plant.

Gray's detractors also charged that Pete was an unsettling influence on the team, causing dissension because of the playing time he took away from more able-bodied men. In fact, open hostility toward Gray was reported to have directly led to the trade of Kreevich and the suspension of pitcher Sig Jakucki, one of Gray's chief antagonists.

While it may be true that other players resented Gray's presence, he can hardly be blamed for that. In fact, Kreevich had his problems with other organizations in the past. He'd signed with the Browns in 1943 after being released by the lowly Philadelphia Athletics for excessive drinking. He joined Alcoholics Anonymous (AA) and cleaned up his act enough to be of use to the Browns, but he was embarrassed about sharing time with a one-armed player and his attitude became a major problem. The Browns actually improved after Kreevich was waived to Washington. He was replaced by veteran outfielder Lou Finney, whose hitting played a major role in the team's stretch run.

Jakucki was another bad actor who openly resented Gray and reportedly tormented him at every opportunity. Ironically, Jakucki was a true "wartime player." He'd flunked a brief trial with the Browns in 1936 and was pitching for a shipyard team when they brought him back to bolster their depleted pitching staff in 1944. A mean, boisterous drunk, Jakucki was suspended and subsequently released for drunkenness more so than his behavior toward Gray.

If Gray's drawing power was a factor in keeping him on the team, at least he put money in the team's coffers by attracting fans and attention — funds that could be used to improve the roster. For example, the purchase of the hardhitting Finney might not have been possible without the additional revenue that Gray generated.

After the 1945 season, the Browns arranged a barnstorming tour to California with Gray as the main attraction. He claimed to have eclipsed his $5,000 salary for the entire 1945 season playing a few games against Pacific Coast League All-Stars.

With the end of World War II and subsequent return of the veteran players who'd been in the service, big league rosters were crowded in 1946. Gray was sent to the Browns' Toledo farm club in the American Association, which had become a Triple A circuit. He hit only .250 in limited duty and dropped out of organized baseball to barnstorm for a year. He returned to the minor leagues in 1948 to hit .290 for Elmira in the Eastern League, but a meager .214 average for Dallas in the Texas League in 1949 convinced him to retire from professional baseball at 34 years of age. He then spent some time barnstorming with the renowned, bearded House of David semipro team before returning to settle in Hanover.

In Hanover, still a village of about 3,000 people, the lifelong bachelor lived in the old 12-room family home where he'd been raised. He shunned writers and reporters and gained a reputation as a recluse, although he was very much a part of the day to day life in Hanover, where he was still admired as a hero. Pete was still afraid people would think of him as a freak and he refused public appearances before strangers.

Gray's means of support after leaving baseball is something of a mystery. Later in life he bragged that he had never worked a day in his life outside of baseball, but admitted that he'd always been pretty good at cards, dice, and pool. He was also a fine golfer, shooting in the low 80s and at times in the high 70s. He played golf well past the age of 70, always open to a side bet.

The cantankerous old-timer seemed to mellow somewhat as the years went by. In 1978 he made a long overdue public appearance, throwing out the first ball at Tim McCarver Stadium in Memphis when the Chicks returned to the American Association after an absence of 17 years. After his season with the Browns, Pete had rejected a $15,000 offer from Hollywood to film his life story and in the interim had turned down requests for television appearances on *I've Got a Secret* and *What's My Line* and more recently *Good Morning America* and *Late Night with David Letterman*. But he finally agreed to a 1986 made-for-television movie about his life entitled *A Winner Never Quits,* which starred Keith Carradine as Pete.

But Gray remained largely forgotten until the Jim Abbott phenomenon of the late 1980s recalled memories of the last one-armed major leaguer. He still refused lucrative offers to appear at baseball card shows or old-timers games, but he did finally give in to the Hall of Fame's repeated requests and donated his old glove to put on display. Later he consented to a biography, entitled *One-Armed Wonder,* which was released in 1995.

In his later years, Pete's headquarters was a small town tavern in Hanover that was owned and operated by a younger cousin Bertha Vedor, his closest remaining relative. He suffered from ulcers and other stomach problems and died on June 30, 2002, at the age of 87

Was Pete Gray a legitimate major league baseball player, as he always wanted to be remembered? It's impossible to tell. Statistically his sole major league season was mediocre at best, but many successful major leaguers struggled as rookies before finding themselves. There are also questions about the way he was used in 1945. He didn't seem to have a defined role, and just when he started to produce consistently, his playing time was reduced. In Pete's biography the author states that the Browns winning percentage was better than .600 with Gray in the lineup and under .425 without him, which would certainly seem to indicate that he improved the club when in the lineup. In addition, Gray was brought to St. Louis largely on the strength of his 68 stolen bases with Memphis, yet he stole only 5 with the Browns. Why wasn't he encouraged to run more?

Gray did apparently have a batting weakness that surfaced against major league pitching. Initially pitchers tried to overpower the lithe left-handed hitter, figuring he couldn't get the bat around in time. But Pete had a good eye and excellent timing and was actually a good fastball hitter. It was breaking balls that gave him trouble. He had to start his swing early to time the fast one and had trouble adjusting to off-speed pitches. With only one arm he wasn't able to check his swing as easily as other players. After word got around, he received a steady diet of the soft stuff.

Although the Browns undoubtedly acquired Pete with an eye on the box office, any player would have gotten a shot after the type a season he had with Memphis in 1944. Gray may have gotten a few breaks along the way because of his gate appeal, but they were nothing compared to the obstacles he faced. In addition, Gray was 30 years old when he got his first chance in the majors, although he'd shaved a few years off for appearances and was listed as 28 years old. His most productive seasons had already been spent on the dusty fields of Pennsylvania's coal mining towns.

In summary, Pete Gray was probably the most seriously disabled player in major league history. The nature of his disability (his arm was missing above the elbow) was even more severe than Abbott or Daily, who had the use of an elbow joint and part of a forearm. In addition, Abbott and Daily were pitchers, which allowed them to mitigate their disability to some extent.

While Pete was with the Browns, Shirley Povich of the Washington Post wrote, "What Gray might have accomplished in the big leagues if blessed with two arms is something for the imagination to play with. Surely he would have been one of the greatest big leaguers of all time."

How good would he have been with two arms? "Who knows?" Pete responded when asked the question. "Maybe I wouldn't have done as well. For one thing, I know I probably wouldn't have tried as hard and practiced as much as I did, and I probably wouldn't have had the same determination to make it to the big leagues."

One thing is certain. Pete Gray beat the odds which relegated most everyone else in the Wyoming Valley to a life in the coal pits. He was never called a great player, but he has been called the most extraordinary ballplayer ever.

PETE GRAY
(born Peter J. Wyshner)
B. March 6, 1915 D. June 30, 2002

YEAR	TEAM	LEAGUE	G	AB	R	H	HR	RBI	AVE	SB	POS
1938	Three Rivers	Provincial	*	60	7	17	1	8	.283	*	OF
1939–41			(Did Not Play Organized Baseball)								
1942	Three Rivers	Can-Amer	42	160	31	61	0	13	.381	5	OF
1943	Memphis	Southern	126	453	56	131	0	42	.289	13	OF
1944	Memphis	Southern	129	501	119	167	5	60	.333	68	OF
1945	ST. LOUIS	AL	77	234	26	51	0	13	.218	5	OF
1946	Toledo	Am Ass'n	48	96	14	24	0	7	.250	2	OF
1947			(Did Not Play Organized Baseball)								
1948	Elmira	Eastern	82	269	37	78	0	14	.290	5	OF
1949	Dallas	Texas	45	56	18	12	0	5	.214	5	OF
MAJOR LEAGUE TOTALS			77	234	26	51	0	13	.218	5	

MONTY STRATTON

An account of ball players who performed with disabilities wouldn't be complete without including the story of Chicago White Sox hurler Monty Stratton, who was still pitching professionally 15 years after losing his right leg in a hunting accident. Stratton's incredible feat was documented in the highly successful 1949 M.G.M. film, *The Stratton Story*, which starred the woefully unathletic Jimmy Stewart as Stratton and June Allyson as Monty's wife, Ethel.

Not surprisingly, the Hollywood writers used some "editorial license" in the movie version of Stratton's career as a one-legged hurler. The movie leaves viewers with the impression that Monty actually resumed his big league career after learning to pitch with an artificial leg. In actuality, Stratton never pitched in an official major league game on one leg, although he did make some exhibition appearances for the White Sox.

Although *The Stratton Story* naturally focused on Stratton's heroic comeback, his early career was also classic Hollywood stuff. Monty Stratton was born May 21, 1912, in Celeste, Texas, and grew up in the tiny community about 50 miles from Dallas. His father was a farmer who died when Monty was young, leaving the boy to help his mother operate the farm.

Pitching for the Celeste town team, Stratton gained local fame as "The Celeste Whirlwind" and was eventually discovered by a White Sox scout. He saw some duty with Chicago in 1934, his first year in professional baseball, and came up to stay late the next season after winning 17 games for St. Paul in the American Association. A right-handed thrower and hitter, the gangly Stratton stood 6'5" and weighed around 180 pounds. He relied primarily on a trick pitch, which he affectionately called the "Gander." The pitch seemed to dart in and out as it approached the strike zone.

Stratton's 1936 season, his first full year in the majors, was a harbinger of the bad luck that would plague him throughout his career. He suffered bouts with both tonsillitis and appendicitis and finished with a disappointing 5–7 won-loss mark in only 16 appearances.

But 1936 was a good year for the White Sox. After 15 years of second division finishes, the Sox fought their way to a lofty third place finish with 81 wins. Jimmie Dykes, who would lead the Sox for another decade, was in only his second full season as manager and also held down third base. The hitters were paced by shortstop Luke Appling's league leading .388 batting average. Outfielder Rip Radcliff at .335, first baseman Zeke Bonura at .330, second baseman Jackie Hayes at .312, and rookie center fielder Mike Kreevich at .307, also enjoyed outstanding seasons at the plate. Sophomore hurler Vern Kennedy won 21 games to lead the staff, but longtime ace Ted Lyons managed only 10 victories. For the first time since the infamous Black Sox scandal of 1920 the White Sox fans were anticipating a run at the American League Pennant in 1937.

For a while in 1937 it looked like they might make it, thanks to the work of 25-year-old Monty Stratton. Stratton pitched spectacularly in 1937, posting a sparkling 15–5 won-lost record. Beginning June 22 he won seven

Monty Stratton — one-legged pitcher

straight games, including three shutouts. In the midst of the streak he was named to the American League all-star squad, but a twisted ankle kept him out of the game. Shortly after the all-star break, the White Sox young ace injured his arm and he pitched only three innings after July 31. With Stratton sidelined, Chicago was no match for the powerful New York Yankees. They finished in third place again, 16 games behind the Bombers, although they improved their record to 86 victories.

Chapter 1—Missing Limbs or Extremities

For the season, Stratton's .750 winning percentage was the second best in the major leagues and his 2.40 earned run average was third best behind future Hall of Famers Lefty Gomez of the Yankees and Carl Hubbell of the New York Giants. In addition, his 2.02 walks-per-game average was the lowest figure in the American League and his 7.76 hits-per-game average was the second lowest. Despite missing about two months of the season, he threw five shutouts, which tied for the second highest total in the big leagues. His 15 wins led the staff and he teamed with Kennedy, Lyons, and newcomer Thornton Lee to form a solid starting rotation. The offense once again featured five .300 hitters. Bonura led the club with a .345 average. Radcliff, Appling and Kreevich chipped in with marks of .325, .317, and .302 respectively, and Dixie Walker took over right field and hit .302.

The White Sox plummeted all the way down to sixth place in 1938 with only 65 victories. Stratton experienced arm problems early in the season and his earned run average rose to 4.01, but his 15 wins against 9 losses was still the best record on the Sox pitching staff, ahead of Lyons, Lee, and Johnny Rigney, who'd replaced Kennedy in the rotation. Furthermore his .625 winning percentage was the fourth best in the league, quite a feat when pitching for a team that finished well below .500. Radcliff and Appling finished over .300 again, as did outfield newcomer Gee Walker. But fancy-fielding, new first baseman Joe Kuhel, who was acquired in exchange for the popular Bonura, batted only .267. The club's leading hitter was outfielder Hank Steinbacher, who batted .331 as a 25-year-old rookie. Steinbacher returned to the minor leagues after his average sunk to .171 the next season and never resurfaced.

Stratton was eagerly looking forward to the 1939 season, confident that his physical problems were finally behind him and that the Sox would rebound. Only 26 years old, he seemed destined for greatness. The crosstown Chicago Cubs manager (and noted grammarian) Charlie Grimm called Stratton, "The nearest pitcher to Grover Cleveland Alexander I ever saw."

But disaster struck in the off-season when Stratton stumbled while hunting rabbits on his mother's farm. A holstered .22 caliber pistol he was carrying discharged into his right leg between the hip and the knee. Monty crawled more than a half of a mile toward the farmhouse before he was able to hail his wife Ethel. He was rushed first to a hospital in nearby Greenville, Texas, and then to Dallas.

Stratton's lousy luck remained true to form. The bullet had pierced the femoral artery behind the knee, cutting off the blood supply to his lower leg. Gangrene quickly set in and the leg had to be amputated the following day. Dr. A. R. Thomasson, the operating surgeon, was quoted as saying, "Monty couldn't have hit that artery if he aimed at it. It probably wouldn't happen more than once in a hundred times."

It looked like the end of a promising career to everyone except Monty Stratton. Equipped with a wooden leg, he doggedly decided to come back. On May 1, 1939, less than six months after the accident, the White Sox played the Cubs in a benefit game on Stratton's behalf. A crowd of more than 25,000 fans paid a dollar each into the "Monty Fund" to watch sore-armed Dizzy Dean pitch against the Sox. The players and umpires even paid their way into the park. The event raised about $28,000 for Monty, who was also presented with an automobile, specially equipped with hand-operated gears and brakes, courtesy of former teammate Tony Piet's Pontiac dealership. In a gut-wrenching pregame ceremony, Stratton took his familiar place on the mound to prove that he could still pitch. Despite a tremendous display of grit and courage it was painfully evident that Monty couldn't pivot on his artificial leg without losing his balance.

According to *The Stratton Story*, Monty became discouraged and depressed during this period. He stopped wearing the prosthesis and became reclusive, spending his time moping around the house. Then one day he watched his infant son's determined efforts to learn to walk. The boy just kept clawing his way back up after each fall. Monty resolved that he wasn't going to stay down either. He strapped on his wooden leg and started helping out with the chores around the farm. Not long afterward, Ethel coaxed him into tossing a few pitches to her, and their was no stopping him after that. Although the Hollywood version has Stratton secretly arranging to pitch in an exhibition contest against topflight minor leaguers and winning the game in dramatic fashion, it's doubtful that Monty resumed his career exactly that way.

In the real world, the White Sox generously offered Stratton a "lifetime job" with the team, and he spent the next few years coaching for them. But he was still a young man and he still wanted to pitch. While going about his coaching duties, he continued to work on his pitching motion to overcome the balancing problem, which was no doubt exacerbated by his lanky frame.

In 1942 Monty managed the Lubbock team in the West Texas League and made a few brief appearances on the mound—his first professional action since the accident. By 1945 he was pitching for a semipro team in Houston, where his stellar performance earned him another chance in organized baseball.

Stratton signed with the Sherman Twins in the Class C East Texas League for the 1946 season. The league permitted Monty to have a "courtesy runner" when he reached base, but he had to reach first on his own.

Otherwise, no special treatment was afforded. Apparently the 34-year-old former All-Star had learned to handle himself adequately in the field because he posted a respectable .974 fielding average in 1946, while winning 18 games and losing 8. In 218 innings he walked only 43 batters. The press quickly got wind of his remarkable efforts and he received national acclaim, culminating with the Most Courageous Athlete of the Year award.

Monty may still have harbored ambitions to return to the White Sox and once again pitch in the big time, but reality set in when he moved up to Waco in the Class B Big State League for the 1947 season. He was hit hard, posting an unsightly 6.55 earned run average while winning seven games and losing the same number.

But the rash of publicity from Stratton's outstanding 1946 season had caught the attention of the film industry, and Monty retired from baseball after the 1947 season to assist in the production of *The Stratton Story*. On the set he was reunited with longtime White Sox manager Jimmie Dykes, who was making one last appearance in a Sox uniform after being dismissed during the 1946 season.

When the movie was finished Monty returned to the farm, although he continued to make occasional minor league appearances as a gate attraction. His last appearance in a regular game was at the age of 41 in 1953, 15 years after the accident that took his leg. He died in 1982 in Greenville, Texas, at the age of 70.

Although Monty Stratton never returned to pitch in a regular season major league game after losing his leg, his ability to successfully compete in the minor leagues is astonishing. His amazing 1946 performance came in the first season after the end of World War II, when the veterans had returned and a glut of talent existed at all levels of professional baseball. Stratton probably pitched under a greater obstacle than any other professional hurler. His leg was amputated above the knee so he didn't have the benefit of a knee joint for mobility and flexibility. This made fielding bunts and covering first base on grounders to the right side extremely difficult. In addition, the righthander lost his right leg, or pivot leg, which made balancing extremely difficult, especially for a man of his height.

Despite his fame, Stratton never strayed far from his "aw shucks" farm boy roots. When asked to comment at the debut of his movie biography he said, "It's my life, all right. I'll just hope folks will think it was worth making into a movie." Apparently they did! *The Stratton Story* was a box office smash and won the Academy Award for best original screenplay.

MONTY FRANKLIN PIERCE STRATTON
B. May 21, 1912 D. September 29, 1982

YEAR	TEAM	LEAGUE	G	IP	SO	BB	W	L	ERA	CG	SHO
1934	Galveston	Texas	9	40	12	11	1	4	4.28	*	*
	Omaha	Western	23	160	108	47	8	10	*	*	*
	CHICAGO	AL	1	3	0	1	0	0	5.40	0	0
1935	St. Paul	Am Ass'n	33	226	120	63	17	9	4.02	*	*
	CHICAGO	AL	5	38	8	9	1	2	4.03	2	0
1936	CHICAGO	AL	16	95	37	46	5	7	5.21	3	0
1937	CHICAGO	AL	22	165	69	37	15	5	2.40	14	5
1938	CHICAGO	AL	26	186	82	56	15	9	4.01	17	0
1942	Lubbock	W Tex-NM	5	9	*	*	0	0	*	*	*
1946	Sherman	E Texas	27	218	108	43	18	8	4.17	*	*
1947	Waco	Big State	15	103	46	30	7	7	6.55	*	*
1949	Temple	Big State	1	4	*	*	0	1	*	*	*
	Vernon	Longhorn	1	9	*	*	1	0	0.00	1	1
1950	Gre-Sherm-Den	Big State	2	18	6	1	2	0	4.50	2	*
	CorCh-Br'sville	Rio Grande	2	18	*	*	2	0	*	2	*
1953	Greenville-Bryan	Big State	1	1	*	*	0	1	*	*	*
	Sherm'n-Denis'n	Sooner St	1	8	*	*	0	1	*	*	*
MAJOR LEAGUE TOTALS			70	487	196	149	36	23	3.71	36	5

BERT SHEPARD

Although Monty Stratton was probably the best one-legged pitcher in baseball history, lefthander Bert Shepard is the only man to actually pitch (and bat) in the major leagues with an artificial leg. And although Shepard appeared in only one official game, he turned in an impressive performance for the Washington Senators that August 4 afternoon in 1945.

Shepard, who'd been a struggling minor league hurler before World War II, is a genuine war hero. His right leg was amputated just below the knee after he was injured in a crash behind enemy lines. Despite this impairment he pitched five and one third innings, giving up only three hits and one run against the Boston Red Sox, in his only big league opportunity.

Bert Shepard was born June 28, 1920, in Dana, Indiana, the second of six boys. His father was a farmhand and the family moved often. When Bert was 10 years old, he went to live with his grandmother in Clinton,

Chapter 1—Missing Limbs or Extremities 41

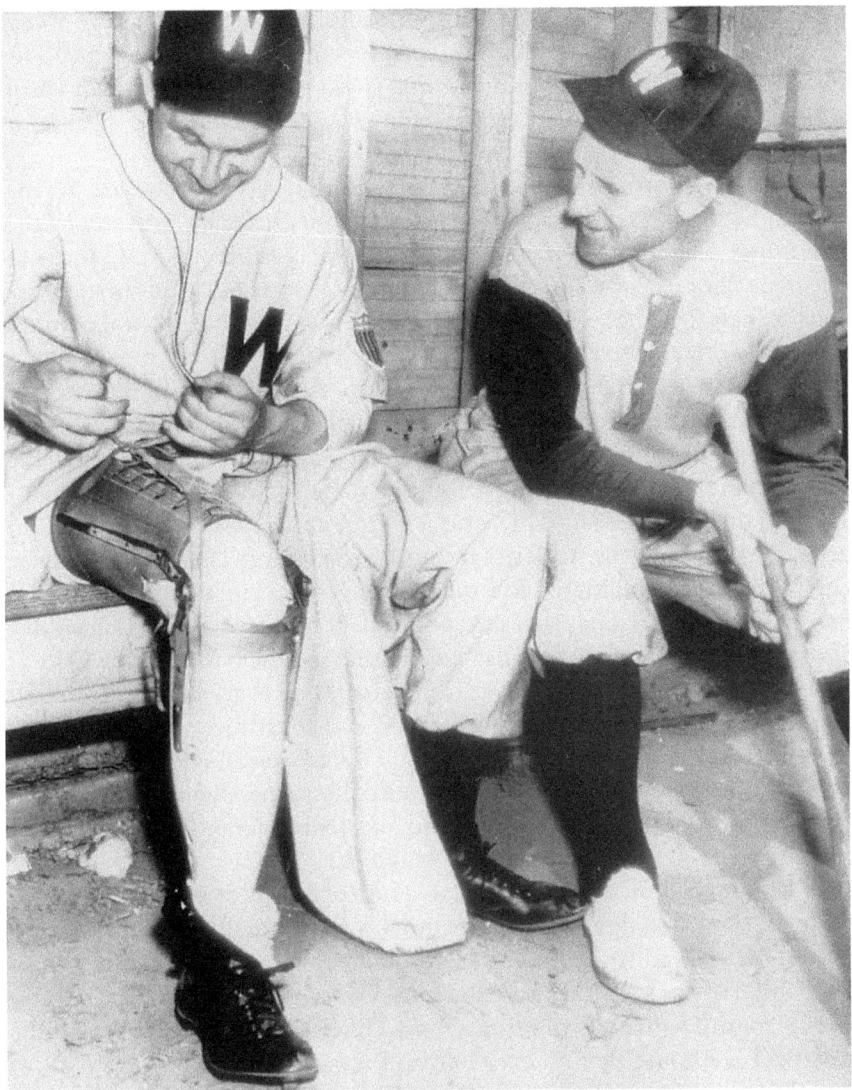

Bert Shepard suits up as Manager Ossie Bluege looks on

Indiana, and soon became a fine sandlot ball player. He played football and basketball in high school, but the school didn't have a baseball team.

After his junior year in high school in 1937 Shepard headed for the West Coast. He'd heard that California was the place to go if you wanted to be a baseball player so he and a buddy hopped freight trains and hitchhiked across the country. They bussed tables and did odd jobs along the way to finance their trip. Once in California, Shepard got a job in a tire retread plant and played baseball wherever he could find a game. The strong-armed 5'11", 185 pound southpaw was playing semipro ball when a Chicago White Sox scout signed him to a $60 per month contract for the 1939 season.

Bert's first professional assignment was short-lived, however. Trying too hard to make an immediate impression, he threw his arm out at the Sox minor league spring training complex in Longview, Texas, and was released. The next year he caught on with the Wisconsin Rapids in the Wisconsin State League, winning three and losing two, but 48 walks in 43 innings led to another release.

Discouraged, but not about to give up, the 20-year-old returned to Clinton in the summer of 1940 to get his high school diploma. By February he was ready for another try and once again headed west. At the Philadelphia Athletics training camp in Anaheim, he talked owner-manager Connie Mack into giving him a tryout and pitched well enough to get a contract with the Athletics minor league club in Anaheim. But once again, control problems led to a quick release. He caught on with the Bisbee team in the Arizona-Texas League, where he lasted a little longer, but was ultimately cut again because he couldn't get the ball over the plate.

Bert was still set on a career in baseball, however, and was thinking about switching to first base. He'd played first for Bisbee when not pitching and had done fairly well. With the United States' entry into World War II, however, many minor league circuits suspended operations and there were few opportunities. Shepard was still looking for a roster spot somewhere when he was drafted in May 1942.

Although he'd never been near an airplane, Bert was accepted for flight training as a fighter pilot and quickly found that he had a talent for flying. He rose to the rank of second lieutenant before shipping out to Scotland. He was soon flying combat missions with the 55th Fighter Group of U.S. Eighth Air Force, piloting a P-38 Thunderbolt. He even flew in the first daytime bombing raid over Berlin, his 34th mission.

By the spring of 1944 Shepard was set to manage the newly organized base baseball team. On May 21, the morning of the first game, a low level bombing and strafing mission over Berlin was ordered. Knowing that as many pilots as possible were needed, Bert volunteered to go even though he wasn't scheduled to fly until the next day. "Besides," he later admitted, "I thought we'd be back in time for the ball game."

But Shepard didn't make it back for his managerial debut. While going in to strafe an aerodrome he was hit by ground fire and crashed his plane. He woke up several days later in a German hospital with his right leg amputated about eleven inches below the knee. In addition, a two-inch-square piece of the frontal sinus bone had been removed from the area above his right eye. Shepard was eventually moved to a Nazi prisoner of war camp where a fellow inmate fashioned an artificial leg for him. He found he could get around pretty well and was soon playing catch and working out on the crude prosthesis. He was repatriated in a trade of prisoners between the Allies and the Axis and arrived back in the States on a Swedish Red Cross ship in February 1945.

While waiting to get a new artificial leg at Walter Reed Hospital, Shepard happened to meet United States Secretary of War Robert Patterson, who was making a visit to lift the morale of the wounded men. Bert told Patterson of his desire to play professional baseball again. When he returned to his desk, the secretary telephoned his old friend Clark Griffith, owner of the Washington Senators (or Nationals as they were called at the time), about Shepard and a tryout was arranged.

Four days after receiving his new leg, Shepard reported to the Senators spring training complex and proved to be a surprisingly good ballplayer. He could throw hard and he moved around so well that it was difficult to tell he wore an artificial leg. Bert became an instant celebrity and the camp was soon full of reporters and photographers anxious to record the exploits of the one-legged war hero. Shepard's actions were widely publicized to inspire other disabled vets returning from the war. His workouts became media events. He threw hours of batting practice, took regular turns at the plate and cavorted around first base in infield practice. He also pitched in several exhibition games against various armed forces teams, whose rosters included veteran professional players.

Shepard didn't let his disability hinder him that much. As a lefthanded pitcher, he landed on the artificial right leg when he threw. As a lefty hitter, his weight stayed back on his good left leg. He reportedly fielded his position adequately and didn't have a major problem with bunts. His old nemesis—poor control—probably held him back more than his severed leg.

The Senators finally signed Bert to be a coach and batting practice pitcher, after he traveled to Atlantic City one day to work out with the New York Yankees. They indicated that they intended to activate him later in the year when he gained better control of his pitches.

Thanks to throwing hours and hours of batting practice, Bert's control gradually improved and he finally got his chance to face a major league lineup on July 10, 1945. The Senators were slated to play the Brooklyn Dodgers in Griffith Stadium as part of a series of exhibition games to benefit the War Relief effort. Two days before the game Washington manager Ossie Bluege told Shepard he would be starting, and the young hurler endured a couple of restless nights. "I felt the pressure, and I knew there were an awful lot of people who thought I couldn't do it," he remembered in an interview in *Once Around the Bases* by Richard Tellis. "If I messed up a bunt or slipped like any other pitcher fielding a ground ball, they'd say it was because of the leg. Mr. Griffith gave me a chance, but there was much more pressure on me because everybody else was afraid I'd fail."

In a pregame interview, Brooklyn manager Leo Durocher publicly threatened a $500 fine for any Dodger who attempted to lay one down against Shepard. Bert resented this stunt because it gave everyone the impression that he couldn't handle bunts.

Although he was no longer an active player, Durocher was in the lineup leading off against Shepard. Leo walked and the next hitter also drew a free pass before Bert settled down and retired the side without further damage. For three innings he shut out the Dodgers on one hit before yielding a couple of runs and being relieved in the fourth.

Shepard was activated after his impressive performance against the Dodgers, but didn't get a chance to pitch in a regular season contest until the second game of an August doubleheader against Boston. Washington was hopelessly behind with two outs in the top of the fourth inning when Bert was summoned to the mound. The Red Sox had already scored 12 times in the inning and still had the bases loaded. Shepard promptly struck out George "Catfish" Metkovich to end the nightmarish inning and went on to finish the game in impressive fashion. On defense he deftly handled two balls hit back at him and at the plate he was hitless in three trips, but made contact twice.

Based on his impressive performance against the Red Sox, Shepard figured to see more action, but the Senators were in a heated battle for the American League pennant which wasn't decided until the last day of the season. Manager Bluege was forced to go with his experienced hurlers, so Shepard didn't get another chance that season or, as it turned out, in succeeding campaigns.

After the 1945 season ended, Shepard kept busy barnstorming and visiting veterans' hospitals across the country. He also made a training film for leg amputees coming back from the war. He reported to the Senators 1946 spring training camp and pitched fairly well in a few exhibition contests. He had little chance, however, to make the pitching staff, which was loaded with returning veterans. When the Senators broke camp, Bert remained with the team as a coach, but later in the year requested an assignment to Washington's Chattanooga farm club in the American Association so he could get some playing time. In one of his first appearances,

Bert shocked everyone by taking an extra base on a hit and then hustling in from second on a subsequent single to left. But he failed to pitch well for Chattanooga, though he was a big crowd favorite.

Bert went back to barnstorming in the Pacific Northwest in the 1946 off-season, pitching and playing first base. Two personal highlights were a strikeout of Stan Musial and a hit off Bob Feller. But in November 1946 Shepard's prospects of reaching the majors again were dealt a devastating blow when complications resulted from additional reconstructive surgery on his leg. The recovery time was originally estimated at six weeks, but four more operations were required that kept him on crutches for two and a half years. In addition to the lost time, his shoulder muscles had tightened so much from using the crutches that he could no longer throw freely.

Finally healthy again, Bert took a job as player-manager for Waterbury in the Colonial League for the 1949 season. He posted a 5–6 won-lost record on the mound and belted four homers in nearly 50 games at first base. Incredibly he also stole five bases and beat out a bunt. The element of surprise was a big factor, of course, but he also showed surprising speed.

As a manager, Shepard was popular with his players. At Waterbury, the owners had to let him go because they couldn't afford his salary, but the players first threatened to strike and then proceeded to raise enough money to rehire him.

Bert left baseball after the year with Waterbury and spent the next two years as a typewriter salesman for IBM. In 1952 he came back and played for teams in four different minor league loops, primarily as a gate attraction. In 1953 he played a few games with Tampa in the Florida International League and finished his professional career two years later with Modesto in the California League. In his final season he hurled a complete game victory in his first start for Modesto, but was hit hard thereafter and released.

After retiring from baseball, Shepard began a career as a safety engineer, working for Hughes Aircraft and Fluor Construction before retiring to Southern California in 1982. An excellent golfer, he won the National Amputee Golf Championship in 1968 and again in 1971. He met his wife Betty while managing a semipro team in North Dakota in the early 1950s. They were married in 1953 and had four children.

Several years after retirement, Bert traveled to the scene of his fateful crash and got a chance to meet the Austrian doctor who saved his life, Dr. Loidl. He was finally able to learn many details of the event. Dr. Loidl had been called to the rural crash site, where he found farmers brandishing pitchforks at an unconscious American pilot. After pulling Shepard from the wreck and treating his wounds, Loidl arranged for him to be properly treated at a German hospital. In fact, Loidl was later interrogated by the Gestapo for his humane treatment of an American P-38 pilot. Shepard only learned of Dr. Loidl when the Austrian asked an English friend to try to find out what happened to the American pilot he'd treated 40 years earlier. The Englishman managed to learn Shepard's identity and track him down.

Bert never felt sorry for himself for his disability. To his way of thinking he wouldn't have met his wife if he'd lived his life any differently. He would have liked to have received more of a chance to pitch for Washington, but he's far from bitter. He may have been used by professional baseball as a publicity gimmick, but unlike Pete Gray, he recognized that he was an inspiration to other disabled individuals and made the best of it.

In truth, Shepard was probably not a legitimate major leaguer. His talent was found wanting by professional baseball before losing his leg and there's no reason to think he would be a better player with the disability, but Bert Shepard definitely had a major league heart.

BERT ROBERT SHEPARD
B. June 28, 1920

YEAR	TEAM	LEAGUE	G	IP	SO	BB	W	L	ERA	GS	H
1939	Tiffin	Ohio State	1	1	0	4	0	1	*	1	1
	Jeanerette	Evangeline	*	*	*	*	0	0	*	*	*
1940	Mt Airy	Big State	*	*	*	*	0	0	*	*	*
	Wisc. Rapids	Wis State	9	43	25	48	3	2	6.07	*	44
1941	Anaheim	California	3	11	*	*	0	1	*	*	*
	Bisbee	Ariz-Texas	30	73	36	51	3	5	8.26	*	102
1942–44		(In Military Service)									
1945	WASHINGTON	AL	1	5	2	1	0	0	1.69	0	3
1946	Chattanooga	Southern	7	29	8	27	2	2	7.45	5	34
1947–48		(Did Not Play Organized Baseball)									
1949	Waterbury	Colonial	20	73	21	44	5	6	6.16	9	65
1950–51		(Did Not Play Organized Baseball)									
1952	Paris	Big State	*	*	*	*	0	0	12.60	*	*
	Hot Springs	Cotton St.	*	*	*	*	1	3	*	*	*
	St. Augustine	Fla State	*	*	*	*	2	2	4.50	*	*
	Corpus Christi	Gulf Coast	*	*	*	*	0	0	*	*	*
1953	Tampa	Fla Intern'l	*	*	*	*	0	0	*	*	*
1954		(Did Not Play Organized Baseball)									
1955	Modesto	California	3	*	*	*	1	1	12.54	*	*
MAJ. LEAGUE PITCHING TOTALS			1	5	2	1	0	0	1.69	0	0

Chapter 1—Missing Limbs or Extremities

YEAR	TEAM	LEAGUE	G	AB	R	H	HR	RBI	AVE	SB	POS
1939	Tiffin	Evangeline	1	0	0	0	0	0	.000	0	P
	Jeanerette	Evangeline	*	*	*	*	*	*	*	*	P
1940	Mt Airy	Big State	*	*	*	*	*	*	*	*	P
	Wisc. Rapids	Wis State	10	9	2	0	0	0	.000	0	P
1941	Anaheim	California	5	6	2	1	*	*	.167	*	P
	Bisbee	Ariz-Texas	30	61	7	13	0	11	.213	0	P-1B
1942–44		(In Military Service)									
1945	WASHINGTON	AL	1	3	0	0	0	0	.000	0	P
1946	Chattanooga	Southern	7	8	0	1	0	0	.125	0	P
1947–48		(Did Not Play Organized Baseball)									
1949	Waterbury	Colonial	69	131	17	30	4	21	.229	5	1B-P
1950–51		(Did Not Play Organized Baseball)									
1952	Paris	Big State	*	*	*	*	*	*	*	*	P
	Hot Springs	Cotton St.	18	28	2	5	0	3	.179	0	P-1B
	St. Augustine	Fla State	10	31	2	5	0	3	.161	0	P-1B
	Corpus Christi	Gulf Coast	*	*	*	*	*	*	*	*	P
1953	Tampa	Fla Intern'l	2	*	*	*	*	*	.000	*	P
1954		(Did Not Play Organized Baseball)									
1955	Modesto	California	3	4	*	*1	*	*	.250	*	P
MAJ. LEAGUE BATTING TOTALS			1	3	0	0	0	0	.000	0	

Two

Severely Damaged Limbs

LOU BRISSIE

While disabled veteran Bert Shepard was captivating the baseball world with his exploits in the spring of 1945, another young war hero was confined to an army hospital bed clinging to a seemingly impossible dream of playing baseball again.

Like Shepard, Lou Brissie was a hard-throwing young left-handed pitching prospect before entering the armed service at the outbreak of World War II. Like Shepard, he was wounded so severely that it didn't seem possible that he would ever play ball again. But Brissie was somewhat luckier than Shepard. Through dogged determination he'd managed to keep his severely damaged left leg intact, overriding army field doctors who recommended amputation. Even as he lay in his hospital bed that spring there was still considerable doubt that the leg could be saved, and even more doubt that it would ever be even marginally functional.

But Brissie persevered, stubbornly keeping his hopes alive through multiple operations to remove bone and shrapnel and implant a metal plate to replace missing bone. Although the leg was saved, doctors told him that his baseball playing days were over. "If God lets me walk again, I'll play, " he answered back.

And play he did! On September 28, 1947, Lou made his major league debut for the Philadelphia Athletics against the pennant-bound Bronx Bombers in Yankee Stadium. He threw seven strong innings in an impressive losing effort.

Less than three years earlier, Army Corporal Lou Brissie of the 351st Infantry, 88th Division lay unconscious in a frozen creek bed in the Apennines mountain range in northern Italy. His legs had been shredded by a German mortar shell and he was barely alive. The 88th Division had been slowly fighting its way across Italy in some of the most grueling combat

Chapter 2—Severely Damaged Limbs 49

of the campaign. Famed war correspondent Ernie Pyle wrote, "Our troops were living in almost inconceivable misery. The fertile black valleys were knee-deep in mud. Thousands of men had not been dry for weeks. Other thousands lay at night in the high mountains with the temperature below freezing and the thin snow sifting over them. They lived like men of prehistoric times, and a club would have become them more than a machine gun."

The morning of December 7, 1944, Brissie's squad suddenly came under intense enemy fire. The first shell exploded near Lou, ripping open his left leg from the knee down and also injuring his other leg. The 20-year-old soldier crawled across the snow-covered ground before collapsing beside a small stream. Nine men in his squad had been killed by the blast and Brissie was the sole survivor. He was so bloodied that several medical corpsmen passed him by before a graves registration team realized that he was still alive.

The badly wounded Brissie was rushed to a field hospital where medics found more than 30 shell fragments in his shattered limb. Doctors felt that amputation of the hopelessly mutilated leg was necessary to save his life. But Lou, barely conscious and with his senses dulled by painkillers, begged them not to. "You can't take the leg off. I'm a ballplayer," he said. The field doctors relented and shipped him to Naples where Dr. W. K. Brubaker immediately performed surgery to save his leg. Brubaker also placed him on around-the-clock treatment with the new wonder drug, penicillin, to ward off infection.

Brissie was shipped back to the States in the spring of 1945, and after 23 operations and extensive rehabilitation he was finally able to leave the hospital in April 1946. He was able to leave under his own power but with the aid of a cane. Back home in Ware Shoals, South Carolina, he contacted a doctor in nearby Greenville who worked with crippled children, and together they devised a brace designed to provide Lou with enough support to pitch again.

After a punishing regimen of running, throwing, and calisthenics to rebuild his strength and stamina, Brissie thought he was ready. His comeback attempt began inauspiciously with the Ware Shoals Riegels, a local semi-pro team. In his first appearance he was rocked for two homers and seven hits and couldn't complete the first inning. For the first time he began to fear that his dream of playing professional baseball might not be possible after all.

Lou's fastball had lost velocity because he couldn't drive hard off his injured leg and fragments of shrapnel in his pitching hand began to hurt him when he threw too many curves. But two weeks later he was back for

Lou Brissie pitches with brace on left leg

another try, this time with more encouraging results. He was learning how to deal with his limitations and was gradually gaining arm strength, control, and — most important — confidence.

Lou Brissie was born in Anderson, South Carolina on June 5, 1924, and was raised in the textile mill area around Greenville where the infamous "Shoeless Joe" Jackson lived and was still a local hero. His high school didn't field a baseball team, but by the age of 14 he was pitching and play-

Chapter 2—Severely Damaged Limbs

ing first base against grown men for the Ware Shoals mill team. After graduation from high school in April 1941 he was reportedly offered a $25,000 bonus by the Brooklyn Dodgers. He elected, however, to sign an agreement with Connie Mack's Philadelphia Athletics that would pay his way to Presbyterian College in Clinton, South Carolina. According to the agreement, he was to report to the Athletics after completing his sophomore year. But Pearl Harbor intervened, and in December 1942 Lou left college and enlisted in the Army as an 18-year-old recruit.

After Brissie's war injury, Connie Mack probably felt guilty about having convinced Lou to forego the Dodgers' bonus offer five years earlier. Providing encouragement, Mack stayed in touch with the young man during his convalescence and monitored his comeback progress. Late in the 1946 season, he invited Lou to Philadelphia to work out with the Athletics. The eager young hurler tried to do too much too soon. He'd developed osteomyelitis in his injured leg and the condition flared up during the workouts. He was admitted to Valley Forge Hospital where he was placed on strong antibiotics for several weeks. After Lou's release from the hospital, Mack regretfully sent him home for the rest of the season—undoubtedly convinced that he'd never see the big lefthander on a baseball field again.

Brissie, however, went home with renewed determination. He continued to work on his mechanics and was fitted for a lighter brace that didn't aggravate his wounded leg as much. When spring training rolled around in 1947 he was ready to go again, and Connie Mack was more than willing to give him another chance. Lou had a decent spring, primarily against minor league competition, and the Athletics offered him a spot on the roster of their Savannah farm team in the South Atlantic League (unofficially known as the Sally League). Connie told Brissie that the Savannah manager would have instructions to keep sending him out to the mound until the young pitcher himself said he had enough.

Old Connie still probably doubted that Brissie could overcome his disability, but the determined southpaw proved otherwise. He turned the league on its ear, winning 12 games in a row at one point and finishing with 23 wins against only 5 defeats and a microscopic 1.91 earned run average. He was summoned to Philadelphia at the end of the season and capped the year with his promising performance against the Yankees in his only appearance. The only downside to his spectacular season was an ominous recurrence of the infection in his leg, which sidelined him for six weeks in mid-season.

But Lou wasn't going to be a one game wonder like Bert Shepard. On April 19, 1948, the 23-year-old rookie lefthander was on the mound for

Philadelphia, all 6'4" and 215 pounds of him — not including the heavy aluminum leg brace. Facing the powerful Boston Red Sox, Lou was cruising along until Ted Williams drilled a vicious liner up the middle that struck his wounded leg just below the knee and ricocheted into the outfield. Williams reached first base and immediately headed to the mound instead of trying for extra bases. As the players gathered around him, Lou looked up at the distressed Williams and said, "Dammit Ted. Why don't you pull the ball like you're supposed to?" Amid the relieved laughter, Lou slowly got to his feet. After hobbling around a little, he resumed pitching and shut the Red Sox down for the rest of the afternoon.

Brissie was the winning pitcher that day and proceeded to become a valued member of the Philadelphia pitching staff. The surprising Athletics challenged the more talented Red Sox, Cleveland Indians, and New York Yankees for the American League pennant before ending up in fourth place. Lou ended up with a fine 14–10 won-lost record for his freshman campaign. Doubling as a starter and a reliever, he completed 11 of 25 starts and tied for the team lead with 5 saves in 14 relief efforts. His 127 strikeouts in 194 innings was the fourth highest total in the league behind all-time greats Bob Feller, Bob Lemon, and Hal Newhouser. In fact, Brissie's strikeouts-per-inning ratio was actually higher than the trio of future Hall of Famers, who pitched more in innings to rack up their higher strikeout totals. In Rookie of the Year balloting (only one award was given for both leagues in 1947 and 1948) he finished in a respectable tie for fourth place with Red Sox infielder Billy Goodman, behind shortstop Al Dark of the Boston Braves, pitcher Gene Bearden of the Indians, and outfielder Richie Ashburn of the Philadelphia Phillies.

In a 1948 *Sport Magazine* article, the legendary Grantland Rice wrote, "Venerable Connie Mack came up with one of the real finds of the year. Lou Brissie ... has captured the hearts of baseball fans everywhere by his courageous triumph over a severe leg injury and by his performance on the mound." Another reporter called him "one of the most courageous and determined players of all time."

Brissie continued his fine pitching in 1949, winning 16 and losing 11 for the fifth place Athletics. He completed 18 starts, again led the team in saves, placed among the league leaders in strikeouts-per-inning, and was named to the American League All-Star Team — although he didn't get in the game.

The Athletics plummeted to last place in 1950, losing 102 games. Primarily due to poor support, Lou's won-lost record fell to 7–19. Despite his poor winning percentage, he was the ace of the staff, leading the club's hurlers in innings pitched, earned run average, strikeouts, and saves. He completed 15 games, compiled a 4.02 earned run average, threw a pair of shutouts, and posted 8 saves. His earned run average was well below the league average and although he was primarily a starting pitcher, he placed fifth in the league in saves.

After 50 years as manager of the Athletics, Connie Mack's reign ended after the 1950 season, and in the first weeks of the 1951 campaign Lou Brissie's remarkable career with the Athletics also came to a close. In a complicated three team deal, Brissie was sent to Cleveland, dashing rookie outfielder Minnie Minoso went from the Indians to the Chicago White Sox, and Sox slugger Gus Zernial ended up with Philadelphia. Several other players were involved, but these three were the key figures in the trade.

Minoso, of course, rejuvenated the White Sox franchise and went on to have a lengthy Hall-of-Fame-type career. Zernial, who'd established the White Sox franchise home run record in 1950, led the league with 33 home runs in 1951 and bashed 191 dingers in a seven-year stint with the Athletics. But Lou Brissie was the man the Indians wanted to bolster their bullpen, and the quality of the other players involved in the transaction was an indication of the high regard for his talent in baseball circles.

Brissie enjoyed an excellent year in his first experience as a full-time reliever, finishing third in the league in saves with nine. He had another solid season in 1952, posting the lowest earned run average of his career. But the strain on his damaged leg was becoming too much to bear and he was forced to retire at the age of 29 after a disappointing 1953 effort.

Since Lou never complained and generally downplayed his disability, fans and even teammates never fully appreciated how much he suffered (Eddie Joost, a Philadelphia teammate for more than three full years, referred to Brissie's leg brace as a "shin guard" in *We Played the Game*). Osteomyelitis, the chronic condition Lou endured, is an infectious, inflammatory bone disease that results in death and separation of the surrounding tissue. It's controllable with proper treatment, but can become aggravated by a bump or bruise and quickly flare up into a full-blown inflection. Lou's awkward, chafing brace constantly aggravated the condition, sometimes sending him to the hospital for treatment between starts and insuring that he pitched in constant agony.

After leaving baseball, Lou was approached about a movie of his life, but he turned Hollywood fame and fortune down with the explanation that he wasn't really a hero and wasn't comfortable with it. Instead he devoted his life to working with young people, becoming Director of American Legion Youth Baseball for several years, where he was honored for his efforts when he stepped down. After leaving the American Legion post he coached youth sports and worked in the insurance industry. He eventually retired to North Augusta, South Carolina and in 1994 was inducted into the Sally League Hall of Fame for his one-year stint in the circuit.

Lou Brissie never enjoyed the type of career he could have had if healthy. His final tally was a mediocre 44–48 won-lost for five full seasons and parts of two others with an ordinary 4.07 lifetime earned run average. But he was iron man, completing almost half of his career starts, an amazing statistic for a man who threw every pitch in pain. In fact, his 45 complete games actually exceed his 33 career victories as a starter. He also excelled when used in relief throughout his career, winning 11 games and saving 29 in that role. In addition, he acquitted himself quite well at the plate and in the field despite his disability. His final batting average was .227, a good mark for a pitcher, and he committed only four errors in his career — none in his first two years.

But, again like Bert Shepard, Lou never felt sorry for himself. In fact, he always felt lucky just to have made it back alive from that icy creek bed in northern Italy.

LELAND VICTOR "LOU" BRISSIE
B. June 5, 1924

YEAR	TEAM	LEAGUE	G	IP	SO	BB	W	L	ERA	CG	SV
1947	Savannah	Sally	35	254	278	100	23	5	1.91	*	*
	PHILADELPHIA	AL	1	7	4	5	0	1	6.43	0	0
1948	PHILADELPHIA	AL	39	194	127	95	14	10	4.13	11	5
1949	PHILADELPHIA	AL	34	229	118	118	16	11	4.28	18	3
1950	PHILADELPHIA	AL	46	246	101	117	7	19	4.02	15	8
1951	PHIL-CLEVE	AL	56	126	53	69	4	5	3.58	1	9
1952	CLEVELAND	AL	42	83	28	34	3	2	3.48	0	2
1953	CLEVELAND	AL	16	13	5	13	0	0	7.62	0	2
MAJOR LEAGUE TOTALS			234	898	436	451	44	48	4.07	45	29

WHITEY KUROWSKI

Whitey Kurowski was another victim of osteomyelitis who had to overcome the disabling effects of the disease to play major league baseball. In Whitey's case, he had to compensate for the loss of four inches of bone in his right forearm to become an all-star third baseman for the St. Louis Cardinals in the 1940s.

It was a miracle that Kurowski was even able to play baseball. When he was seven years old, he fell off of a fence and landed in a pile of broken glass. His right arm was badly cut and he developed blood poisoning which turned into osteomyelitis. There were fears that the arm would have to be amputated, but instead doctors removed about four inches of infected bone and tissue from his ulna, the inside and longer of the two bones in the forearm. The operation saved Whitey's arm, but resulted in a deformed, misshapen limb that was several inches shorter than his left arm when he grew to adulthood.

George "Whitey" Kurowski was born on April 19, 1918, in Reading, Pennsylvania. He got his nickname early in life because his hair was already snow white as a kid. After his injury, he simply wouldn't allow his wounded arm to keep him from playing ball and developed powerful muscles to compensate for the missing bone. He played softball five nights a week and then played baseball on weekends from morning till night. In high school and American Legion baseball he started concentrating on third base despite the fact that the position requires a better throwing arm than most others.

Because his right arm was shorter than his left, the right-handed hitter had difficulty reaching pitches on the outside part of the plate. Therefore he had to crowd the dish, which caused him to frequently be plunked by inside pitches. The disfigurement also forced him to turn his right wrist over when he swung the bat, making him a dead left field hitter. He was such a pull-hitter that second basemen often played him on the shortstop side of the base when he reached the major leagues.

Kurowski's hometown of Reading was in the middle of the Pennsylvania coal mining region, and like many other young men raised in the area, Whitey wanted no part of the mines. His incentive to escape life as a miner was reinforced when his brother Frank was killed in a mine cave-in when Whitey was a teenager. Baseball seemed to be his ticket out, but professional organizations were leery of Whitey's maimed throwing arm and he initially didn't get any offers after high school. Finally in 1937 the manager of the Caruthersville team in the Class D North East Arkansas League, who was from the Reading area, gave the 19-year-old youngster a shot. A .339 batting average started him on his way and a league leading .386 mark the next year for Portsmouth in the Mid-Atlantic League solidified his status as a prospect in the St. Louis farm system.

Whitey, who'd developed into a stocky 5'11", 193-pounder with thick legs and surprising speed, spent the next three years as the regular third

Whitey Kurowski makes the play despite a disfigured right arm

baseman for the Class AAA Rochester Red Wings in the International League. In the closing weeks of the hotly contested 1941 pennant race he was called up along with Rochester teammate Stan Musial to join the parent Cardinals for the stretch run. Musial's .426 average and Kurowski's .333 mark in limited action weren't enough to enable the Cards to catch the Brooklyn Dodgers, but the two youngsters established themselves as genuine major leaguers.

In the spring of 1942, while Whitey was fighting to win his first big league job, his father died of a heart attack. The 24-year-old had to leave the team to attend to funeral arrangements in the middle of spring training, but he returned to wrestle the third base job from veteran Jimmy Brown. With Musial taking over in left field, the two rookies helped drive the Cardinals to the National League pennant and a World Series victory over the heavily favored New York Yankees.

In fact, Kurowski was the Series hero. He blasted a home run off future Hall of Famer Red Ruffing in the top of the ninth inning to break a 2–2 tie in the seventh game. After the Cardinals' victory, Whitey led the celebration by playfully ruffling the proud white mane of the Commissioner of Baseball, Judge Kenesaw Mountain Landis, and tearing National League President Ford Frick's hat to shreds. He also led the team in a rousing chorus of "Pass the Biscuits Miranda," the team's victory anthem that season.

Whitey was an integral part of a Cardinal dynasty that would bring the World Championship to St. Louis in 1942, 1944, and 1946. He was part of the first wave of young stars who emerged from the organization's vast farm system in the early 1940s, a group that included Musial, Marty Marion, Walker and Mort Cooper, Max Lanier, Ernie White, Johnny Beazley, Murray Dickson, Howie Pollet, Johnny Hopp, Ray Sanders, Harry Walker, Harry Brecheen, and others. From 1943 through 1947 Kurowski established himself as one of the finest third baseman in baseball and made the National League All-Star Team every year except 1945. He would have made it that year too, but there wasn't an All-Star Game because of World War II. He was, however, named to the Major League All-Star Team selected by the Sporting News at the end of the season.

The 1947 season was Whitey's best year, although the Cardinals had to settle for a second place finish. With future Hall of Fame teammates Musial, Schoendienst, and Enos Slaughter having off seasons, Kurowski had to carry the Cards offense much of the time. In 146 games he hit for a .310 batting average and compiled a .420 on-base percentage, second highest in the league behind batting champ Harry Walker of the Philadelphia Phillies. Whitey also slammed 27 homers, scored 108 runs, drove in 104, and walked 87 times—all career highs. In the National League Most Valuable Player voting that year, Boston Braves third baseman Bob Elliott won the league's award with figures that were remarkably similar to Kurowski's numbers. Elliott batted .317, hit 22 homers, scored 93 runs, drove in 113, and drew 87 bases on balls for the third place Braves. In addition, Elliott's .956 fielding average was only slightly better than Kurowski's .954 percentage, but for some reason Whitey finished a distant ninth in the MVP balloting.

Unfortunately, 1947 was to be Whitey's last full season as a big league baseball player. Although it was not publicized, his patched-up throwing arm had bothered him throughout his career. The condition caused pinched nerves and muscle damage and he underwent 13 operations on the arm during his career so that he could continue playing. But in 1948 his arm problems became so severe that he was limited to just 65 games in the field and a disappointing .214 batting average.

Kurowski gave it another try in 1949, but more arm problems ended his big league career at 31, an age when most players are in the midst of their prime. The Cardinals, mindful of his value to the team, kept him around for a while as a pinch hitter and utility infielder, but Whitey just couldn't throw anymore. He spent most of the 1949 season trying to rehabilitate his arm with Houston in the Texas League. When the arm failed to come around, he accepted an offer to manage the Cards' Lynchburg farm club in the Piedmont League for the 1950 season and began a long and successful career as a minor league manager and coach.

Kurowski managed in the Cardinals farm system and was a coach for the parent club for more than a decade before moving to the New York Mets organization. His career in organized baseball included a stint as skipper of his hometown Reading club in the Cleveland Indians system and ended after a few disappointing seasons in the Carolina League in 1972. After leaving baseball, he worked for Berks County as a sealer of weights and measures, retiring from that post in 1980. In retirement, Kurowski lived in Shillington, a suburb of Reading. He was an avid golfer and a tireless autograph signer, who actually took great pleasure in signing for fans. Whitey died on December 9, 1999. He was the father of four children and was survived by his wife, Joan.

For his entire major league career, Kurowski never played on a team that finished lower than second place. His lifetime batting average was a fine .286, with a career high of .323 in 1945 that tied for the fourth highest mark in the major leagues. From 1943 through 1947 he finished among the top ten in the league in home runs each season, and from 1945 through 1947 he finished among the top ten hitters in batting average, on-base percentage, slugging, total bases, and runs batted in every year. He led National League third sackers in putouts three times, in fielding twice, and in assists and double plays once. He forged a 22-game hitting streak in 1943 and was a hero of the 1946 playoff. Although known as a free swinger throughout his career, he posted respectable base on balls totals. Despite these accomplishments he was overshadowed by more illustrious teammates, and his best finish in balloting for the National League Most Valuable Player Award was a fifth place finish in 1945.

Kurowski also held the Cardinals' record for most homers in a month with twelve until Mark McGwire came along. His three years with Rochester resulted in his selection as the third baseman on the all-time Rochester Red Wing squad. Although he was basically through as an active player after the 1949 season, he made occasional minor league appearances up until the 1959 season. That year his successful pinch-hitting appearance for Billings at the age of 41 resulted in a 1.000 batting average for his final season as a player.

But Whitey's value to the Cardinals was more than just raw statistics could describe. The gritty, underrated third baseman was considered the consummate team player. Before the 1946 season, Kurowski was holding out for more money and had been approached by Mexican League representatives. The Mexican League was in the process of "raiding" major league rosters to stock a new league south of the border. Whitey took it upon himself to call a team meeting and tell his teammates that he felt honor-bound to play in St. Louis. He urged them to put the Mexican League business behind them and concentrate on winning the pennant, which they did.

Kurowski's favorite saying, "Putting 'We' ahead of 'I,'" was put to the test in the spring of 1949. During his injury-plagued 1948 season, word had filtered down through the Cardinals farm system that sore-armed Whitey Kurowski couldn't hold down the hot corner much longer.

One of the Cardinals top prospects for the job was minor leaguer Eddie Kazak, who was already a veteran of six minor league campaigns and three years of military service. Kazak, however, had been a second baseman most of his career and had only shifted to third in 1948 when Kurowski started to falter. Despite the fact that Kazak was after his job, Whitey worked hard to teach the hardhitting rookie the finer points of third base play. The Cardinals and Kurowski were rewarded when Kazak was named the National League's starting third baseman in the 1949 All-Star Game.

GEORGE JOHN "WHITEY" KUROWSKI
B. April 19, 1918 D. December 9, 1999

YEAR	TEAM	LEAGUE	G	AB	R	H	HR	RBI	AVE	SB	POS
1937	Caruthersville	Neb-Ark	107	433	125	147	3	59	.339	20	3B
1938	Portsmouth	Mid Atl	129	542	133	209	14	112	.386	34	3B
1939	Columbus	Am Ass'n	18	60	5	19	2	8	.317	2	3B
	Rochester	Internat'l	124	519	102	151	11	68	.291	13	3B
1940	Rochester	Internat'l	133	520	85	145	15	73	.279	13	3B
1941	Rochester	Internat'l	142	500	96	144	13	69	.288	21	3B
	ST. LOUIS	NL	5	9	1	3	0	2	.333	0	3B
1942	ST. LOUIS	NL	115	366	51	93	9	42	.254	7	3B
1943	ST. LOUIS	NL	139	522	69	150	13	70	.287	3	3B
1944	ST. LOUIS	NL	149	555	95	150	20	87	.270	2	3B
1945	ST. LOUIS	NL	133	511	84	165	21	102	.323	1	3B
1946	ST. LOUIS	NL	142	519	76	156	14	89	.301	2	3B
1947	ST. LOUIS	NL	146	513	108	159	27	104	.310	4	3B
1948	ST. LOUIS	NL	77	220	34	47	2	33	.214	0	3B
1949	ST. LOUIS	NL	10	14	0	2	0	0	.143	0	3B
	Houston	Texas	*	*	*	*	2	33	.233	*	3B
1950	Lynchburg	Piedmont	*	*	*	*	1	6	.286	*	3B
1953	Peoria	Three I	*	*	*	*	0	0	.200	*	PH

YEAR	TEAM	LEAGUE	G	AB	R	H	HR	RBI	AVE	SB	POS
1955	Peoria	Three I	*	*	*	*	0	0	.000	*	PH
1959	Billings	Pioneer	*	*	*	*	0	0	1.000	*	PH
MAJOR LEAGUE TOTALS			916	3229	518	925	106	529	.286	19	

EDDIE KAZAK

It's possible that Whitey Kurowski was so willing to help Eddie Kazak because they shared similar backgrounds. Kazak was also from a mining community. He was born in Steubenville, Ohio, but grew up in Muse, Pennsylvania, a tiny town outside of Pittsburgh. He and his parents and five siblings lived in a company-owned house. As a youngster, Eddie played baseball and worked in the mines along with his friend Andy Seminick, who would eventually become a star catcher for the Phillies. When Eddie was offered a contract by the Boston Braves, he had doubts about signing because he knew his family depended on the money he earned in the mines. But his father admonished him to "take anything to get out of the mines."

But the similarities between Whitey Kurowski and Eddie Kazak don't end with their mining backgrounds, their Polish ancestry, and their fair hair. Both players also shared serious problems with their throwing arms, although the origins of their ailments were very different.

Eddie Kazak, who was born Edward Tkaczuk on July 8, 1920, was actually less than two years younger than the more experienced and accomplished Kurowski. Eddie started his professional baseball career in 1940 with a perfectly sound throwing arm. During World War II, however, Eddie served as a paratrooper and combat infantryman and was bayoneted by a Nazi soldier in hand-to-hand combat in France. Later he had a part of his right elbow blown off by a shell fragment. A plastic patch was surgically inserted into his elbow to replace missing bone, but the arm was never the same.

After his release from the military Kazak worked his way up the Cardinals' minor league chain, playing for Columbus and then Rochester before joining St. Louis for a six game trial late in the 1948 season. He'd always been a solid hitter, but his fielding had held him back—particularly his throwing. His throwing arm remained stiff and he could never straighten it out despite 18 months of rehabilitation in army hospitals and years of work on the baseball field.

Under Kurowski's tutelage, Eddie beat out highly regarded Tommy

Glaviano for the Cardinals third base job in spring training. The 29-year-old rookie burned up the league at the start of the season, hitting at a .350 clip for the first two months. He not only started at third base for the National League in the All-Star Game, but also banged out two hits in two trips to the plate. Eddie faded in the second half of the season as injuries took their toll. Nevertheless, he finished with an excellent .304 batting average in 92 games.

Eddie's damaged throwing arm, however, would never be major league caliber, and the next season Glaviano captured the regular job and went on to have a solid season. But Kazak was a productive hitter off the bench in 1950, leading the league in pinch-hitting appearances. In 1951 however, he found himself back in the minor leagues. Like his predecessor, Whitey Kurowski, his major league career was over at the age of 31 due to a bum arm.

Except for a brief big league trial in 1952, Eddie Kazak found himself playing out the string as a career minor leaguer. He found a home in San Diego and became a Pacific Coast League legend, playing in the minor leagues until he was 40 years old. After retirement he lived in Austin, Texas, where he died on December 15, 1999, less than a week after his mentor Whitey Kurowski's death.

Whitey Kurowski and Eddie Kazak were two similar players from similar backgrounds whose lives were ironically intertwined. Both managed to beat the odds and overcome severe disabilities that would have stopped most men and both managed to enjoy long and rewarding professional baseball careers.

Kurowski probably spoke for both of them when he said, "I was fortunate enough just to be able to play. It's the dream of every kid, and I was able to fill that dream. That was enough for me."

EDWARD TERRANCE KAZAK

(born Edward Terrance Tkaczuk)
B. June 18, 1920 D. December 15, 1999

YEAR	TEAM	LEAGUE	G	AB	R	H	HR	RBI	AVE	SB	POS
1940	Valdosta	Ga-Fla	130	528	83	154	4	101	.292	7	2B
1941	Albany	Ga-Fla	135	584	133	221	2	113	.378	5	2B
1942	Houston	Texas	118	424	44	109	5	51	.257	4	2B
1943-45	ST. LOUIS	NL	(In Military Service)								
1946	Columbus	Sally	124	483	74	144	14	73	.298	7	2B
1947	Rochester	Internat'l	12	32	2	4	0	1	.125	0	3B

YEAR	TEAM	LEAGUE	G	AB	R	H	HR	RBI	AVE	SB	POS
	Omaha	Western	93	347	83	113	20	88	.326	4	2B
1948	Rochester	Internat'l	142	508	72	157	12	85	.309	6	3B
	ST. LOUIS	NL	6	22	1	6	0	2	.273	0	3B
1949	ST. LOUIS	NL	92	326	43	99	6	42	.304	0	3B-2B
1950	ST. LOUIS	NL	93	207	21	53	5	23	.256	0	3B
1951	ST. LOUIS	NL	11	33	2	6	0	4	.182	0	3B
	Houston	Texas	*	*	*	*	13	65	.304	*	INF
1952	ST. LOU-CINC	NL	16	17	2	1	0	0	.059	0	3B-1B
	Buffalo	Internat'l	*	*	*	*	6	16	.315	*	INF
1953	Buffalo	Internat'l	*	*	*	*	13	59	.267	*	INF
1954	Beaumont	Texas	*	*	*	*	19	104	.344	*	INF
1955	San Diego	Pac Coast	*	*	*	*	12	67	.302	*	INF
1956	San Diego	Pac Coast	*	*	*	*	18	83	.305	*	INF
1957	San Diego	Pac Coast	*	*	*	*	4	50	.289	*	INF
1958	SD-Seattle	Pac Coast	*	*	*	*	7	50	.334	2	INF
1959	Seattle	Pac Coast	*	*	*	*	4	38	.256	*	INF
	Miami	Internat'l	*	*	*	*	0	0	.346	*	INF
1960	Austin	Texas	*	*	*	*	0	0	.250	*	INF
MAJOR LEAGUE TOTALS			218	605	69	165	11	71	.273	0	

CHARLEY GELBERT

Another St. Louis Cardinal infielder, a predecessor to Whitey Kurowski at third base, also performed with a significant portion of bone missing from one of his limbs. Charley Gelbert played major league baseball for several years after a shotgun blast blew away several inches of bone, nerve, and posterior artery from his left leg. In fact, his accomplishment was considered so incredible it was featured in *Ripley's Believe It or Not.*

The fateful accident occurred in November 1932 when the 26-year-old Gelbert and several companions were hunting near his Fayetteville, Pennsylvania, home. Near the end of the day Charley snagged his foot on a vine and stumbled to the ground. His shotgun discharged into his left leg about four inches above the ankle. Fortunately the gun was pressed right up against his leg when it fired. If it had been a few inches away, Charley's foot would have been blown off. As it was, the charge went all the way through his leg, almost completely destroying the sheath of tendons extending down from the upper leg muscles to the ankle and shooting away a section of the fibula, the smaller of the two leg bones.

It was initially feared that amputation would be necessary, but Charley fought tenaciously to keep the leg. Everything depended on how much circulation was left. The first night was critical — if the foot grew cold, it would have to come off to prevent gangrene. Charley's wife Jerri spent a long, sleepless night massaging the injured foot to make sure it stayed warm. Fortunately the little bit of artery that remained intact was enough to provide an adequate supply of blood.

Charley remained hospitalized for more than three months. Four inches of posterior artery and nerve were completely destroyed and the leg was supported only by the big bone and the single remaining blood-supplying tendon. The fibula hung suspended from the knee area, totally disconnected from the foot. It was almost two years before he could walk without the aid of a cane or crutches and he limped around with an open wound for two and a half years.

At the time of the injury, Gelbert was one of the top shortstops in the National League. The right-handed hitting infielder had joined the Cardinals in 1929 after a sensational season at Rochester. The Cards had won the 1928 National League pennant with aging future Hall of Famer Rabbit Maranville at the key shortstop position, but Rabbit was dispatched to the Boston Braves to make room for Gelbert. Although somewhat error prone, Charley's fielding was spectacular overall, and his .262 batting average in 1929 wasn't bad for a rookie.

The Cardinals fell to fourth place in Gelbert's first season as their regular shortstop, but they rebounded to recapture the pennant in his second year. Manning the important second spot in the batting order, Charley improved his batting average to .304, scored 92 times, and drove in 72 runs. He starred in the World Series with a .353 batting average and a perfect fielding mark, although the Cardinals were downed in six games by the powerful Philadelphia Athletics.

In 1931 Gelbert hit .289 and drastically reduced his errors in the field, but he really came of age in the World Series rematch with the Athletics. While teammate Pepper Martin was earning the nickname "The Wild Horse of the Osage" by belting out a Series record 12 hits and running wild on the bases, Gelbert took charge on defense. He set records for shortstops in a seven game series by accepting 42 chances, including six double plays, without an error as the underdog Cardinals denied the mighty Athletics their third straight championship.

The 1932 season was a disappointing one for Gelbert and the Cardinals. Charley's average fell to .268 and St. Louis tumbled all the way to seventh place. But the outlook was far from grim. The club was undergoing a facelift. Dizzy Dean had been called up from Houston to solidify the pitching staff. Ripper Collins supplanted veteran Jim Bottomley at first base, and Joe Medwick came up late in the year to take over left field. Gelbert figured to be a key man in the anticipated resurgence. He was still

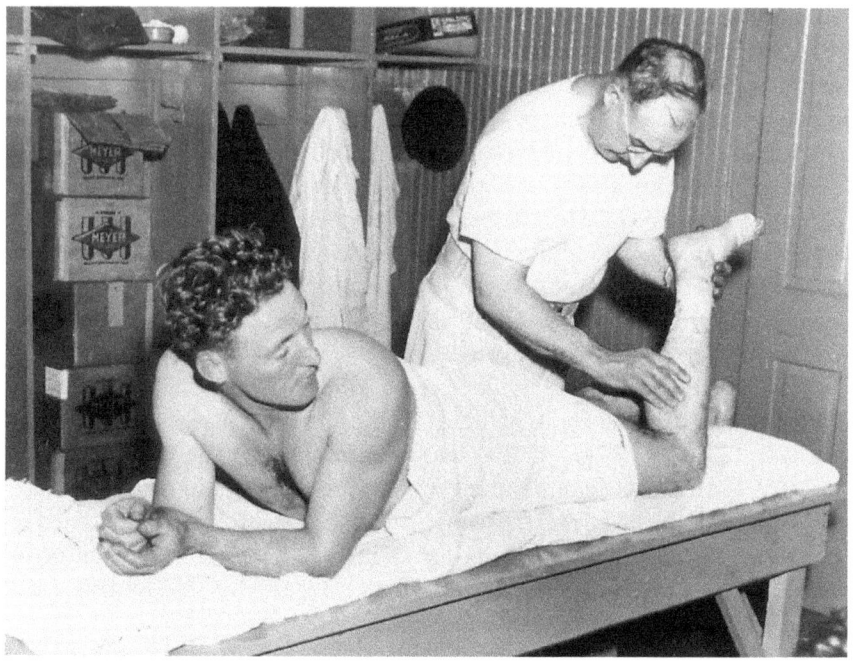

Charley Gelbert receives therapy on his damaged leg

only 26 years old and was already established as one of the game's elite shortstops. His future appeared brilliant until the unfortunate hunting mishap.

After the accident, physicians gave Gelbert "a chance" of regaining full use of his injured leg. But that meant walking without the use of a cane — not resuming a career as a professional baseball player. No one really believed he would play ball again.

But Charley was made of tough stuff. His father had been an All-American football star at the University of Pennsylvania and had even been picked by the legendary Walter Camp as an end on Camp's all-time All-American Team. Charley's given name was Magnus Ott Gelbert, but he decided to use his father's name. Young Charley, who was born January 26, 1906, in Scranton, Pennsylvania, was also a football star in college at Lebannon Valley, despite packing only about 170 pounds on his 5'11" frame. He signed with the Cardinals in 1926 while still in college and made it to the big leagues after only two years in the minors.

The loss of their brilliant young shortstop was a tremendous blow to the Cardinals that probably cost them the 1933 National League pennant. When Gelbert went down, the Cardinals tried to replace him by moving star second baseman Frankie Frisch to shortstop and plugging veteran slugger Rogers Hornsby, who they had signed in the off-season, in at second. The flaw in the plan soon became painfully apparent. Although still a great hitter, the leg-weary 37-year-old Hornsby could no longer handle second base, while the versatile Frisch, who was 34 years old himself, was clearly out of place at shortstop.

On May 17, 1933, the Cardinals made one of the most significant trades in their history. They acquired flashy-fielding, loudmouthed Leo Durocher from the Cincinnati Reds along with a couple of minor leaguers for reliable starting pitcher Paul Derringer and two lesser lights, infielder Sparky Adams and pitcher Allyn Stout. The antagonistic Durocher had been jettisoned to Cincinnati, baseball's Siberia at the time, by the New York Yankees after the 1929 season. There were rumors that the young infielder had run afoul of Babe Ruth by stealing from the Babe. He'd spent three seasons in obscurity with the second division–dwelling Reds and his career was going nowhere. But that quickly changed when the desperate Cardinals engineered the deal for the 27-year-old shortstop. Although Derringer won 161 games in 10 years with the Reds, Durocher expertly filled the Cardinals' shortstop void. The flamboyant infielder enjoyed being in the public eye again and his combative nature earned him a reputation that would ultimately gain him access to the managerial ranks. Eventually "Leo the Lip" would become one of the most famous, successful, and widely despised managers of all time.

After a disastrous start the Cardinals came on strong after Frisch replaced Gabby Street as manager in the second half of the 1933 campaign. They finished in fifth place, but were only nine games behind the pennant-winning New York Giants.

Of course the Cardinals won it all in 1934. In a thrilling pennant race they nosed out the Giants with the help of the Brooklyn Dodgers. Before the season, Giants manager Bill Terry had responded to a question about the Dodgers' pennant chances with the flippant response, "Is Brooklyn still in the league?" The Dodgers, who never really needed an excuse to despise their crosstown rivals, exacted revenge by beating the Giants at home the last two games of the year to hand the pennant to St. Louis. The Cardinals then beat the Detroit Tigers in a wild seven game World Series, which featured angry Tiger fans showering left fielder Joe Medwick with debris in the late innings of the final game.

All but forgotten amid all the excitement was former teammate Charley Gelbert, who was quietly recovering from his wounds and slowly working to regain strength in his all-but-ruined leg.

But after being away from the game for two years, the 29-year-old

Gelbert was a surprise participant when the Cardinals' 1935 spring training camp got underway. He sported a special rubber stocking, which he had designed himself, to provide support for the damaged leg. He cavorted around the infield with the scrubs, pitched batting practice, and hustled his head off—doing anything to make himself useful.

The 1935 edition of the Cardinals was a different team than the underachieving 1932 squad Gelbert had last played for. The defending World Champions were called the "Gashouse Gang," a colorful, enduring nickname earned with their aggressive, down-and-dirty style of play. Veteran second baseman Frisch was now the manager, and the Dean brothers, Dizzy and Paul, anchored the pitching staff. Young Bill DeLancey did most of the catching, while Frisch, Medwick, Collins, Martin, Ernie Orsatti and Jack Rothrock supplied the offensive firepower.

Of course, Durocher was firmly entrenched at shortstop, but after an impressive spring performance the Cardinals decided to carry the stouthearted Gelbert as a utility infielder. Because of his damaged leg, Charley still had trouble starting and stopping quickly and he didn't have enough spring in the remaining leg muscles to jump well. But he still had a great pair of hands and a strong accurate throwing arm.

Early in the year, however, the decision to keep Gelbert looked like little more than an act of compassion. In his first regular season action, his seventh inning error allowed the winning run in a Cardinal loss to the Philadelphia Phillies. But Charley refused to give up and the leg gradually got stronger. He generally filled in for Durocher, who was frequently pulled for a pinch hitter, but his range was limited at shortstop. Gelbert finally got a chance to shine when third baseman Pepper Martin came down with a sore arm in midseason. Charley begged for the chance to fill in for Pepper and performed brilliantly at the hot corner where range is not as critical as it is at shortstop. After Martin returned, Charley backed him up for the rest of the season, often replacing him for defensive purposes. With his strong arm and sure hands he fielded everything hit his way and turned in many spectacular plays. He also contributed several clutch hits and left many observers with the opinion that he was actually a better hitter than before the injury. For the 1935 season he hit a solid .292 in 62 games as a utility infielder and was selected as the "Most Courageous Athlete" in the country by the Philadelphia Sport Writer's Association.

Charley's play in 1935 was so impressive that the Cardinals allowed Pepper Martin to return to the outfield the next year, where he was more comfortable, and installed the 30-year-old hero at third base. Gelbert was more-or-less the regular third baseman in 1936 and also filled in some at shortstop, but the increased demands of regular duty on his gimpy leg dropped his batting average to .229 for 93 games.

Prior to the 1937 season, Gelbert was sold to the Cincinnati Reds where he backed up young Billy Myers at shortstop. His hitting was awful and he was waived to Detroit late in the year. His composite average was a paltry .161 for the season and he was sent to the minor leagues by the Tigers after the season.

But Charley Gelbert had another comeback left in him. The 1938 season found the 32-year-old infielder manning third base for the Toledo Mud Hens, where he hit .284 and drove in an impressive 91 runs. His outstanding performance led to another major league chance in 1939 with the Washington Senators in the American League. He served the Senators as a valuable sub and even did a little pitching for them until the contending Boston Red Sox acquired him late in the 1940 season to fill at third base. Charley was through as a major leaguer after the 1940 season, but hung on for two more seasons in the high minors.

During his playing career, Charley had devoted his off-seasons to coaching at Gettysburg College in Pennsylvania. After he retired from the active ranks, he turned to working with youngsters fulltime and became a highly successful baseball coach for Lafayette College in Pennsylvania. Over a 21-year stretch his team took seven postseason tournaments and five District II titles. Of course, Charley still wanted to be on the field. During his career at Lafayette he battled for and eventually won the right to allow college coaches to man the coaching lines during games. Gelbert died on January 13, 1967, in Easton, Pennsylvania.

Although Charley Gelbert never regained his pre-injury status as a major league star, his comeback to play five seasons at the major league level after his devastating injury was nothing short of miraculous.

In 1941 he was billed in *Ripley's Believe It or Not* as the man who "played 239 major league games with a broken leg."

CHARLES MAGNUS GELBERT
(born Magnus Ott Gelbert)
B. January 26, 1906 D. January 13, 1967

YEAR	TEAM	LEAGUE	G	AB	R	H	HR	RBI	AVE	SB	POS
1926	Syracuse	Internat'l	1	4	*	1	*	*	.250	*	SS
1927	Syracuse	Internat'l	5	*	*	*	*	*	.333	*	SS
	Topeka	Western	45	161	30	46	*	*	.286	6	SS

YEAR	TEAM	LEAGUE	G	AB	R	H	HR	RBI	AVE	SB	POS
1928	Rochester	Internat'l	164	573	145	195	*	*	.340	30	SS
1929	ST. LOUIS	NL	146	512	60	134	3	65	.262	8	SS
1930	ST. LOUIS	NL	139	513	92	156	3	72	.304	6	SS
1931	ST. LOUIS	NL	131	447	61	129	1	62	.289	7	SS
1932	ST. LOUIS	NL	122	455	60	122	1	45	.268	8	SS
1933-34	ST. LOUIS	NL (Did Not Play — Voluntarily Retired Due to Injury)									
1935	ST. LOUIS	NL	62	168	24	49	2	21	.292	0	3B-SS
1936	ST. LOUIS	NL	93	280	33	64	3	27	.229	2	3B-SS
1937	CINCINNATI	NL	43	114	12	22	1	13	.193	1	SS-2B
	DETROIT	AL	20	47	4	4	0	1	.085	0	SS
1938	Toledo	Am Ass'n	143	490	99	137	8	91	.284	7	3B
1939	WASHINGTON	AL	68	188	36	48	3	29	.255	2	SS-3B
1940	WAS-BOSTON	AL	52	145	16	38	0	15	.262	0	3B-SS-P
1941	Louisville	Am Ass'n	40	74	8	20	0	10	.270	1	SS-P
1942	Montreal	Internat'l	*	*	*	*	2	23	.217	*	INF
MAJOR LEAGUE TOTALS			876	2869	398	766	17	350	.267	34	

BO JACKSON

    Bo Jackson always seemed to be doing the impossible. Whether on the gridiron or the diamond, Bo was always doing things no one had done before. For an incredible six year period from 1985 to 1990, Jackson was the most spectacular athlete in the world. During that period, Bo won the Heisman Trophy in college and was named to both Major League Baseball and the National Football League All-Star Teams.

    Yet Bo's most amazing athletic accomplishment was returning from total hip replacement surgery to play major league baseball for two seasons with an artificial hip.

    In 1986 the skeptics winked when the Heisman Trophy winner said he was going to play professional baseball instead of football. But by the end of the year he was in the major leagues with the Kansas City Royals. The next season he was in the Royals regular lineup and two years later he was the Most Valuable Player in the Major League All-Star Game.

    In 1987 the experts scoffed when Bo announced that he was going to play football as an off-season "hobby." But he rushed for more than 200 yards in his fifth game and was named to the All-Rookie team despite playing in only seven contests. By the end of his third season he'd become the first National Football League player to make two 90-yard touchdown runs from the line of scrimmage, and the next year he was named to the Pro Bowl team.

Chapter 2—Severely Damaged Limbs

In 1992, when Bo vowed that he would resume his professional baseball career after hip replacement surgery, the doubters should have known better. After all, Bo had made a habit of doing the impossible. But playing a demanding professional sport on an artificial joint just didn't seem possible, even for Bo Jackson.

Jackson was the first athlete to star in two major sports simultaneously. As a running back he was often compared to the legendary Jim Brown. As a baseball player he was an original. No one played the game like Bo. He simply overpowered a game normally ruled by timing, reflexes, and coordination. His hitting couldn't be compared to sweet-swinging Hank Aaron. Bo just smashed the ball. His fielding or base running couldn't be compared to the instinctive Willie Mays. Bo just outran the ball.

When Bo first talked about becoming a professional baseball player after his senior year at Auburn University, most of the sporting world assumed he was just posturing to gain a more lucrative pro football contract. Not that he wasn't a promising baseball player. He'd been drafted in the second round by the New York Yankees out of high school, but opted for college football. As a junior, the right-handed hitting outfielder batted .401 for the Auburn baseball squad. However, he quit in the middle of his senior season with a mediocre .246 batting average, casting additional doubts about the depth of his interest in the national pastime.

But Bo was serious about a career in baseball. He turned down a guaranteed $2 million offer from football's Tampa Bay Buccaneers to sign a $200,000 baseball contract with Kansas City. He started his baseball career with the Memphis Chicks, a Kansas City farm club, in 1986 and was promoted to the parent Royals late in the season after only 53 minor league games.

Bo won the Royals regular left field job in the spring of 1987 and had a surprising total of 18 homers at the all-star break when he announced that he intended to play football for the Los Angeles Raiders in the fall. The press howled at his decision, as well as his unfortunate choice of words. Bo told reporters that his number one priority was still baseball; he'd just be adding football to his many off-season hobbies—like fishing and hunting.

More than a few pro football players were deeply offended. A Washington Redskins linebacker threatened, "I'll put a good lick on him and see how he likes his new hobby." Even his new Raiders teammate Howie Long remarked, "Bo must have had a frontal and rear lobotomy."

The reaction of the baseball world was even more intense. They were afraid they'd lost Bo, who had already developed into a terrific gate attrac-

Bo Jackson hitting with an artificial hip

tion. Thomas Boswell, considered one of the most insightful sportswriters around, wrote, "To be a great baseball player you need a little humility. And that, to be blunt, is why Bo Jackson is heading for the door. If he has any significant success in cleats, you'll never see him back in spikes."

Baseball writers and officials became more convinced that Bo would abandon baseball when he slumped during the second half of the 1987 season and lost his regular left field job. He finished his first full campaign in the majors with an impressive 22 homers, but hit a lowly .235 and struck out 158 times in only 396 at-bats.

The fear that Bo would not return to the Royals continued to grow when he experienced immediate success in professional football. He gained 14 yards on his first carry and ran for 98 yards and a touchdown in his first home game. The next week in Seattle, his defining moment as a professional football player occurred when he simply ran over highly touted linebacker Brian Bosworth for a touchdown. He also had a run of 91 yards from scrimmage and finished with 221 yards rushing in 18 carries for the day. Although a sprained ankle ended his season early, he averaged almost seven yards per carry and received considerable support for the league's Rookie of the Year honor despite playing less than half of the schedule.

But Bo was true to his word. He returned to the Royals and concentrated on baseball. His batting average and slugging percentage improved every year from 1986 through 1990 as did his ratio of homers per at-bat.

His popularity crested in 1989 when a spectacular first half made him an overwhelming choice for the American League All-Star Team. He led off the classic with a tremendous 448-foot home run and was named the game's Most Valuable Player. Bo's all-star feats coincided with the introduction of the fabulously successful "Bo Knows" advertising campaign. Bo had already become a marketing icon the year before when he signed a lucrative contract to promote Nike shoes. The "Bo Knows" campaign capitalized on the young star's habit of referring to himself in the third person. It became his signature phrase and part of the era's pop vocabulary.

Until slowed by nagging leg injuries later in the 1989 season, it looked like Bo might join Jose Canseco as the only major leaguer to hit 40 homers and steal 40 bases in the same season, but he missed significant playing time in the last half of the year and finished with 32 homers and 26 steals. He also drove in 105 runs in only 135 games. The next year, more injuries limited him to 111 games, but he raised his batting average to .272 and belted 28 homers. His slugging average and home run percentage were both the fourth highest in the league.

Jackson's progress in professional football was equally impressive. When he made the 1990–1991 Pro Bowl team, he became the first athlete to be selected as an All-Star in two major sports. Unfortunately, he would never play in professional football's all-star extravaganza.

Bo Jackson's illustrious career as a two-sport star ended suddenly on January 13, 1991 when he injured his left hip on routine play during a Raiders playoff victory over the Cincinnati Bengals. Initially the injury wasn't considered that serious, but it didn't respond to treatment. A condition known as a vascular necrosis developed which caused the cartilage and bone around the partially crushed hip joint to deteriorate.

The severity of the injury didn't really register with the public until the Royals unconditionally released Bo in the spring of 1991. The Chicago White Sox subsequently signed him as a long-term rehabilitation project and publicity magnet. He even managed to get into 23 late season games with the Sox in 1991, but the results were disappointing.

In the off-season, Bo undertook a rigorous conditioning program designed to build up the surrounding muscles to compensate for the damaged hip. It was another advertising coup as Nike built a campaign around Bo's rehabilitation efforts. But when he reported to the White Sox 1992 spring training camp, it soon became painfully evident that his damaged hip would not permit him to perform at the big league level.

Bo returned to the disabled list and underwent an operation to replace his ruined hip joint with an artificial ball and socket device. The *New York Times* carried an article thanking Bo for the memories and bidding him a warm farewell. Even Bo had doubts. In the *Times* article he was quoted as saying he may have had his last at-bat in the major leagues.

Hip replacement surgery is a commonplace modern medical procedure, usually performed to restore mobility for senior citizens. The medical prognosis was that Bo would probably be able to run with the artificial hip, but not like a major leaguer. There were encouraging stories of beer league softball players and ballet dancers continuing to perform after hip replacement, but no one had ever exposed an artificial hip joint to the rigors of professional sports.

The 6'1" 225-pound Jackson would put the prosthesis to the ultimate test. His new rehabilitation program consisted of more than 10,000 pushups, 15,000 sit-ups, and 35,000 hip exercise repetitions in the five months before he reported to the White Sox 1993 spring training camp.

The 30-year-old superstar made the roster, and his first regular season appearance with his bionic hip was one of the most dramatic events in the annals of sports. Bo came to the plate as a pinch hitter in the sixth inning of the Sox home opener against the Yankees and blasted a home run over the right field fence with his first swing of the bat. Fireworks exploded overhead and pandemonium reigned as Jackson triumphantly circled the bases. The roaring crowd demanded a curtain call and Bo came out of the dugout for another standing ovation. He recovered the home run ball and later had it bronzed and affixed to his mother's gravestone.

Bo always maintained that the death of his mother in 1992 gave him the strength to overcome his disability. She was the backbone of the family which lacked a father figure much of the time. Bo was born and raised in the small town of Bessemer, Alabama. He came into the world on November 30, 1962, the eighth of ten children. His real name is Vince Edward Jackson, named after the star of the Ben Casey soap opera, Vince Edwards. As a youngster he was so wild he was called "boar hog" which was eventually shortened to "Bo."

The heroic home run was the highlight of Bo's comeback. Although he'd lost his tremendous speed, his power was still imposing and he became a valuable part-time player. Even with two good hips Bo had never been a polished outfielder, yet he played 47 games in the outfield in 1993 and managed to post the highest fielding average of his career. He also served as the designated hitter in 36 contests and ended up with 16 homers in 284 trips to the plate. His batting average, however, was only .232 and he fanned 106 times.

The White Sox captured the 1993 American League Western Division Championship and faced the Toronto Blue Jays in the League Championship Series. The Sox lost in six games, due partly to Bo's abysmal performance. He was hitless in ten at-bats and struck out six times. The scouting report was that the artificial hip made him too stiff at the plate and he wasn't able to bend down enough to hit the low strike.

Bo became a free agent and signed with the California Angels for the 1994 season. Platooning in left field with rookie Jim Edmonds, he enjoyed a highly productive year. He hit a career high .279, despite striking out more than a third of the time, and blasted 13 homers in only 201 plate appearances. His power totals projected to 39 homers and a gaudy 129 runs batted in over a full season of 600 at-bats.

In contrast to the rest of his incredible career, Bo's retirement from professional baseball was a nonevent. The 1994 season was suspended at the two-thirds point by a labor strike which spilled over into spring training and wasn't settled until shortly before the traditional opening day. Amid the furor over arranging a new schedule, hastily organizing mini training camps, and negotiating of a backlog of contracts, 32-year-old Bo Jackson officially retired to pursue, among other things, an acting career.

Jackson ended his baseball career with a .250 lifetime batting average and 147 home runs in 694 major league games. But Bo could never be adequately measured by mere statistics. In the introduction to Bo's autobiography *Bo Knows Bo*, which came out just before his devastating injury in 1990, Royals great George Brett starts out with the statement, "Bo Jackson is my hero." Brett goes on to explain, "When he's at the top of his game, it's a sight to see. It's beyond your wildest dreams. It's beyond *my* wildest dreams." Noteworthy praise, coming from a man who won American League batting titles in three different decades and was elected to the Baseball Hall of Fame in his first year of eligibility.

The only Hall of Fame honor that has come Bo's way, however, is a 1998 selection to the College Football Hall of Fame. His aborted baseball career is a monument to unfulfilled promise. His successful comeback to play baseball at the major league level with an artificial hip shows how great he could have been.

Bo was the first to man to play professional baseball with an artificial hip and will probably remain the only one for some time. The medical profession is now cautioning hip replacement candidates that the artificial joints do not last forever and are not designed for twisting, turning, high impact activities. At a press briefing for the 2002 annual meeting of the American Academy of Orthopedic Surgeons, Dr. Arlen Hanssen of the Mayo Clinic said that when Jackson "hit a home run in his first at-bat after having total hip replacement, it was an orthopedic surgeon's worst nightmare."

Although promising new materials are being developed, 10 to 20 years is still considered a reasonable estimate for the life expectancy of an artificial hip under optimal conditions. Re-replacements are performed, of course, but the problem with them is that more bone is lost with each procedure so the life of the succeeding joint is shortened every time another replacement procedure is performed.

"Surgically implanting replacement hips or knees in elite athletes and sending them back to the playing field is questionable medical practice and most orthopedic surgeons will not do it," said Dr. Hanssen.

Although there's been no official announcement, Jackson is presumed to no longer be on his first replacement joint. Star outfielder Albert Belle recently developed a hip condition similar to Bo's and elected to retire from the game at the age of 34 rather than undergo replacement surgery. He reportedly consulted with Bo before making the decision.

When Bo chose baseball coming out of college, he said it was because he liked the idea of a long career and hated the idea of a crippling injury.

If only Bo had known.

VINCENT EDWARD "BO" JACKSON
B. November 30, 1962

YEAR	TEAM	LEAGUE	G	AB	R	H	HR	RBI	AVE	SB	POS
1986	Memphis	Southern	53	184	30	51	7	25	.277	3	OF
	KANSAS CITY	AL	25	82	9	17	2	9	.207	3	OF
1987	KANSAS CITY	AL	116	396	46	93	22	53	.235	10	OF
1988	KANSAS CITY	AL	124	439	63	108	25	68	.246	27	OF
1989	KANSAS CITY	AL	135	515	86	132	32	105	.256	26	OF
1990	KANSAS CITY	AL	111	405	74	110	28	78	.272	15	OF
1991	Sarasota	Fla State	2	6	1	2	0	2	.333	0	DH
	Birmingham	Southern	4	13	2	4	0	0	.308	1	DH
	CHICAGO	AL	23	71	8	16	3	14	.225	0	DH
1992	CHICAGO	AL	(Did Not Play — Disabled List)								
1993	CHICAGO	AL	85	284	32	66	16	45	.232	0	OF-DH
1994	CALIFORNIA	AL	75	201	23	56	13	43	.279	1	OF-DH
MAJOR LEAGUE TOTALS			694	2393	341	598	141	415	.250	82	

DAVE DRAVECKY

Although it was to be short-lived, Dave Dravecky of the San Francisco Giants made one of the greatest comebacks of all time. He came back to pitch in the major leagues less than a year after undergoing radical cancer surgery in which half of the deltoid muscle was removed from his pitching arm.

Dravecky underwent the operation to remove a cancerous tumor from his left arm on October 7, 1988. The operating surgeon was brutally frank with Dave about his chances of returning to professional baseball after the operation. "My greatest hope is that after intensive therapy you will regain a normal range of motion and be able to play catch with your son in your backyard," he said.

Yet on August 10, 1989, Dravecky returned to the mound to face the Cincinnati Reds and shut them down for seven innings, giving up a single bloop hit. He finally tired in the eighth and was chased from the mound, but the Giants hung on to win 4 to 3 and preserve his victory. Veteran Giants manager Roger Craig, who'd earned his baseball spurs during some exciting times with the legendary Brooklyn Dodgers, called it the most emotional baseball game he'd ever seen.

Unfortunately, Dave's next appearance on the mound would end in tragedy. On August 15 he started against the Montreal Expos under their domed stadium and after five innings he'd held them to three hits and hadn't allowed a run. But in the top of the sixth, the weakened humerus bone in his left arm snapped on a pitch to Tim Raines. At the time, doctors thought that the bone just hadn't had enough time to return to full strength and with time it would heal and allow Dravecky to return to the mound. But the 33-year-old lefthander would never take the mound again.

Dave Dravecky was born in Youngstown, Ohio, on February 14, 1956. He was raised in Youngstown, met his future wife Janice there while in high school, and attended Youngstown State University. He'd become a Californian while with the San Diego Padres, but moved back to his hometown after the 1987 season.

Though many considered it a miracle that Dravecky was able to resume pitching after his surgery, Dave always considered the fact that he made the major leagues at all to be a minor miracle in itself. He was never considered a top prospect. The 6'1", 195-pound southpaw originally signed with the Pittsburgh Pirates organization, but didn't see his first big time action until he was traded to San Diego in 1982. After pitching effectively in relief his rookie season, Dravecky joined the Padres starting rotation in 1983 and won a career high 14 games.

Dave Dravecky — cancer survivor

The next season, Dave played a key role in the Padres first National League pennant. He started 14 times and made 36 appearances out of the bullpen, winning 9 games and finishing with a strong 2.93 earned run average. He starred in postseason play, pitching 10 scoreless innings in relief.

Dravecky returned to the Padres rotation in 1985, winning 13 games and posting another 2.93 earned run average in a career high 214 innings. His won-lost mark fell to 9–11 in 1986, but he still finished with a fine 3.07 earned run mark. In 1987 he was being used primarily in relief and his won-lost record was only 3–7

Chapter 2—Severely Damaged Limbs

when he was traded to the Giants in a mid-season swap along with outfielder Kevin Mitchell and pitcher Craig Lefferts for enigmatic third baseman Chris Brown, future Cy Young winner Mark Davis, and a couple of lesser lights.

The trade keyed the Giants charge to the 1987 Western Division title as Mitchell starred in place of Brown at third base and Dravecky helped stabilize the starting rotation with seven victories against five losses and a 3.20 earned run average. In the League Championship Series against the St. Louis Cardinals, Dravecky fired a masterful two-hit shutout to win game number two and even the series. But he was the loser in game six despite giving up only one run in six innings, and the Giants lost in seven games.

Dave began the 1988 season full of optimism after a solid spring training performance. He got the opening day honors and fired a three-hitter, but his season quickly turned sour as his shoulder began to ache and he had trouble getting his arm loose. He pitched only six times after his opening day masterpiece before undergoing arthroscopic shoulder surgery in June.

The previous year Dravecky had noticed a small lump on his throwing arm about the size of a quarter. Late in the season he'd brought it to the attention of the Giants trainer who told him not to worry about it. Nevertheless, Dave decided to have it tested in the off-season, but a magnetic resonance image (MRI) procedure indicated that the growth was benign. He'd been advised to have it checked again in six months. Amazingly, the medical team paid scant attention to the mysterious lump while treating Dravecky's shoulder problem, a circumstance that would later prove disastrous.

Dave began rehabilitation immediately after surgery, but something was still wrong. His arm was killing him and he couldn't throw hard enough to break a pane of glass. Later that season, he attempted to pitch on a minor league rehab assignment, but was shut down for the year when the arm failed to come around.

By the end of the 1988 season, the lump on Dravecky's arm had grown to the size of about half of a golf ball. The Giants trainer told Dave that he thought the lump only looked bigger because the surrounding muscles had atrophied from the enforced layoff. Fortunately, Dravecky decided to have it looked at again and got his first indication that the curious mass could be cancerous. A follow-up biopsy identified the growth as a fibrous desmoid tumor. It was not considered life threatening, but it was certainly a threat to Dravecky's baseball career.

News of Dravecky's ailment was a severe blow to the Giants. With

Dravecky on the disabled list for most of the 1988 season, the Giants tumbled to fourth place in National League Western Division. They'd been heavily counting on a comeback by the lefty starter in 1989.

Instead, Dravecky underwent off-season surgery for the removal of the tumor. Along with the tumor, the surgeon would have to remove at least half of the deltoid muscle, rendering the remaining muscle almost useless. The deltoid is one of the three most powerful muscles in the arm. It's the muscle at the front of the upper arm, the one that body builders clench to show off their strength. Due to the position of the tumor and the need to ensure that every single cancerous cell was destroyed, a wide margin around the tumor had to be removed. The tumor actually sat on the humerus bone, so a procedure was used whereby the bone was scraped and frozen with liquid nitrogen to kill all living cells—including bone cells. As a result, the bone would be brittle for a time, but it was believed that the destroyed cells would eventually regenerate and the bone would regain full strength.

Nearly eleven hours after he'd been wheeled into the operating room Dravecky was moved to recovery, but his ordeal wasn't over. Complications arose due to the length of the surgery and he had to undergo the knife again to restore circulation in his leg. Afterward the surgeon repeated his grim prognosis to Dave's wife, Janice. "Short of a miracle," he said, "he will never pitch again."

The "miracle" started two weeks after surgery when Dravecky displayed a remarkable range of motion in his arm. The virtual loss of the deltoid muscle had been expected to drastically effect certain kinds of movement. It was only hoped that he would eventually be able to lift his arm over his head, but to the doctor's surprise Dave was able to lift his left arm straight over his head two weeks after surgery. A few weeks later he was able to duplicate his pitching motion and he began to feel the first faint stirring of hope that he would actually pitch again someday

The doctors were still understandably cautious. It wasn't until mid-March, about two weeks before the start of the 1989 baseball season, that Dave was permitted to pick up a baseball for the first time. He made it to Arizona for the last two days of the Giants spring training and the appearance of his mangled arm immediately attracted the morbid fascination of his teammates. "Man, you look like Jaws took a bite out of you!" exclaimed Kevin Mitchell, welcoming him back.

The medical experts were dumbfounded. They couldn't understand how Dave was managing to throw with the same motion he'd used before the operation. The only explanation they could venture was that with Dravecky's muscular build the other muscles had somehow adapted and were compensating for the loss of the deltoid muscle function.

Chapter 2—Severely Damaged Limbs 79

Dave's explanation for the phenomena was much simpler. He attributed it to "a miracle of God." Throughout his career, Dravecky had been a deeply religious man. He was known to roll back the eyes of sportswriters with biblical quotations rather than baseball clichés and to occasionally send less devout teammates fleeing with his proclamations of faith. In San Diego he was associated with a collection of devout Christian players, some of whom gained notoriety as members of the ultraconservative John Birch society.

Whether Dravecky's incredible progress was made possible by the heavens or the overdeveloped muscles of his left arm, he was soon pitching in simulated games. In late July he began a successful rehabilitation assignment in the Giants farm system that culminated with three complete game minor league victories.

The "Dravecky Miracle" reached its climax when Dave jogged to the mound to face the Reds in front of 34,810 wildly cheering Giants fans. The Candlestick Park scoreboard in center field flashed "WELCOME BACK, DAVE!" in gigantic letters.

The game would not be an easy test for Dave. The Giants held a scant two game lead in the National League Western Division race. The Reds, who'd been picked by many to take the flag, were dying to gain a game on the front runners.

Before the game, Cincinnati manager Pete Rose was asked what he thought about Dravecky's upcoming comeback effort. His response was typically introspective and succinct: "He's back, and it's great for him. I hope he loses."

Dave's stirring victory over the Reds gave the Giants a tremendous shot in the arm. They were hoping he could slide back into his old number two spot in the rotation behind "Big Daddy" Rick Reuschel. In his next turn he looked ready to do just that as he held the Expos scoreless through five innings. But in the dugout after the top of the fifth, Dave's arm felt strange. His medical advisors were still nervous about his fragile humerus bone and had warned him to stop immediately if anything didn't feel right. But the veteran southpaw was intent on his pitching and ignored the signs.

Dravecky went out to pitch in the top of the sixth inning and surrendered a leadoff homer before hitting the next batter with a pitch. The first pitch to Tim Raines, the third hitter of the inning, was the last ball Dave would ever throw with his tortured left arm. He took his stretch, pivoted on his left leg, raised his arm and fired. In his autobiography, *Comeback*, Dravecky described the pitch this way: "Next to my ear I heard a loud popping noise. The sound was audible all over the field. It sounded as though someone had snapped a heavy tree branch. It felt as though my arm had separated from my body and was sailing off toward home plate."

To the horror of onlookers, Dravecky tumbled headfirst to the ground as the ball flew high over the catcher's head. He clutched his left arm and screamed in pain as he did a complete somersault and landed flat on his back. Despite the tremendous pain, Dave refused to be taken off the field lying down and was carried off sitting up on a stretcher. The grisly action, as well as his heroic exit was captured on film and rolled endlessly before television audiences for days thereafter. Relievers protected the Giants' lead so that Dave was able to go out with a win.

Of course, Dravecky was through for the year, but the medical experts considered it just a setback at the time. They expected the bone to fully heal and finish regaining strength, possibly allowing Dave to return to action the next spring.

In the meantime, the Giants were on their way to the 1989 National League pennant and Dave stayed with the team to cheer them on even though he couldn't pitch. After the Giants won the deciding game of the League Championship Series from the Chicago Cubs, he couldn't resist joining his teammates in a postgame celebration on the field and refractured his arm during the ensuing melee.

Although the second break itself was not considered serious, the resulting x-rays revealed that a mass had formed in the area where the tumor had been removed. Dravecky had been warned that a desmoid tumor was the most likely type to come back after an operation. Further testing revealed that the worst had happened, the tumor had grown back. This time Dravecky was through with baseball. He underwent two more surgical procedures before his left arm was amputated in June 1991 due to chronic infection and nerve damage.

Dravecky's record stood at 64 victories and 57 defeats with a solid 3.13 career earned run average when his pitching career suddenly and tragically ended. He distinguished himself both as a starter and reliever. In 146 starts he completed 28 games and threw 9 shutouts. In 80 relief appearances he recorded 10 saves. Although his stats aren't overwhelming, he was a clutch pitcher who rose to the occasion when his team needed him the most. In almost 26 League Championship and World Series innings he gave up only one earned run for a microscopic postseason earned run average of 0.35 and he also pitched two scoreless innings in the 1983 All-Star Game.

After his ordeal, Dave faced the question of whether the comeback had been worth it. Had it been worth the year of rehabilitation and the excruciating pain to pitch only twice more at the major league level?

His answer came without hesitation: "Yes, it was worth it a million times over.... I got to live out the greatest boyhood dream of all. I got to do what the experts said was impossible, to come back from cancer and pitch a major league baseball game. Without a deltoid muscle in my pitching arm, I won a game in a pennant drive in front of tens of thousands of screaming fans. What more would anybody want out of baseball?"

DAVID FRANCIS DRAVECKY
B. February 14, 1956

YEAR	TEAM	LEAGUE	G	IP	SO	BB	W	L	ERA	CG	SV
1978	Charleston	W Car'lina	20	52	31	32	4	2	4.15	*	*
1979	Buffalo	Eastern	35	114	81	59	6	7	4.26	*	*
1980	Buffalo	Eastern	27	161	64	60	13	7	3.35	*	*
1981	Amarillo	Texas	30	172	141	45	15	5	2.67	*	*
1982	Hawaii	Pac Coast	16	36	26	14	4	1	2.48	*	*
	SAN DIEGO	NL	31	105	59	33	5	3	2.57	0	2
1983	SAN DIEGO	NL	28	184	74	44	14	10	3.58	9	0
1984	SAN DIEGO	NL	50	157	71	51	9	8	2.93	3	8
1985	SAN DIEGO	NL	34	215	105	57	13	11	2.93	7	0
1986	SAN DIEGO	NL	26	161	87	54	9	11	3.07	3	0
1987	SAN DIEGO	NL	30	79	60	31	3	7	3.76	1	0
	SAN FRANCISCO	NL	18	112	78	33	7	5	3.20	4	0
1988	SAN FRANCISCO	NL	7	37	19	8	2	2	3.16	1	0
	Phoenix	Pac Coast	1	3	1	0	0	1	16.88	0	0
	San Jose	California	2	16	8	1	2	0	1.69	1	0
	Phoenix	Pac Coast	1	9	3	0	1	0	2.00	1	0
1989	SAN FRANCISCO	NL	2	13	5	4	2	0	3.46	0	0
MAJOR LEAGUE TOTALS			226	1063	558	315	64	57	3.13	28	10

Three

Maimed or Disfigured Extremities

MORDECAI "THREE FINGER" BROWN

Most ballplayers with disabilities don't seem to think of themselves as having a disability. To them the disability is just something they have to compensate for like a weak throwing arm or lack of speed. There's one case, however, where a player's disability may actually have been an advantage on the baseball diamond.

Mordecai Brown got his nickname, "Three Finger," because his throwing hand was badly mangled as a boy. His index finger was cut off leaving only a nub, his middle finger was badly misshapen and bent severely to the right, and he couldn't straighten his pinky finger which curled in toward his palm. After one look at Brown's useless looking right hand, a person who wasn't familiar with his accomplishments would probably have concluded that he couldn't possibly grip a baseball at all.

Yet Mordecai always contended that his disfigured hand actually gave him a better grip on the ball for throwing his vaunted curve — and his performance backed it up. Although he wasn't overpowering, Brown won 239 games while losing only 129 times in 14 major league seasons. He won more than 20 games six years in a row and posted a minuscule 2.06 career earned run average, third lowest in baseball history. He was also strong and durable, completing 271 out of 332 starts while also relieving 149 times and leading the league in saves four straight seasons. These efforts earned him a place in the Baseball Hall of Fame.

Mordecai Peter Centennial Brown was born in the tiny mining town of Nyesville, Indiana, on October 19, 1876. Since the year of his birth was the hundredth anniversary of the country's independence from Great Britain, the extra name "Centennial" was tacked on.

Chapter 3—Maimed or Disfigured Extremities

Now you just can't call a professional baseball player Mordecai, and while "Three Finger" Brown sounded good in the sports pages, it wasn't really a workable moniker. Since Brown hailed from a mining community and had actually worked in the mines as a teenager, the more practical nickname of "Miner" was bestowed on him early in his professional career.

Brown injured his right hand at the age of seven when he stuck it in a corn chopping machine while visiting his uncle's farm. A few weeks later the impetuous youth further damaged the same hand when he fell chasing a hog around the barnyard.

Despite his disfigurement, Mordecai grew up to be a pretty fair athlete. By 1898 the strong-armed, 21-year-old was playing third base for Coxville, a semipro team made up of local miners. One afternoon, he was forced to take the mound against a team from Brazil, Indiana, when the regular Coxville hurler injured his arm and he pitched his team to victory. When Brazil offered him more money to pitch for them, he grabbed the opportunity and his pitching career was fully, if somewhat belatedly, underway.

In 1901 Brown signed his first professional contract with nearby Terre Haute in the Three-I League, so called because it consisted of teams from the states of Indiana, Illinois, and Iowa. He earned his $60 per month salary and began a meteoric rise through the minor league ranks by leading the league with 23 wins. It was with Terre Haute that he was first referred to as "Three Finger" Brown, although nobody knows why the name stuck since only one digit was actually missing.

The following season he moved to Omaha in the Western League and won 27 games while completing every game he started. At the end of the year he was sold to the National League St. Louis Cardinals.

The 26-year-old rookie had a decent freshman season for St. Louis in 1903. He won 9 and lost 13 with a fine 2.60 earned run average for a woeful team that finished with a dismal 43–94 won-lost record. After the season he was traded to the Chicago Cubs for Jack "Brakeman" Taylor, a solid veteran starter who'd won more than 20 games the previous two seasons and would win another 21 for the Cardinals in 1904. At the time of the trade it was rumored that the Cardinals thought that Brown's hand was too much of an obstacle for him to develop into a star.

It was a huge break for Brown and the Cubs. Chicago was in the midst of building a dynasty that would dominate the league for much of the decade, and Mordecai Brown was a critical addition. Key parts were already in place when he arrived. Frank Chance had been with the club since 1898 as a second string catcher and outfielder before finally settling in as the regular first baseman in 1903. He would be named manager in 1905 and quickly earn the title "The Peerless Leader." Catcher Johnny Kling arrived in 1900, freeing Chance for duty in the field. Joe Tinker moved in at shortstop in 1902 and was joined by second baseman Johnny "Crab" Evers late the same season. Pitcher Carl Lundgren and center fielder Jimmy Slagle were also already in place.

The Cubs had finished a solid third in 1903 and moved up to second the next year with the addition of Brown and outfielders Frank "Wildfire" Schulte and "Circus Solly" Hofman. Replacing Taylor in the rotation, Mordecai won 15 games. He improved to 18 wins in 1905 and another important piece was added to the puzzle when "Big Ed" Reulbach was added to the pitching staff. The Cubs, however, slipped to third place.

Everything finally came together in 1906. Before the season Chicago obtained speedy veteran Jimmy Sheckard from Brooklyn to play left field and hard-hitting Harry Steinfeldt from Cincinnati to take over third base. They also added pitcher Jack Pfiester who'd failed in a couple of trials with Pittsburg but became an instant success with the Cubs. During the season they bolstered their pitching staff with the acquisition of young Orval Overall from the Cincinnati Reds and the reacquisition of "Brakeman" Jack Taylor from the Cardinals.

The Cubs won 116 games while losing only 36 in 1906, the best regular sea-

Mordecai "Three Finger" Brown of the Cubs

son record of all time. The Tinker-to-Evers-to-Chance combination became famous for turning sensational double plays, Kling performed brilliantly behind the plate, and Schulte, Steinfeldt and company chipped in with timely hitting. But it was the spectacular pitching that made the Cubs great, and Miner Brown was the undisputed ace of the staff. His 26 wins included nine shutouts and five one-hitters, and his 1.04 earned run average still stands as the second lowest post-1900 mark for a starter. In the World Series against the crosstown White Sox he lost the first game 2 to 1 and pitched a 1 to 0 shutout in game four. But he was knocked out in the second inning of the sixth and final game after yielding seven runs as the heavily favored Cubs suffered a humiliating loss to the "Hitless Wonders" from the South Side.

The Cubs rebounded to capture the pennant again in 1907. Brown, who posted a 20–6 won-lost record during the regular season, atoned for his failure in the previous Classic by blanking the Detroit Tigers 2–0 to clinch the Cubs' first World Championship.

In 1908 the Cubs captured a third straight National League title thanks to the infamous "Merkle Boner" episode. It was one of the most dramatic pennant races in baseball history with the Cubs battling John McGraw's New York Giants right down to the wire. In the closing weeks of the season the Giants had seemingly beat the Cubs on a ninth inning, two-on, two-out single to center. The runner on third scored easily, but the runner on first, a 19-year-old rookie named Fred Merkle, neglected to touch second base before heading to the clubhouse. After a confusing appeal by the Cubs, he was ruled out on an inning-ending force at second base. Therefore, the run didn't count. But the New York fans had already swarmed the field in celebration, so the game ended in a tie.

When the Giants and Cubs finished the season with identical 93 and 55 won-lost records, the tie game was scheduled to be replayed in New York, the first official pennant playoff in history. The Giants and their fans were furious. They felt that they were being robbed and the pennant should already be theirs. One of the largest and nastiest crowds in history mobbed the Polo Grounds for the replay. The game was an early sellout so ticketless fans perched on the elevated tracks overlooking the field which kept the trains from running. The fire department was called in to drive them away with water hoses, but the angry mob then set fire to the outfield fence in an unsuccessful attempt to break into the park. Things weren't much better inside as unruly fans lined the inside of the outfield fence and the Cubs dugout had to be surrounded by policemen to keep the unruly spectators at bay.

Because Brown had pitched so much in the closing weeks of the season, Chicago sent Jeff Pfiester to the mound to face the Giants ace, Christy Mathewson. But when Pfiester started poorly, the Cubs' overworked ace righthander was called in to relieve him. The courageous Brown, who'd received death threats from New York's notorious "Black Hand" criminal organization, had to fight the overflow crowd on his way in from the bullpen to face Art Devlin with two runners on, two outs, and a run already in. He promptly fanned Devlin to end the inning and held the Giants in check the rest of the way to beat Mathewson by a score of 4–2. The Cubs headed to Detroit for the World Series the next morning under a police escort. The Series was somewhat anticlimactic as the Cubs prevailed in five contests. Brown won two games without yielding an earned run.

The controversy surrounding the Merkle incident, as well as the brilliance of Christy Mathewson, overshadowed Miner Brown's sensational performance in 1908. He finished second in the league to Mathewson in the following categories: games won (37 to 29), lowest earned run average (1.43 to 1.47), shutouts (12 to 9), and fewest walks per game (0.97 to 1.41). And, in an era when top starters doubled as closers, the two aces also tied for the lead in saves with five apiece. In addition, Brown's winning percentage of .763 was third best in the league, barely behind teammate Ed Reulbach's .774 and Matty's .771 mark.

Unfortunately, Brown was destined to play second fiddle to Mathewson throughout his entire career. Matty, who was actually four years younger than Mordecai, was the classic hero. He was tall, fair-haired, and handsome with a reputation for clean living and sportsmanship. He'd been a football star and president of his class at Bucknell University and was deemed a model for America's youth. His nickname was "The Big Six" after a legendary railroad train of the era that always came through. Brown, on the other hand, was a poorly educated working type with an unsightly disfigurement. He stood a modest 5'10" tall and weighed a sturdy 175 pounds. Although American Monthly, a national magazine, ran photos of his rugged exercise program when he was 38 years old, he was not physically imposing in appearance. And of course, Mordecai was unflatteringly called "Three Finger" and "Miner" compared to Matty's magnificent nickname.

During his prime, Mathewson was acclaimed as the greatest pitcher of his era and had the record to support it, but in head-to-head confrontations no pitcher matched up against the great Matty like Miner Brown. Between July 12, 1905, and October 8, 1908, Brown beat Mathewson nine straight times, no small factor in the Cubs success over their arch rivals during that period.

Although the Cubs fell to second place behind the Pirates in 1909,

Brown pitched as well as he had the previous year. He led the league with 27 wins, 32 complete games, 342 innings pitched, and 7 saves. In addition his fabulous 1.31 earned run average was second best to—who else?—Christy Mathewson. He enjoyed another great season in 1910, winning 25 games with a 1.86 earned run average to lead the Cubs back to the top of the standings. At 34 years of age in 1911 he was still good for 21 victories as the Cubs dropped to second place. But his earned run average climbed to a more pedestrian 2.80 after being under 2.00 for five consecutive seasons.

Clearly Mordecai was starting to fade. In 1912 he suffered a leg injury which limited him to 15 games and a 5–6 won-lost mark. After the season there was major uproar when the Cubs tried to send the veteran workhorse back to the minor leagues. He finally ended up in Cincinnati where he came back to win 11 games in 1913 and lead the Reds staff with six saves.

In 1914 Brown jumped to the newly formed Federal League, accepting an offer to manage and pitch for the St. Louis entry. He was relieved of his managerial responsibilities in July and shipped to the Brooklyn Federals in August. He posted a combined 14–11 won-lost record for the season.

The next season found Miner Brown back in "Chi Town" with the Federal League Chicago Whales. The 38-year-old veteran posted a fine 17–8 won-lost mark and his 2.09 earned run average was the third best in the league. But the Federal League folded after the 1915 season and under the terms of surrender, Brown found himself returning to the Chicago Cubs along with former teammate Joe Tinker and a bevy of other ex-Federal Leaguers.

Approaching 40 years old in 1916, Mordecai was pretty well finished as a major league hurler and didn't pitch much for the Cubs, but he still had one day in the sun left. On Labor Day, he hooked up with his old adversary, Christy Mathewson, one last time. Matty wasn't his former self either. His arm was gone and he'd been traded to Cincinnati in July to take over as the Reds manager. He'd removed himself from the active ranks, but consented to take the mound one more time against "Three Finger" Brown to boost attendance. The match resembled two washed-up old fighters stumbling around the ring, too proud and stubborn to quit. Both veteran warhorses went the distance, with Matty finally staggering off with a sloppy 10–8 victory. It was the last appearance in the major leagues for both of them and left Brown with a 13 to 11 edge over Mathewson in 24 career match-ups.

Although he was through in the big leagues, Miner Brown continued pitching in the minor leagues for several years. In 1917 and 1918 he pitched for his old teammate Joe Tinker who was managing Columbus in the American Association. As a grizzled 42-year-old in 1919, he returned to Terre Haute where he'd begun his professional career eighteen years earlier and won 16 games while dropping only 6 decisions. He also served as the Terre Haute manager that year, as well as the next, his last in professional baseball.

After his professional baseball career was over, Mordecai managed a semipro team in Lawrenceville, Illinois, sponsored by the Indiana Refining Company. Later he opened up a gas station in Terre Haute and ran it until 1946. The old righthander occasionally pitched as late as 1931 when he appeared in an old-timers game in Cincinnati. Regretfully, he didn't live to enjoy his induction into the recently established Baseball Hall of Fame in Cooperstown in 1949. When he died on February 14, 1948, the words kindly, courageous, charitable, and honest were chosen to describe him.

Given Mordecai Brown's sensational career, it's difficult to see how he could have been any better with a perfectly formed pitching hand. In fact, after his retirement he declared, "The old paw served me pretty well in its time. It gave me a firmer grip on the ball, so I could spin it over the hump. I gave me a greater dip." Convincing himself and others that he could pitch with his disfigured hand was probably the biggest obstacle that Brown had to overcome. He got a late start on his career because he never tried pitching until he was 21 years of age.

Brown was certainly not self-conscious about his injury. During his heyday people came from miles around to see the infamous chopping machine which his uncle loved to show off. Eventually Mordecai acquired the machine himself and set it up in his garage for curious sightseers to view.

MORDECAI PETER CENTENNIAL "THREE FINGER" BROWN
B. October 19, 1876 D. February 14, 1948

YEAR	TEAM	LEAGUE	G	IP	SO	BB	W	L	ERA	CG	SV
1901	Terre Haute	Three I	*	*	*	*	23	8	*	*	*
1902	Omaha	Western	*	*	*	*	27	15	*	*	*
1903	ST. LOUIS	NL	26	201	83	59	9	13	2.60	19	0
1904	CHICAGO	NL	26	212	81	50	15	10	1.86	21	1
1905	CHICAGO	NL	30	249	89	44	18	12	2.17	24	0
1906	CHICAGO	NL	36	277	144	61	26	6	1.04	27	3
1907	CHICAGO	NL	34	233	107	40	20	6	1.39	20	3

YEAR	TEAM	LEAGUE	G	IP	SO	BB	W	L	ERA	CG	SV
1908	CHICAGO	NL	44	312	123	49	29	9	1.47	27	5
1909	CHICAGO	NL	50	343	172	53	27	9	1.31	32	7
1910	CHICAGO	NL	46	295	143	64	25	13	1.86	27	7
1911	CHICAGO	NL	53	270	129	55	21	11	2.80	21	13
1912	CHICAGO	NL	15	89	34	20	5	6	2.64	5	0
1913	CINCINNATI	NL	39	173	41	44	11	12	2.91	11	6
1914	S.L.-BR'KLYN	FL	35	233	113	61	14	11	3.52	18	0
1915	CHICAGO	FL	35	236	95	64	17	8	2.09	17	3
1916	CHICAGO	NL	12	48	21	9	2	3	3.91	2	0
1917	Columbus	Am Ass'n	30	185	61	51	10	12	2.77	*	2
1918	Columbus	Am Ass'n	12	50	13	9	3	2	2.70	*	*
1919	Indianapolis	Am Ass'n	6	*	*	*	0	3	*	*	*
	Terre Haute	Three I	*	*	*	*	16	6	*	*	*
1920	Terre Haute	Three I	*	*	*	*	4	6	*	*	*
MAJOR LEAGUE TOTALS			481	3172	1375	673	239	129	2.06	271	48

CHARLEY "RED" RUFFING

Like Mordecai Brown, Pete Gray, Whitey Kurowski and scores of other major leaguers, Red Ruffing grew up in mining country. Like the others he escaped the mines to play major league baseball, but Red didn't escape without a constant reminder of life in the mines.

The loss of four toes from his left foot due to a mining accident when he was 16 years old provided Red with all the incentive he would ever need to get away from the mines. The teenager, who was a promising slugger with professional baseball ambitions at the time, was forced to convert to pitching to continue in baseball. Though he pitched in constant pain from the damaged foot throughout his career, Ruffing won 273 games in a big league career that spanned 24 years and was inducted into the Baseball Hall of Fame in 1967.

Charles "Red" Ruffing was born in Granville, Illinois, on May 3, 1904, and grew up in Nokomis, a mining village in southern Illinois. Red's father was a company man, a supervisor of operations above ground for the Reliance Coal Company. He also served as mayor of Coaltown, the company town on the outskirts of Nokomis, and managed the company's baseball team. Young Red was one of five children. One of his brothers, John was signed as pitcher by the Cardinals in 1924, but quit baseball to get married. The Ruffing family was made up of big broad shouldered folks, and Red was no exception. He grew to almost 6'2" in height and weighed more than 200 pounds. His weight would become a constant concern throughout his professional baseball career. He had a big stomach and tended to gain weight if he didn't watch his diet and exercise carefully.

At the age of 15 the strapping young man left school to work in the mines. The accident that cost him part of his foot occurred in March 1921. By that time, he had already had a 20-year-old cousin die in a mine mishap and seen a brother's kneecap and fingers smashed in another mining accident. Years earlier his father had been brought to the surface with a broken back. On that fateful day Red was working deep in the mines as a coupler, hooking together empty coal cars for loading, when the miner driving the string of cars suddenly jammed on the brakes causing the heavy vehicles to pile up. Red's left foot was crushed beneath a wheel. Four toes had to be amputated and when blood poisoning set in a few days later it looked like he would lose the entire foot. But somehow the strong young man managed to pull through, although he would spend the next six months on crutches.

Red had begun playing baseball for the company team when he was only 14 years old, not because his father was coach, but because he could hit the ball a ton. As a long ball hitting first baseman and outfielder, he'd been promised a minor league job for the upcoming 1921 season. Now those plans were dashed. He didn't even know how well he'd be able to walk, much less run. Red figured his professional baseball career was over before it started and so did everyone else in Nokomis, except a former minor league player named Doc Bennett, who was running a local pool hall and managing a semipro team on the side.

Bennett saw Ruffing fooling around pitching to the neighborhood kids while still on crutches and couldn't help noticing his strong throwing arm. Doc approached him about pitching for his club when he got off the crutches. Red, who'd never pitched before, thought Bennett was crazy, but quickly agreed to the offer. When the foot healed, Red found that he could pitch with his disability. As a righthander, he landed on his left leg, so he had to learn to land on the side of his mutilated left foot. It hurt like crazy, of course, but it might be a way out of the mines.

As a pitcher, Red had only raw talent going for him at first. He simply reared back and fired the ball as hard as he could for as long as he could. He piled up strikeouts, but also got cuffed around quite a bit pitching for Doc Bennett's team. But even then he had the ability to rise to the occasion. He pitched his best games against the Hillsboro nine, Nokomis' bitter rival.

The experience landed Ruffing a job with Danville in the Three-I League for the 1923 season. His pitching style was still crude and he lost more than he won, but his high hard fastball soon attracted the attention

Chapter 3—Maimed or Disfigured Extremities 91

Red Ruffing, hitter turned pitcher after maiming foot

of big league scouts. He was sold to the Boston Red Sox at the end of his first season in professional baseball.

After splitting a season between Boston and their Dover farm club in the Eastern Shore League Ruffing joined the Red Sox to stay in 1925 and remained with them until he was traded to the Yankees in 1930. In the five full seasons Red spent with the Red Sox, they finished in last place each year and averaged more than 101 losses annually. Ruffing's record for that period was a miserable 39 wins against 93 losses. He lost a league-leading 25 games while winning 10 in 1928 and just to prove it wasn't a fluke, he led in losses again in 1929 with 22. Things were going so bad for him on the mound that the Sox seriously considered converting him to the outfield and even tried him there for two games in 1929.

Everything turned around for Ruffing on May 7, 1930, when the financially strapped Red Sox sent him to the New York Yankees in exchange for $50,000 and reserve outfielder Cedric Durst. In those days, the Red Sox made a habit of supplying the Yankees with quality pitching. Over the years they'd provided Carl Mays, Sam Jones, Herb Pennock, Waite Hoyt, and Joe Bush, not to mention Babe Ruth, who was still a pitcher when they sold him to the Yankees in 1919. To the Yankees credit, they'd recognized Ruffing's potential early and had been trying to acquire him for years. The Red Sox didn't really want to give up their young workhorse, but they had bills to pay.

Ruffing became an immediate winner with New York. After losing three games for the Red Sox, he posted a 15–5 won-lost mark in Yankee pinstripes for the rest of the 1930 campaign. The Yankees finished third in 1930, but moved up to second place in 1931 as an eccentric young hurler named Lefty Gomez joined Ruffing in the rotation. The free-spirited Gomez and the stoic Ruffing would form a deadly left-right combination throughout the remainder of the 1930s as the Yankees transitioned from the Ruthian period to the DiMaggio era while dominating the American League. An ever popular controversy among Yankee fans was which one of the two brilliant starters was manager Joe McCarthy's ace. Gomez supporters would always bring up the fact that the lefty was selected to start five of the first seven All-Star Games from 1933 to 1939. Meanwhile, Ruffing backers were quick to point out that the redhead was named to open four of the five World Series that the Yankees participated in during that time.

As the years went by Ruffing became a polished hurler, expanding his repertoire to include a variety of off-speed pitches. He racked up his first 20-win season in 1936 at the age of 32 and enjoyed it so much that he did it again the next three years. Red was still going strong when World War II started. In 1942 he won 14 and lost 7 for the pennant-winning Yankees but received a surprise summons from Uncle Sam after New York's World Series loss to the St. Louis Cardinals.

At the time, Ruffing was 38 years old with a wife and kids and a mother-in-law to support—not to mention the four missing toes from his left foot. But the draft board was going through another wave of criticism about special treatment for professional athletes and other celebrities. Some ballplayers had apparently received preferential treatment and obtained questionable deferments. So the board was in the process of trying to right one wrong with another.

Due to the condition of his foot, Red flunked all the physical examinations. But an army doctor wrote that what he could do on the outside, he could do on the inside, and okayed him for active duty. So on December 29, 1942, crippled, old Red Ruffing went off to play baseball in defense of his country, while many younger and more able-bodied players retained their deferments and their spots on major league rosters. In the fall of 1943 Ruffing pitched his Long Beach squad to victory over Camp Pendleton for the Southern California service championship.

After the surrender of Germany, the military started sending soldiers home. Ruffing was released on June 5, 1945, and rejoined the Yankees a month later. He was 41 years old and 30 pounds overweight, but he could still pitch well enough to handle wartime major league lineups. Down the stretch, he won seven games and lost three for the Yankees with a tidy 2.89 earned run average.

There's no telling how long Ruffing would have kept going if he hadn't broken his kneecap early in the 1946 campaign. Despite holding out all spring, he got off to a tremendous start that year—winning five of six decisions, including two shutouts and four complete games, and compiling a 1.77 earned run average. The injury curtailed his season and the Yankees released him at the end of the year. Red caught on with the Chicago White Sox for the 1947 season, but re-injured his knee in spring training and was out of action until midseason. He made an effort to return, but the knee just couldn't hold up and he finally had to call it quits at the ripe old age of 43.

Ruffing did some scouting and managed in the minor leagues after his retirement from the active ranks. In 1962 he had the dubious distinction of serving as the first pitching coach for the fledgling New York Mets under the leadership of the legendary Casey Stengel. With the great Rogers Hornsby serving as hitting coach, the Mets had more talent on the sidelines than on the field as they lost a record 120 games. The experience with the Mets must have reminded Red of his early years with those feeble Boston teams. In fact, veteran hurler Roger Craig brought back memories of Red Ruffing in his Red Sox days by dropping 24 decisions in 1962 and following up with 22 losses the next year. Undaunted, Red continued to coach for a few more years before retiring to the Cleveland area where he and his wife Pauline had settled while he was scouting for the Indians. He was elected to the Hall of Fame in 1967, his final year of eligibility. A stroke in 1973 left him confined to a wheelchair, but he was still sound of mind and was an annual visitor to Hall of Fame ceremonies until his death on February 17, 1986, in Mayfield Heights, Ohio.

In a career that spanned 24 years, Ruffing won 273 times and lost on 225 occasions with a final 3.80 earned run average. He finished 335 of 536 starts. His 21–7 won-lost record led the league in wins and winning percentage in 1938. He also led the league in strikeouts in 1932 and in shutouts in 1938 and 1939. He won more games for the Yankees than any other pitcher until Whitey Ford came along and Red actually has more career victories than Whitey when his Boston and Chicago years are taken into account. In seven fall classics Ruffing won seven games while losing two, placing second all-time behind Ford in career World Series victories. Although detractors often criticize his lack of success in his early years with Boston, it wasn't all Red's fault. For example, he posted a respectable 3.86 earned run average and led the league in complete games in 1928 while losing a league-leading 25 decisions.

Ruffing was also one of the greatest hitting pitchers of all time. For much of his career he was the Yankees' top right-handed pinch hitter, going to the plate more than 250 times in that role. His lifetime batting average is a solid .269 and his 36 homers remains the third highest career total for a pitcher behind Wes Ferrell and Bob Lemon.

Red Ruffing managed to overcome his physical disability through sheer determination and willpower. Although his maimed foot always pained him, he was a great believer in building a pitcher's stamina by running, both as performer and later as pitching coach. In his glory days it was not unusual for him to keep pitching and running even though the sock on his left foot was soaked with blood.

Along the way, Red overcame another significant barrier — his limited education and social skills. One would have thought that a local boy from a small village like Nokomis who reached the major leagues would own the town. However, Nokomis' already had a local favorite in the big leagues before Ruffing got there. "Sunny Jim" Bottomley, a slugging first baseman for the St. Louis Cardinals, also grew up in Nokomis. He was four years Red's senior and was already established as a star when Red was breaking in with the Red Sox. Bottomley, a future Hall of Famer in his own right, managed to eclipse Ruffing in his own backyard, with a great

Chapter 3—Maimed or Disfigured Extremities 95

deal of help from Red's dour personality. Red, however, finally managed to win the home folk over when he returned to Nokomis to claim Pauline Mulholland, a local girl, for his bride in 1934. The local Chamber of Commerce even erected a banner on the main road east of town proclaiming Nokomis as the home of Charley Ruffing. It matched the one to the west of town that had flown for several years advertising the home of Jim Bottomley.

In 1942 a magazine did a feature story about Red's reading habits, listing the 24 weighty books that he'd read that year while leading the Yankees to the pennant. The once crude young man, who never completed his formal education, had grown to be regarded as a well read and well-spoken gentleman. The proud, rugged competitor, who commanded respect on and off the field, was a classic symbol of the New York Yankees' success.

CHARLES HERBERT "RED" RUFFING
B. May 3, 1904 D. February 17, 1986

YEAR	TEAM	LEAGUE	G	IP	SO	BB	W	L	ERA	CG	SHO
1923	Danville	Three I	39	239	88	89	12	16	*	*	*
1924	BOSTON	AL	8	23	10	9	0	0	6.65	0	0
	Dover	Eastern	15	94	72	23	4	7	*	*	*
1925	BOSTON	AL	37	217	64	75	9	18	5.01	13	3
1926	BOSTON	AL	37	166	58	68	6	15	4.39	6	0
1927	BOSTON	AL	26	158	77	87	5	13	4.66	10	0
1928	BOSTON	AL	42	289	118	96	10	25	3.89	25	1
1929	BOSTON	AL	35	244	109	118	9	22	4.86	18	2
1930	BOST-NY	AL	38	222	131	68	15	8	4.38	13	2
1931	NEW YORK	AL	37	237	132	87	16	14	4.41	19	1
1932	NEW YORK	AL	35	259	190	115	18	7	3.09	22	3
1933	NEW YORK	AL	35	235	122	93	9	14	3.91	18	0
1934	NEW YORK	AL	36	256	149	104	19	11	3.93	19	5
1935	NEW YORK	AL	30	222	81	76	16	11	3.12	19	2
1936	NEW YORK	AL	33	271	102	90	20	12	3.85	25	3
1937	NEW YORK	AL	31	256	131	68	20	7	2.98	22	5
1938	NEW YORK	AL	31	247	127	82	21	7	3.31	22	4
1939	NEW YORK	AL	28	233	95	75	21	7	2.93	22	5
1940	NEW YORK	AL	30	226	97	76	15	12	3.38	20	3
1941	NEW YORK	AL	23	186	60	54	15	6	3.54	13	2
1942	NEW YORK	AL	24	194	80	41	14	7	3.21	16	4
1943-44	NEW YORK	AL			(In Military Service)						
1945	NEW YORK	AL	11	87	24	20	7	3	2.89	8	1
1946	NEW YORK	AL	8	61	19	23	5	1	1.77	4	2
1947	CHICAGO	AL	9	53	11	16	3	5	6.11	1	0
MAJOR LEAGUE TOTALS			624	4344	1987	1541	273	225	3.8	335	48

HAL PECK

Another player who suffered a similar injury to Ruffing's and went on to a major league career is outfielder Hal Peck.

On September 3, 1942, Peck accidentally shot the second and third toes off his left foot while shooting rats in the henhouse of his farm outside of Milwaukee. Hal was 25 years old at the time and considered a topflight major league prospect. The promising young left-handed hitter was just completing a tremendous season with the Milwaukee Brewers, batting .333 for the independent minor club in the Class AAA American Association owned by Bill Veeck.

Harold Arthur Peck was born April 20, 1917, in Big Bend, Wisconsin. He began his career in professional baseball hitting .331 for Hopkinsville in the old Kitty League and joined Milwaukee in 1940 after a season with Bloomington in the Three I League.

Several major league organizations were pursuing the 5'11", 175 pound speedster before the accident. Veeck, who always referred to Hal as his favorite player, was on the verge of selling his contract to the Chicago White Sox, but after the mishap there was serious doubt that he would be able to compete again, and interest in the young outfielder was greatly reduced. Veeck ended up selling him to the Brooklyn Dodgers on a trial basis for the 1943 season, but Peck was having a problem with small growths or plantar's warts on the sight of the wound and could barely run. Veeck ended up getting him back. He missed most of the 1943 season after undergoing additional surgery to remove the growths, but came back to hit a resounding .345 for Milwaukee in 1944 and demonstrate that he still had good speed by swiping 18 bases.

Philadelphia's Connie Mack was never afraid to take another look at damaged goods, so Peck was sold to the Athletics during the 1944 season. He enjoyed a fine rookie year in 1945, batting .276 in 112 games for the Athletics. Although the injury slowed him down considerably, he still slammed 9 triples and stole 5 bases. By 1947 Veeck had purchased the Cleveland Indians and he immediately reacquired his "favorite player." Hal platooned in right field that year and hit a solid .293 in 114 games for the Indians. The next season he was part of the Indians' 1948 World Championship team, leading the league in league pinch hits and batting .286 overall. The next year, the 32-year-old Peck's role was reduced almost entirely to pinch-hitting and he retired at the close of the season after hitting .310 in limited duty.

Hal Peck died in Milwaukee on April 13, 1995, a week shy of his 78th birthday.

HAROLD ARTHUR PECK
B. April 20, 1917 D. April 13, 1995

YEAR	TEAM	LEAGUE	G	AB	R	H	HR	RBI	AVE	SB	POS
1938	Hopkinsville	Kitty	*	*	*	*	6	69	.331	*	OF
1939	Bloomington	Three I	*	*	*	*	0	33	.286	*	OF
1940	Milwaukee	Am Ass'n	136	527	76	155	9	66	.294	11	OF
1941	Milwaukee	Am Ass'n	144	561	79	150	8	64	.267	8	OF
1942	Milwaukee	Am Ass'n	141	568	90	189	10	94	.333	9	OF
1943	BROOKLYN	NL	1	1	0	0	0	0	.000	0	PH
	Milwaukee	Am Ass'n	23	45	11	20	1	15	.444	0	OF
1944	Milwaukee	Am Ass'n	148	579	140	200	13	83	.345	18	OF
	PHILADELPHIA	AL	2	8	0	2	0	1	.250	0	OF
1945	PHILADELPHIA	AL	112	449	51	124	5	39	.276	5	OF
1946	PHILADELPHIA	AL	48	150	14	37	2	11	.247	1	OF
1947	CLEVELAND	AL	114	392	58	115	8	44	.293	3	OF
1948	CLEVELAND	AL	45	63	12	18	0	8	.286	1	PH-OF
1949	CLEVELAND	AL	33	29	1	9	0	9	.310	0	PH-OF
MAJOR LEAGUE TOTALS			355	1092	136	305	15	112	.279	10	

CARLOS MAY

Of the players who've overcome significant disabilities to perform at the major league level, Carlos May could be the one whose accomplishments are the least recognized and appreciated.

In the middle of an outstanding rookie season with the Chicago White Sox, May lost most of his right thumb in a freak accident while on military reserve duty. A few weeks earlier he'd been named to the American League All-Star Team and at the age of 21 became one of the youngest players ever to perform in the classic. At the time of his injury, he was the leading candidate for the American League Rookie of the Year Award and looked like a future superstar.

Several players have enjoyed successful major league careers despite the loss one or more fingers, most notably the great pitcher Mordecai Brown. However, the loss of a thumb is a different matter all together. Many anthropologists consider the opposable human thumb to be one of the key features that distinguished the evolution of man from other species. Without a fully functional right thumb it seemed impossible that the lefty hitting, right-handed throwing May would be able to hold the bat firm enough to hit major league pitching or grip the ball well enough to throw like a big leaguer.

But Carlos May refused to accept what seemed to be inevitable. After four operations and months of rehabilitation Carlos opened the 1970 season playing left field and hitting in the third spot in the White Sox batting order. For the year, he played 150 games and batted a solid .285, the second highest average among Sox regulars and a slight improvement over his pre-injury mark. He was also second highest on the club in runs scored and runs batted in, led in walks, and shared the lead in stolen bases. He went on from there to enjoy a solid major career that lasted through 1977.

Carlos May was born on May 17, 1948, in Birmingham, Alabama, the younger of two boys. His brother Lee, who is five years older, was a slugging first baseman whose major league career spanned 18 seasons. Carlos began playing baseball in the sandlots of Birmingham. He started attracting attention when he batted an incredible .735 as a high school sophomore and had advanced to the topflight semipro Birmingham Industrial League by the time he was signed by the White Sox at the age of 18.

The solidly built 5'11" 200-pound phenom quickly advanced through the Sox farm system. After hitting a sensational .426 in the Gulf Coast Rookie League in 1966, he advanced to Appleton of the Midwest League and batted .338 the next season. In 1968 he hit a league-leading .330 for Lynchburg in the Class A Carolina League and finished the year with a 17 game trial in Chicago.

In the late 1960s the White Sox were a pitching-rich, but power-hungry, team. In 1968 they finished ninth in the ten team American League despite a 2.75 staff earned run average. Offensively they produced a meager .228 team batting average and slugged only 71 home runs, the lowest team figure in the league. Their leading hitter was left fielder and former two-time National League batting champ Tommy Davis, who hit a mediocre .268. Their big home run threat was third baseman Pete Ward, with a mere 15 circuit shots. May was by far the best looking hitter to come up through the White Sox farm system in decades. The *Baseball Digest* scouting report on 1969 rookies raved, "Outstanding batting credentials. Looks like the slugger the White Sox have been waiting for. If he sticks and plays every day could be a Rookie of the Year candidate."

When Tommy Davis was claimed by the Seattle Pilots in the 1969 expansion draft, the White Sox decided to give their precocious young slugger a shot at the regular left field job. The jump from Class A to the American League is difficult enough, but May would have the added burden of leading the team's offense. But Carlos was everything the White Sox could have hoped for. For 100 games he was batting .281 with 18 homers

Chapter 3—Maimed or Disfigured Extremities 99

Carlos May using special batting glove due to missing right thumb

and 62 runs batted in when he reported to Camp Pendleton, California for Marine Corps reserve training.

On August 11, 1969, May and his reserve unit were on the firing range practicing with live mortars. There were about a dozen guns in use, each loaded with six rounds of ammunition. In the deafening din, it was impossible to tell which guns were firing. When Carlos' gun wouldn't fire anymore, he assumed it was empty and shoved a ramrod down the barrel to swab it out. However, there was still an unfired shell in the barrel that was forced against the firing pin by the ramrod. Fortunately the shell didn't explode, but it shot out of the tube, shearing May's right thumb off at the first joint. The nail bed and the knuckle were gone, leaving a stub of flesh and gristle which was bent grotesquely back and embedded in Carlos' wrist. He also had powder burns on his left hand and face. Although the missing section of thumb was found about 50 feet away and rushed to the hospital, there was no way it could be re-attached.

Over the next four months, May underwent four surgical procedures. In the first operation, the stump that used to be his thumb had to be removed from the wrist and reseated in its proper position. The second procedure was to graft skin from his thigh onto the truncated digit. In October, while the baseball world was watching the Miracle New York Mets beat the heavily favored Baltimore Orioles in the World Series, Carlos was undergoing the first step of a complicated skin graft procedure which involved surgically attaching his right hand to his abdomen. The procedure was designed to facilitate the transfer of skin from his stomach to build up the remaining portion of his thumb.

A final operation was needed to disengage his hand, including the transplanted skin, from his stomach. With the cast still on his hand, Carlos began rehabilitation by tossing objects back and forth with his wife Margaret. After the cast was removed, his rehab routine often consisted of lobbing the ball or playing pepper with Margaret. This helped him keep his weight down and get used to handling a ball and bat with his partially reconstructed thumb.

That Christmas in Birmingham his brother Lee, a star with the Cincinnati Reds at the time, got his first look at Carlos' new thumb and was immediately filled with apprehension. "How can he throw a ball with that?" the older brother thought to himself.

But Carlos never had any doubt. He reported early to the White Sox spring training camp in Sarasota and quickly convinced Sox manager Don Gutteridge that he could handle the left field job. The White Sox had generously given May a new contract with a substantial raise and a guarantee that he would be paid for the full season even if he couldn't play. Carlos repaid their faith with interest with his solid 1970 comeback year. In 1971 he raised his average to a team-leading .294 and switched to first base to cut down on the long throws he had to make. He led the league's first sackers in total chances per game, although his 18 errors at first also led the league.

The 1972 season found the agreeable May moving back to left field to make room for newly acquired superstar Dick Allen at first base. With the enigmatic Allen capturing the Most Valuable Player Award, the Sox were in the race for the pennant for the first time in Carlos' career and ended up finishing second behind the Oakland A's. Carlos contributed a .308 batting average to the effort, a fraction of a point lower than Allen's team-best mark, and also swiped a career high 23 bases.

In the three seasons following his injury-shortened rookie campaign, May's batting average had improved each year, but his home run totals of 12, 7, and 12 were disappointing compared to his rookie output of 18 circuit blasts in less than two thirds of a season. Carlos' decrease in power was certainly understandable. For a left-handed batter the right thumb keeps the bat firmly locked in the lower hand. Before his injury, the sweet-swinging May was able to generate power by opening up his hips and letting go of the bat with his left (top) hand during his follow-through. After the injury, holding onto the bat during his follow-through was more difficult even with the aid of a special batting glove and he was forced to become more of a "hacker" or contact hitter at the plate.

Despite this limitation, May consciously decided to go for the fences in 1973 and managed to raise his output to 20 homers. He also drove in a career best 96 runs, but the cost was a 40-point drop in his batting average. It was the last really productive year at the plate for the 25-year-old outfielder.

Over the next four years, May's playing time decreased each season as he bounced from left field to first base to designated hitter. His high marks were an ordinary .271 batting average in 1975 and a mere eight homers in both 1974 and 1975. During the 1976 season the White Sox traded him to New York, where he got his first taste of postseason play. But he missed out on the Yankees World Championship in 1977 when he was sold to the California Angels late in the campaign. His big league days were over in the United States after the 1977 season, but he went overseas to extend his career another four years in Japan.

The Carlos May story is one of baseball's "Would've Been" tragedies, ranking right up there with the misfortunes of Pete Reiser, Herb Score, Monty Stratton, Tony Conigliaro, and other surefire future Hall of Famers who never reached the heights predicted of them due to unfortunate injuries. Carlos came up in the era when the pitcher was king, when team batting averages hovered around the .230 mark and anything approaching .300 was outstanding. As a raw rookie he joined one of the weakest hitting teams of the time and played his home games in a notorious "pitcher's park." Yet, before injury curtailed his freshman season, his stats projected to 27 homers, 96 runs batted in, and 87 walks in 550 plate appearances. Even though he missed more than a third of the season he still finished second on the team in homers and runs batted in behind Bill Melton and second in batting average to Walt "No Neck" Williams. His combination of consistency, power, and selectivity at the plate was rare for an established veteran — unheard of for an inexperienced 21-year-old kid. He also had good speed, a decent throwing arm, and a winning disposition.

Although *The Sporting News* named Carlos the American League's top rookie in 1969, he was denied the more prestigious Baseball Writer's Association Rookie of the Year Award when the scribes selected outfielder Lou Piniella of the Kansas City Royals for the honor. It was certainly a puzzling choice. Piniella had 493 official at-bats to May's 367, but hit 7 fewer homers, scored 19 fewer runs, and drew 25 fewer walks. Lou did drive in 6 more runs than Carlos, but it took him 126 more chances to do it. On defense, neither rookie was anything to write home about, but May's .982 fielding percentage was higher than Piniella's .977 average. In fact, the only area where Piniella's stats were better than May's was in batting where his .282 average was a point higher than May's .281 mark. Ironically May and Piniella ended up teammates and good friends, sharing the designated hitter spot for the Yankees in 1976 and 1977.

Even after the injury took away much of his power, May was still one of the better hitters in baseball. He finished seventh in the league in hitting in 1971 and fourth in 1972. He also finished among the league leaders in on-base percentage, runs, hits, total bases, and bases on balls in 1972, triples and stolen bases in 1971, and runs batted in in 1973. In 1972 he was selected to the American League All-Star Team for the second time.

Although his defense was often maligned, his glove was good enough that he continued to play in the field after the designated-hitter rule was adopted in 1973. His development probably suffered because he willingly shifted positions several times in the prime of his career for the good of the team. He would probably never have been considered an accomplished fielder, but there's no doubt that his throwing was hampered after his injury by his inability to grip the ball properly. It's the end of the thumb,

Chapter 3—Maimed or Disfigured Extremities

which Carlos was missing, that guides the ball when throwing and makes it possible for the thrower to aim it accurately.

For his career, May spent nine full seasons and part of a tenth as a major leaguer. He was a regular for seven of those years. In 1,165 games, his lifetime batting average was a respectable .274 and he blasted 90 homers and stole 85 bases. Late in his career he became an excellent pinch hitter, batting .375 in that role in his final two years. He played in the 1976 World Series with New York, but went hitless as the Yankees were swept in four straight games by the Cincinnati Reds.

Carlos still enjoys several distinctions. The White Sox were one of the first clubs to put the player's name on the back of their jersey, so he was the first player to wear his birthday (May 17) on his back when he was issued number 17. In 1969 Carlos and his brother Lee became the fourth brother combination to play in the All-Star Game together. They were actually the first pair to compete against each other since the previous duos, Joe and Dom DiMaggio, Harry and Dixie Walker, and Felipe and Matty Alou, were all on the same side when they appeared together. The May brothers' combined total of 56 homers that year is the third highest total by a brother duo in baseball history behind Joe and Vince DiMaggio's 59 in 1937, and Jason and Jeremy Giambi's combined 61 in 2002. They are currently in a fourth place tie with the Boyer brothers, behind Hank and Tommie Aaron, the three DiMaggio's, and Eddie and Rich Murray for career homers by a sibling contingent.

When his days as an active player came to an end, Carlos went to work for the Post Office, but has stayed involved in the game. He's still with the White Sox as a community relations representative with their Speaker's Bureau and serves as a batting instructor in their minor league system. He's often described as a genuinely nice guy. Indicative of his general good nature and positive outlook is that he actually considered himself lucky because he wasn't standing directly in front of the barrel when the gun fired.

During his time in the Camp Pendleton and Long Beach Naval hospitals, Carlos saw enough misfortune and misery to keep from ever feeling sorry for himself. In an interview before his successful comeback he said, "Everywhere I went, I saw kids worse off than I was.... All fresh back from Vietnam, those kids were. They had nothing. So what the hell right do I have to squawk about losing a little-bitty tip off the end of my thumb."

CARLOS MAY
B. May 17, 1948

YEAR	TEAM	LEAGUE	G	AB	R	H	HR	RBI	AVE	SB	POS
1966	Sarasota	Gulf Coast	16	47	11	20	0	10	.426	*	OF
	Winter Haven	Fla State	37	118	8	18	0	4	.153	*	OF
1967	Appleton	Midwest	63	207	45	70	10	48	.338	*	OF
1968	Lynchburg	Carolina	113	397	62	131	13	74	.330	*	OF
	CHICAGO	AL	17	67	4	12	0	1	.179	0	OF
1969	CHICAGO	AL	100	367	62	103	18	62	.281	1	OF
1970	CHICAGO	AL	150	555	83	158	12	68	.285	12	OF
1971	CHICAGO	AL	141	500	64	147	7	70	.294	16	1B
1972	CHICAGO	AL	148	523	83	161	12	68	.308	23	OF
1973	CHICAGO	AL	149	553	62	148	220	96	.268	8	DH-OF
1974	CHICAGO	AL	149	551	66	137	8	58	.249	8	OF
1975	CHICAGO	AL	128	454	55	123	8	53	.271	12	1B-OF
1976	CHIC-NY	AL	107	351	45	91	3	43	.259	5	DH
1977	NY-CAL	AL	76	199	21	47	2	17	.236	0	DH
1978-81	Japanese Leagues		*	*	*	*	*	*	*	*	*
MAJOR LEAGUE TOTALS			1165	4120	545	1127	290	536	.274	85	

GIL COAN

If young Carlos May wanted some first-hand advice on how to play baseball without a thumb he could have contacted former major league outfielder Gil Coan. A childhood injury had left Coan with little more than a stump for a left thumb, but he played nine full seasons and parts of two others in the major leagues, mostly with the Washington Senators.

Coan was a lefty hitter and right-handed thrower like May, but since it was his left thumb that was severed, he faced a different set of obstacles. In the field, Coan's throwing wasn't affected, but he sometimes had trouble squeezing the ball in his glove because of the thumb. At bat, Coan's impaired hand was the top one, which reportedly didn't affect his hitting in the least. If that's true, it's a mystery that May didn't turn around and hit from the right side after his injury since he was a switch-hitter when he originally signed with the White Sox.

Born May 18, 1922, in Monroe, North Carolina, Gilbert Fitzgerald Coan starred for the Ecusta Paper Corporation team in Brevard, North Carolina. He'd turned down earlier offers to turn pro to stay in Brevard and get married. But he soon found his job at the paper mill hazardous and unpleasant and accepted an offer to play in the Senators farm system in 1944. After splitting his first season between Kingsport of the Appalachian League and Chattanooga of the Southern Association, he hit .372 and stole 37 bases for Chattanooga in 1945 and was named the Minor League Player of the Year.

In 1946 the fleet, 6 foot tall, 180-pound rookie was billed by the Senators as the American League's next great star. He was said to be faster than George Case, Washington's longtime center fielder who had led the American League in stolen bases five straight years from 1939 to 1943 and would lead again in 1946 after being traded to the Cleveland Indians to make room for Coan.

But Gil never approached the stardom predicted of him. He reported to training camp overweight and out of shape in the spring of 1946 and hit a dismal .209 in 59 games for the year. After another spectacular season at Chattanooga in 1947, he finally broke into the Senators regular lineup in 1948 and stole 23 bases, the second highest total in the league. But his average was only .232 in 138 games. Coan finally compiled a respectable batting average in 1950 when he registered a .303 mark in part-time duty and enjoyed his best season in 1951 when he again hit .303 and scored 85 runs in 135 games, but he was no longer a stolen base threat by that time and was error-prone in the outfield due to his disability.

A poor 1952 season cost Gil his regular spot with the Senators and he was swapped to the Baltimore Orioles in 1954. He was sent to the White Sox and subsequently waived to the New York Giants in 1955. He returned to the minors in 1956 after a brief trial with the Giants and finished out the season with Minneapolis in the American Association. He retired from baseball after that season with a modest .254 career batting average — another performer whose rich promise was never fulfilled.

GILBERT FITZGERALD COAN
B. May 18, 1922

YEAR	TEAM	LEAGUE	G	AB	R	H	HR	RBI	AVE	SB	POS
1944	Kingsport	Appalach	72	267	76	98	13	64	.367	17	OF
	Chattanooga	Southern	48	194	47	65	0	15	.335	9	OF
1945	Chattanooga	Southern	140	540	126	201	16	117	.372	37	OF
1946	WASHINGTON	AL	59	134	17	28	3	9	.209	2	OF
1947	Chattanooga	Southern	151	585	126	199	22	92	.340	42	OF
	WASHINGTON	AL	11	42	5	21	0	3	.500	2	OF

YEAR	TEAM	LEAGUE	G	AB	R	H	HR	RBI	AVE	SB	POS
1948	WASHINGTON	AL	138	513	56	119	7	60	.232	23	OF
1949	WASHINGTON	AL	111	358	36	78	3	25	.218	9	OF
1950	WASHINGTON	AL	104	366	58	111	7	50	.303	10	OF
1951	WASHINGTON	AL	135	538	85	163	9	62	.303	8	OF
1952	WASHINGTON	AL	107	332	50	68	5	20	.205	9	OF
1953	WASHINGTON	AL	68	168	28	33	2	17	.196	7	OF
1954	BALTIMORE	AL	94	265	29	74	2	20	.279	9	OF
1955	BALT-CHICAGO	AL	87	160	18	36	1	12	.225	4	OF
	NEW YORK	NL	9	13	0	2	0	0	.154	0	OF
1956	NEW YORK	NL	4	1	2	0	0	0	.000	0	OF
	Minneapolis	*Am Ass'n*	*	*	*	*	12	54	.286		*OF
MAJOR LEAGUE TOTALS			918	2877	384	731	39	278	.254	83	

JIM MECIR

    Pitcher Jim Mecir, a current major leaguer with a serious permanent disability, is an example of a modern day player who wouldn't have stood a chance of competing in professional baseball before the advent of modern medical techniques. In fact, he defied a lot of medical opinions by reaching the major leagues and staying there. Mecir, who pitches for the Oakland A's, was born with a pair of club feet, a condition that was only partially corrected by surgical procedures. Despite this disability, the righthander is ranked as one of the top relief specialists in the game, a righthanded setup man who's also effective against lefthanded hitters. The 2003 campaign was his ninth year in the major leagues.

    A club foot is a malformation of the bones, joints, muscles, and blood vessels in the foot caused by abnormal prenatal development. In appearance the foot is somewhat kidney shaped with a high mid-foot arch. The condition is characterized by the turning in of the back part of the foot and the turning under of the forefoot. In addition, the heel is drawn up due to the tightened Achilles tendon, resulting in an inability to bring the foot to a flat standing position.

    Clubfoot is a relatively common birth defect, occurring in approximately one out of 735 births. The affliction is ancient; Egyptian mummies have been discovered with club feet. The disfigurement occurs roughly twice as often in boys as in girls and affects both feet about 50% of the time. Although the condition appears to be genetic, it seems to often be repressed and can skip many generations. The severity of the condition varies widely. Several world class athletes have been born with the deformity including Olympic figure skater Kristi Yamaguchi, pro-bowl quarterback Troy Aikman, and Mia Hamm, a star of women's professional soccer and fiancé of baseball star Nomar Garciaparra.

Mecir's left foot was straightened when he was an infant by the insertion of a bar between his feet. Another operation at the age of eight to fix his right foot wasn't as successful. Jim's calf muscle atrophied after the procedure, resulting in his right leg being an inch shorter than the left, which caused a pronounced limp.

Despite his disability, Mecir developed into an outstanding athlete. In addition to baseball, he also played basketball and actually ran track in high school. In fact, when Jim first joined the A's during the 2000 season, his new teammate (at the time) Jason Gambi recalled their first meeting in the 1994 Arizona Fall League. "I guarantee you he's one of the fastest guys on this team," Giambi stated. "He can fly."

Jim Mecir, a contemporary story of courage

Jim Mecir was born on May 16, 1970, in Bayside, New York, and grew up Smithtown on Long Island. His father is a firefighter, who was on vacation at the time of the World Trade Center terrorist attack, but rushed to the site to help search for missing co-workers and friends. Long Island is "Carl Yastrzemski" territory, and as an 18-year-old, Mecir won the award bearing Yaz's name that goes to the outstanding high school baseball player in Suffolk County. Other winners of note include current relief ace Bill Koch and infielder Tony Graffanino of the Chicago White Sox, former major leaguers Tom Veryzer and Neal Heaton, and former National Football League quarterback Boomer Esiason.

After high school, Jim attended Eckerd College in St. Petersburg, Florida, where his pitching coach was former major leaguer Rich Folkers. Initially, Folkers was dubious about Mecir's ability to play with his condition based on input from other coaches, but he was quickly impressed with Jim's all around athletic ability once he saw him in action. While at Eckerd, Mecir learned to throw a screwball from watching the left-handed Folkers work with a lefty teammate. The screwball is an unusual pitch that breaks in the opposite direction from the arm movement. Folkers wasn't trying to teach it to Mecir because it's usually a pitch that lefthanders develop to break away from right-handed batters. The most renowned screwballer was former 1930s New York Giants lefthander Carl Hubbell, although legendary righthander Christy Mathewson threw it. More recently, record-breaking righty relief ace Mike Marshall was a master of the pitch. Mecir, who was struggling with traditional breaking pitches, seemed to pick it up quickly and with Folker's encouragement incorporated it into his arsenal to complement his fastball.

In the third round of the 1991 amateur draft, Mecir was selected by the Seattle Mariners and began his professional career as a starting pitcher with San Bernardino in the California League that year. After three mediocre seasons as a starter, he switched to relief with Jacksonville in 1994. The results were outstanding. He posted an excellent 2.69 earned run average and compiled 13 saves. Jim's days as a starter were over. He's never started another game since except for a one inning minor league rehab assignment in 2001. After another fine performance in relief for Tacoma in 1995, Mecir was called up to the Mariners for a late season audition.

In the off-season, Jim was sent to the New York Yankees along with first baseman Tino Martinez and reliever Jeff Nelson for pitcher Sterling Hitchcock and third baseman Russ Davis. He spent the 1996 and 1997 seasons bouncing between the Yankees and their Columbus affiliate, pitching well in the minors, but failing to establish himself in the big leagues.

After the 1997 campaign, Mecir caught a break when he was selected by the newly formed Tampa Bay Devil Rays in the expansion draft. Finally getting an opportunity to pitch regularly, he won 7 games while losing only 2, posted a fine 3.11 earned run average, and struck out 77 batters in 84 innings in 1998. He got off to a great start the next year, appearing in 17 of Tampa Bay's first 34 games, but fractured his right elbow in a freak collision with a teammate during pregame conditioning exercise to end his season prematurely.

Jim came back from the arm injury to post a fine 7–2 won-lost record for Tampa Bay before being swapped to Oakland in July 2000. Although it was exciting to move from a cellar dwelling club to a contender, the Tampa Bay area had become Mecir's adopted home. It's where he attended college and where he'd met his wife Pamela, a Tampa native. Jim was drafted by Tampa Bay while the couple was honeymooning and they'd set up housekeeping in nearby Gulfport, so it was difficult to leave. But Mecir quickly became an integral part of the A's bullpen corps, setting up for closer Jason Isringhausen. He even closed some games and racked up four saves when Isringhausen hit a rough spell. For the season, Mecir's combined won-lost record for Tampa Bay and Oakland was 10 wins against 3 losses, which gave him the second highest winning percentage in the league. The A's made it to the Division Series as the wildcard club. They lost to the Yankees, but Mecir was outstanding, pitching five and one-third scoreless innings in three appearances and yielding only one hit.

Jim also pitched well in 2001 as the A's again captured the American League West wildcard berth. But the year was not without some disconcerting physical problems for Mecir. His disfigured right leg started to give him trouble and for the first time, his disability actually put him on the disabled list.

Throughout his career, Jim had steadfastly followed the universal mantra of athletes with disabilities—claiming that his condition didn't really put him at a disadvantage. He had always stubbornly maintained that his limp was the sole manifestation of his disfigurement and it only affected his walking. But the reality is that Jim's whole pitching motion is unconventional because of the foot. He isn't able to keep his left shoulder closed the way pitchers are generally taught. Instead the shoulder flies open when he delivers the ball because he can't drive off the mound properly with his defective right leg. Therefore, his delivery is largely dependent on the torque generated from his upper body. Of course, Mecir claims that this actually helps him by making his pitches more difficult for the batter to pick up. In addition, he contends that his upper body delivery allows him to throw his vaunted screwball more naturally.

But finally, even Jim had to accept the fact that his condition was having an adverse impact on his body. Mecir is a big man, packing 230 pounds on a 6'1" frame. Over the years the constant wear and tear, which was intensified by the misalignment of his right leg, destroyed the cartilage in his knee. Complicating the problem is that in addition to clubfeet, Jim was born without an anterior cruciate ligament. Now that he has almost no cartilage left, the bone grinding on bone causes muscle problems as well.

In August 2001 Mecir's knee became so painfully inflamed that he had to undergo arthroscopic surgery. During the procedure, a jelly-like material harvested from the back of a rooster's head was injected into the knee to lubricate the joint and rebuild the damaged meniscus or fibrous cartilage. Jim was activated in early September and posted a sensational 1.46 earned run average over his final 12 appearances to help Oakland land a postseason spot. But he was not as effective in the Division Series as the

A's were again eliminated by the Yankees, this time after capturing the first two games.

Mecir's 2002 season was similar to the previous campaign. He pitched well, but as the season wore on his knee wore out. He ended up with a 6–4 won-lost mark in 61 games, but his activity was greatly reduced in the closing months of the season because of soreness in his right knee. The damaged right knee was simply making it impossible for him to plant his foot and deliver the ball with the same velocity he once had. In the past, Jim's fastball approached the mid-90s, but now he struggled to reach the 90 mph mark. Down the stretch, Mecir served a three game suspension after he precipitated a brawl by hitting White Sox shortstop Royce Clayton with a pitch. The A's won the division title outright, but they were once again eliminated in the first round, this time by the California Angels. Mecir pitched only a single scoreless inning in the Division Series.

Going into the 2003 season, Mecir's career won-lost record stood at 26 wins and 23 losses and his earned run average was 3.70 for 316 major league games, all of them in relief. But in postseason play his earned run average was a sparkling 1.88 for six appearances. He's considered one of the best middle relievers at stranding baserunners as evidenced by the fact that during his career he's held batters to a .224 composite batting average with runners in scoring position. His elusive screwball gives him an uncanny ability to get lefthanded batters out. In 2002 southpaw swingers batted only .204 against him, the eighth lowest figure among all American League pitchers. In fact, he's held lefties to a .214 batting average for his career. Jim's also stingy with the long ball. He went 35 games without giving up a homer until Seattle's Mike Cameron belted one off him in September 2002.

Although Mecir, who now lives in Kildeer, Illinois, still had two years to go on his contract with the A's, the 32-year-old-year-old veteran's career was in jeopardy due to his ailing right knee. The problem was compounded when he injured his left knee in the off-season while playing with his children. In November 2002, he underwent surgery to repair a torn patella tendon and was expected to miss the first two months of the 2003 season. Oakland desperately needs a healthy Mecir, especially since last year's closer Billy Koch was dispatched to the White Sox. The financially constrained A's have been an amazingly resilient team. In 2002 they finished first in the American League West despite the loss of slugging first baseman and former Most Valuable Player Giambi, ace reliever Isringhausen, and star outfielder Johnny Damon through free agency. They hope that their valuable setup specialist is equally resilient.

Jim's former pitching coach with the Tampa Bay, Rick Williams, had

Chapter 3—Maimed or Disfigured Extremities 111

this to say about Mecir while he was with the Devil Rays: "Courage is the first word that comes to mind. Guts ... Perseverance.... Not listening to anyone tell him what he could not do and proving that he can.... It's just not a factor with him. It really isn't a limitation. He's turned it into a non-factor. "

Unfortunately, Jim Mecir's disability has become a factor. But don't bet against him turning it into a non-factor again.

JAMES JASON MECIR
B. May 16, 1970

YEAR	TEAM	LEAGUE	G	IP	SO	BB	W	L	ERA	GS	SV
1991	San Bernardino	California	14	70	48	37	3	5	4.22	12	1
1992	San Bernardino	California	14	62	53	26	4	5	4.67	11	0
1993	Riverside	California	26	145	85	58	9	11	4.33	26	0
1994	Jacksonville	Southern	46	80	53	35	6	5	2.69	0	13
1995	Tacoma	Pac Coast	40	70	46	28	1	4	3.10	0	8
	SEATTLE	AL	2	5	3	2	0	0	0.00	0	0
1996	NEW YORK	AL	26	40	38	23	1	1	5.13	0	0
	Columbus	Internat'l	33	48	52	15	3	3	2.27	0	7
1997	NEW YORK	AL	25	34	25	10	0	4	5.88	0	0
	Columbus	Internat'l	24	27	34	6	1	1	1.00	0	11
1998	Tampa Bay	AL	68	84	77	33	7	2	3.11	0	0
1999	Tampa Bay	AL	17	21	15	14	0	1	2.61	0	0
2000	Tampa Bay	AL	38	50	33	22	7	2	3.08	0	1
	Oakland	AL	25	35	37	14	3	1	2.80	0	4
2001	Oakland	AL	54	63	61	26	2	8	3.43	0	3
	Sacramento	Pac Coast	1	1	0	0	0	0	0.00	1	0
2002	Oakland	AL	61	68	53	29	6	4	4.26	0	1
MAJOR LEAGUE TOTALS			316	400	342	173	26	23	3.70	0	9

Four

Impaired Organ Function or Chronic Illness

WILLIAM "DUMMY" HOY

William Hoy was known to the baseball world as "Dummy Hoy" throughout his lifetime. He was the first baseball player with a major disability to achieve stardom. Hoy played in the big leagues from 1888 until 1902 and was rated one of the top defensive center fielders of the era. In 1,796 major league games he scored 1,424 runs and banged out more than 2,000 hits. His lifetime batting average was .287 and he stole 594 bases, which was the fourth greatest career total at the time he retired.

Hoy was a deaf mute who played in a time when insensitive and sometimes cruelly descriptive nicknames were common. Players from rural areas were often called Rube and players with Indian heritage were invariably referred to as Chief. Then there was "Piano Legs" Hickman, "Jumbo" McGinnis, "Grasshopper" Whitney, "One Arm" Daily, and "Wee Willie" Keeler to name a few players whose uncomplimentary nicknames were based on physical traits. A deaf player, of course, would automatically be called "Dummy." In fact, if Hoy hadn't been deaf, he probably would have been called "Shorty" or "Kid" or even "Wee Willie" due to his diminutive stature. Although the *Baseball Encyclopedia* lists Hoy's height as 5'6" and weight at 160 pounds, other references put him in the 5'4", 145-pound range. His size may have been as much of a hindrance to getting a chance in baseball as his deafness.

William Ellsworth Hoy was born on May 23, 1862, in the small Ohio town of Houcktown. He completely lost his hearing at the age of three during a bout of meningitis. He mastered sign language and also became a proficient lip reader. The meningitis also affected his speech, but he was able to communicate in a strained, squeaky voice that was sometimes difficult for strangers to understand.

Chapter 4—Impaired Organ Function or Chronic Illness

As a youngster, Hoy attended the Ohio State School for the Deaf in Columbus, Ohio, completing grade school and high school in six years and graduating as class valedictorian. He apprenticed as a cobbler, a common occupation for the deaf at that time, and eventually opened a small shoe repair shop in his hometown of Houcktown. On weekends he played semi-pro baseball, usually as a catcher.

Hoy didn't get his start in professional baseball until 1886 when he was 24 years old. His performance as a semipro caught the attention of Frank Selee, manager of the Oshkosh club in the Northwestern League, and he was given a contract. Selee, who would later manage in the major leagues for 16 years, stood behind his protégé when he got off to a poor start and was rewarded with an excellent .328 first year batting average and a gaudy .367 mark in 1887. After that, Selee sold Hoy's contract to the Washington team in the National League.

In 1888 Hoy enjoyed a sensational rookie year for last place Washington. His .274 batting average was the highest on the team and he led the entire league with 82 stolen bases. The young outfielder quickly became a fan favorite for his exciting style of play. He was affectionately called "The Amazing Dummy" and when he made an outstanding play, the crowd would show their appreciation by standing up and wildly waving their hats. Hoy was a fleet, daring baserunner and combined tremendous range with a strong arm in the outfield. He played a shallow center field and was expert at charging the ball and getting it back in fast to nab or hold runners. In the outfield, fellow fly chasers knew that it was Hoy's ball and they should back off when they heard his throaty, squawking call. At the plate, the little left-handed hitter didn't have much power, but he had a good eye and walked frequently. He usually batted in the leadoff spot to take advantage of his speed and high on-base percentage.

Hoy's career could be called a case study in the evolution of the major leagues in the late 1800s through the turn of the century. After a fine sophomore season with Washington, he jumped to the newly formed Players League for the 1890 season and hit .298 for Buffalo, his third last place team in his first three years. The Players League folded after one season and Hoy signed with St. Louis in the American Association, which had been formed in 1882 and was considered a major league at the time. With second-place St. Louis in 1891 Hoy finally got a chance to play with a winning team, but the American Association was absorbed by the National League after the season and he found himself back with Washington and back in the depths of the National League. Despite Hoy's fine play, Washington finished tenth in the twelve team National League in 1892 and returned to the cellar in 1893.

"Dummy" Hoy's 1888 Old Judge Cabinet Card

Chapter 4—Impaired Organ Function or Chronic Illness 115

In 1894 Hoy returned to his home state to play for Cincinnati and stayed there for four seasons, hitting a combined .292 but never cracking the .300 mark. The Reds ranked among the worst teams in the league when he first reported but had climbed into the first division by the time he moved to Louisville in 1898. Louisville finished ninth in both of Hoy's seasons with the club, but he hit over .300 for the first time in 1898. For the 1899 season, he registered a career high .306 average in a league-leading 633 at-bats at the age of 37.

Hoy seemed to be getting better with age, although the baseball world really didn't know exactly how old he was. During his first season with Oshkosh back in 1886, a local newspaperman went through the clubhouse taking down each player's age, height, and weight. Probably because of Hoy's affliction, the reporter didn't interview him and just put him down as 20 years old rather than his correct age of 24. The young outfielder elected to let the new number stand, figuring it wouldn't hurt if the big leagues thought he was a little younger than he really was.

At the age of 38 Hoy decided to start the new century in a new league and signed on with the Chicago White Stockings in the fledgling American League for the 1900 season. Although Chicago finished in first place, the American League wasn't technically considered a major league until 1901. The White Stockings celebrated the American League's inaugural season as a recognized major league by again finishing in first place. The 39-year-old Hoy, who batted .294, led the league in walks, and scored more than 100 runs for the ninth time, was finally on a pennant winner in the major leagues.

In 1902 Hoy was back with Cincinnati, as Chicago elected to go with Fielder Jones in center field. Hoy batted .290 for the year but lost his spot in the regular lineup when Cincinnati acquired Cy Seymour and Joe Kelley from Baltimore in mid-season. The 41-year-old star finished his professional career in 1903 with Los Angeles in the Pacific Coast League, where he played in all 211 games of the expanded Pacific Coast League schedule and swiped 46 bases.

After his retirement from baseball, Hoy lived on an Ohio farm with his wife, Anna Maria, who he'd met in Cincinnati. Anna was also a deaf mute and a teacher for the deaf. Their son, Carson, became a prominent Cincinnati jurist.

In 1961 Hoy was asked to throw out the first ball for the third game of the 1961 World Series between the Cincinnati Reds and the New York Yankees, the first game in Cincinnati. Upon hearing that Hoy was 99 years old, announcer Joe Garagiola wondered if that was his real age or his baseball age. Hoy died a little more than two months later on December 15,

1961. At the time of his death he had lived longer than any other major leaguer.

During his career, Hoy managed to collect some interesting and remarkable accomplishments. He is said to be one of only three outfielders to nail three baserunners at the plate in one game. The year was 1889 and the catcher was none other than the legendary Connie Mack according to reports. Hoy is also one of a small handful of men who played in four different circuits that were considered major leagues. Although he slugged only 40 homers in his career, he hit the first gram slam home run in American League history in 1901. In addition, he was something of an iron man despite his small stature. He never appeared in fewer than 100 games until his last season with Cincinnati.

Hoy's name often comes up for Hall of Fame consideration when they start talking about admitting more 19th-century stars, but thus far his credentials have not been considered quite good enough. But Hoy was first in the hearts of his fellow deaf Americans, at least in the realm of sports. While he was playing, he was a model for deaf students at Gallaudet College in Washington, D.C. They often went to see him play, and he visited the campus at every opportunity. In 1951 the American Athletic Association of the Deaf established its own Hall of Fame to honor outstanding deaf athletes and sports leaders. By unanimous vote, the first person to be enshrined was William Hoy.

OTHER DEAF PLAYERS

Contrary to popular opinion, William Hoy was not the first deaf player in the big leagues. That distinction belongs to Ed "Dummy" Dundon a pitcher for Columbus in the old American Association in 1883 and 1884. In fact, although Hoy is often given credit for the innovation, it may have been Dundon who initiated the use of hand signals to indicate balls and strikes. Dundon reportedly umpired a game in Mobile, Alabama, in 1886 and used hand signals to communicate his decisions. It may have been due to Hoy's longevity, however, that the practice caught on and became standard at all levels.

Edward Joseph Dundon was born July 10, 1859, and attended the Ohio State School for the Deaf with William Hoy, who was three years his junior. Primarily a pitcher, he posted a record of 3 wins and 16 losses as a rookie in 1883, but improved to 6 and 4 in his second and last season. He also played the outfield, hitting for a paltry .151 lifetime batting average. Dundon was from Columbus and died there at the age of 34 in 1893.

It was William Hoy's success at the major league level that paved the way for another deaf mute, Luther Taylor. Taylor, who also endured the nickname "Dummy," was a right-handed pitcher whose big league career began as Hoy's was winding down. Taylor was born on February 25, 1875, and hailed from Oskaloosa, Kansas. He attended the Kansas School for the Deaf before beginning his professional baseball career with the Albany, New York team in the Eastern League in 1900. The slender hurler, who stood 6'1" and weighed only 160 pounds, soon caught the eye of the New York Giants and finished the season with them. In 1901 Taylor led the league in games pitched and losses for the seventh place Giants.

Taylor jumped to the American League at the beginning of the 1902, but soon returned to New York. With Hoy moving over from the American League to finish out his career with Cincinnati in 1902, it was the only season that two deaf players competed against each other in the major leagues. The Giants ended up in last place in 1902, but that was the year that the legendary John McGraw began his 30-year reign as manager of the Giants.

Under McGraw the Giants quickly built a National League dynasty. McGraw traded away everyone except Taylor, future Hall of Fame great Christy Mathewson, and catcher Frank Bowerman. From 1903 through 1907 Luther teamed with Mathewson and Joe McGinnity in the Giant's starting rotation and won 78 games, including 21 wins in the 1904 championship season.

Taylor was a big favorite of manager McGraw. McGraw knew sign language, and the two often coached the bases together, clowning around and baiting umpires in sign language to the delight of the fans. In fact, there's an anecdote about Taylor getting tossed from a game for silently insulting an umpire who happened to be fluent in sign language, but the identity of the umpire varies. At the height of his career, Luther was so popular in New York that Broadway celebrities like the famous Lillian Russell often attended Giants games just to see him perform. Taylor's unusual windup and delivery, described as a "corkscrew turn," also pleased the fans and moved one writer to compose an often reprinted poem about the deaf mute hurler.

When his fastball began to fade, Luther fell to only eight victories in 1908 and was sent back to the minor leagues. The team was so sorry to see the colorful 34-year-old pitcher go that they presented him with a solid gold medal decorated with 20 diamonds. Taylor pitched another six years in the minors before his 40-year-old arm finally gave out. He spent some time umpiring in the Midwest, probably the first deaf umpire in pro baseball, before beginning a career working with hearing impaired young people. He successfully coached baseball and football for the Kansas School for the Deaf and then joined the staff of the Illinois School for the Deaf in Jacksonville. In retirement he scouted for the Giants and in 1952 the American Athletic Association of the Deaf made him the second inductee into their Hall of Fame, preceded only by William Hoy.

Luther Taylor died on August 22, 1958, but not before leaving a legacy. At the Illinois School for the Deaf, one of his charges was a kid named Dick Sipek, who developed into an outstanding baseball, football, and basketball player under Taylor's tutelage. Taylor managed to hook Sipek up with the Cincinnati Reds following graduation, and after two seasons in the minors, Sipek spent the 1945 season with the Reds. He thus became the first deaf player in the major leagues since Luther Taylor left the Giants almost 40 years earlier. After one Reds game, the 22-year-old Sipek was surprised to find 83-year-old "Dummy" Hoy, a former Cincinnati player, waiting outside the clubhouse to meet him.

Dick Sipek, who was born January 16, 1923, in Chicago, lost most of his hearing in an accident at the age of five, but was able to speak. The 5'9", 175-pounder was a right-handed throwing, lefty batting outfielder like Hoy. He broke in with a sensational .424 average and 42 runs batted in in 37 games with Erwin in the Appalachian League in 1943 and hit .319 with 85 runs batted in for Birmingham in the Southern Association in 1944. He hit .244 in 82 games for the Reds in 1945, his only major league season, but went on to play another six seasons in the minors. In 1951, his last season in organized baseball, Sipek hit .322 for Reidsville in the Carolina League.

Years after his retirement from baseball, Sipek was playing in a golf tournament at a convention for the deaf, when he noticed another golfer pointing him out and signing that "he was the last deaf player in professional baseball." Dick approached the man in the clubhouse afterward and told him that he didn't want to be remembered as the last deaf player. He wanted to see another deaf ballplayer reach the big leagues.

Sipek's wish was realized in 1993 when Montreal Expos outfielder Curtis Pride became the first deaf major leaguer in almost 50 years. Pride's first major league hit was greeted with a five-minute standing ovation from a capacity crowd at Montreal's Olympic Stadium. Like Sipek, Pride was also an accomplished multi-sport athlete. In high school in Washington, D.C., he excelled in soccer, basketball, wrestling, swimming, track, and gymnastics, as well as baseball. Curtis was the only American named as one of the top 15 youth soccer players in the world and was a member of the U.S. National All-Star Soccer Team which competed for the 1985 Junior World Cup in China. He was a *Parade Magazine* high school All-American in basketball and became a four-year starter at point guard for the College of William and Mary.

When Sally Pride was pregnant with Curtis in 1968 she contracted German measles. Curtis was born December 17 and by the age of nine months, the infant was diagnosed as congenitally deaf with a 95% hearing loss. But unlike the deaf baseball players who preceded him, Pride was "mainstreamed" in the fourth grade after spending three years in special education classes. From the beginning he'd refused to learn sign language, instead developing lip reading skills. He graduated from high school with a 3.6 grade point average (on a 4.0 scale) and earned a full college basketball scholarship.

But baseball had been Pride's first love since T-ball. He was drafted by the New York Mets out of high school and worked out a deal whereby he played professional baseball during the summer while attending William and Mary the rest of the year. Curtis graduated in 1990 with a degree in finance, but he was not making as much progress in baseball, partially due to missing so much time while in college. After seven years in the minor leagues he'd only advanced to Double A ball.

Before the 1993 season, Curtis became a free agent and signed with the Expos, who promised him more playing time. He caught fire in the Expos' system, going from Class AA to Class AAA to the National League in one year. For the season, he batted a combined .324 with 21 homers and 50 stolen bases. Pride spent the strike-shortened 1994 campaign in the minor leagues and didn't return to the Expos until June 1995. He had only 63 at-bats with the Expos before returning to minors to help Ottawa win the International League championship.

In 1996 the 27-year-old outfielder signed with the American League Detroit Tigers and his career finally seemed to take off. He appeared in 95 games for the Tigers and hit .300 with 10 homers and 11 stolen bases, but the following season, his average sagged to .210 before he was released in August. The Boston Red Sox signed Curtis to a minor league contract later that month and recalled him in September. He managed to hit a home run in his first time at bat for the Red Sox but only got one more plate appearance that season.

Prior to the 1998 season, Pride signed with the Atlanta Braves and played in 70 games that year as a reserve outfielder and pinch hitter. He returned to the minor leagues the next season and has spent most of the next four seasons in the minors except for brief trials with the Red Sox in 2000 and the Expos in 2001.

Like Hoy and Sipek before him, Pride bats from the left side and throws right-handed. He's an even six feet tall and tips the scales at a muscular 205 pounds. He's characterized as a powerful, aggressive player and a good fastball hitter who has some problems with off-speed pitches.

Pride has been a spokesman for the Better Hearing Institute and makes numerous appearances on behalf of children with disabilities. In the off-season he works as a special education instructor with physically and learning disabled children and volunteers as a youth soccer coach.

In recognition of his achievements and community service, Curtis has been honored with the National Council on Communicative Disorders' Youth Achievement Award and the *Washington Post's* All-Met Distinguished Alumni Award and was also named one of 1995s Ten Outstanding Young Americans by the U.S. Junior Chamber of Commerce.

Curtis Pride played in the Pittsburgh Pirates minor league system in 2002. At the age of 34, his chances of making it back to the big leagues appear slim. But Curtis says that his disability taught him not to quit and not to need sympathy from people or expect them to treat him differently. So don't count him out yet and don't feel sorry for him.

WILLIAM ELLSWORTH "DUMMY" HOY
B. May 23, 1862 D. December 15, 1961

YEAR	TEAM	LEAGUE	G	AB	R	H	HR	RBI	AVE	SB	POS
1886	Oshkosh	Northwest	71	232	69	76	*	*	.328	*	OF
1887	Oshkosh	Northwest	116	531	108	195	*	*	.367	*	OF
1888	WASHINGTON	NL	136	503	77	138	2	29	.274	82	OF
1889	WASHINGTON	NL	127	507	98	139	0	39	.274	35	OF
1890	BUFFALO	PL	122	493	107	147	1	53	.298	39	OF
1891	ST. LOUIS	AA	139	559	134	163	5	64	.292	59	OF
1892	WASHINGTON	NL	152	593	108	166	3	75	.280	60	OF
1893	WASHINGTON	NL	130	564	106	138	0	45	.245	48	OF
1894	CINCINNATI	NL	128	495	114	148	5	70	.299	27	OF
1895	CINCINNATI	NL	107	429	93	119	3	55	.277	50	OF
1896	CINCINNATI	NL	121	443	120	132	4	57	.298	50	OF
1897	CINCINNATI	NL	128	497	87	145	2	42	.292	37	OF
1898	LOUISVILLE	NL	148	582	104	177	6	66	.304	37	OF
1899	LOUISVILLE	NL	154	633	116	194	5	49	.306	32	OF
1900	Chicago	Am Ass'n	137	547	115	139	1	*	.254	32	OF
1901	CHICAGO	AL	132	527	112	155	2	60	.294	27	OF
1902	CINCINNATI	NL	72	279	48	81	2	20	.290	11	OF
1903	Los Angeles	Pac Coast	211	804	156	210	*	*	.261	46	OF
MAJOR LEAGUE TOTALS			1796	7104	1424	2042	40	724	.287	594	

LUTHER HADEN "DUMMY" TAYLOR
B. February 21, 1875 D. August 22, 1958

YEAR	TEAM	LEAGUE	G	IP	SO	BB	W	L	ERA	CG	SO
1900	Albany	Eastern	*	*	*	*	10	8	*	*	*
	NEW YORK	NL	11	62	16	24	4	3	2.45	6	0
1901	NEW YORK	NL	45	353	136	112	18	27	3.18	37	4
1902	CLEVELAND	AL	4	34	8	8	1	3	1.59	4	1
	NEW YORK	NL	26	201	87	55	7	15	2.29	18	0
1903	NEW YORK	NL	33	245	94	89	13	13	4.23	18	1
1904	NEW YORK	NL	37	296	138	75	21	15	2.34	29	5
1905	NEW YORK	NL	32	213	91	51	16	9	2.66	18	4
1906	NEW YORK	NL	31	213	91	57	17	9	2.20	13	2
1907	NEW YORK	NL	28	171	56	46	11	7	2.42	11	3
1908	NEW YORK	NL	27	128	50	34	8	5	2.33	6	1
1909-14			(Minor League Records Not Available)								
MAJOR LEAGUE TOTALS			274	1916	767	551	116	106	2.75	160	21

EDWARD JOSEPH "DUMMY" DUNDON
B. July 10, 1859 D. August 18, 1893

YEAR	TEAM	LEAGUE	G	AB	R	H	HR	RBI	AVE	BB	POS
1883	COLUMBUS	AA	26	93	8	15	0	*	.161	3	P-OF-2B
1884	COLUMBUS	AA	26	86	6	12	0	*	.140	5	OF-P-1B
MAJ. LGE. BATTING TOTALS			52	179	14	27	0	*	.151	8	

YEAR	TEAM	LEAGUE	G	IP	SO	BB	W	L	ERA	CG	SHO
1883	COLUMBUS	AA	20	167	31	38	3	16	4.48	16	0
1884	COLUMBUS	AA	11	81	37	15	6	4	3.78	7	0
MAJ. LGE. PITCHING TOTALS			31	248	68	53	9	20	4.25	23	0

RICHARD FRANCIS SIPEK
B. January 16, 1923

YEAR	TEAM	LEAGUE	G	AB	R	H	HR	RBI	AVE	BB	POS
1943	Erwin	Appalach	*	*	*	*	2	42	.424	*	OF
	Birmingham	Southern	*	*	*	*	2	25	.336	*	OF
1944	Birmingham	Southern	*	*	*	*	4	85	.319	*	OF
1945	Reds	NL	82	156	14	38	0	13	.244	9	PH-OF

YEAR	TEAM	LEAGUE	G	AB	R	H	HR	RBI	AVE	BB	POS
1946	Syracuse	Internat'l	*	*	*	*	1	22	.245	*	OF
1947	Columbia	S Atlantic	*	*	*	*	4	57	.272	*	OF
1948	Reidsville	Carolina	*	*	*	*	13	78	.318	*	OF
1949	Reidsville	Carolina	*	*	*	*	14	71	.321	*	OF
1950	Reidsville	Carolina	*	*	*	*	2	20	.246	*	OF
1951	Reidsville	Carolina	*	*	*	*	11	67	.322	*	OF
MAJOR LEAGUE TOTALS			82	156	14	38	0	13	.244	9	

CURTIS JOHN PRIDE
B. December 17, 1968

YEAR	TEAM	LEAGUE	G	AB	R	H	HR	RBI	AVE	SB	POS
1986	Kingsport	Appalach	27	46	5	5	1	4	.109	5	OF
1987	Kingsport	Appalach	31	104	22	25	1	9	.240	14	OF
1988	Kingsport	Appalach	70	268	59	76	8	27	.284	23	OF
1989	Pittsfield	NY-Penn	55	212	35	55	6	23	.259	9	OF
1990	Columbia	S Atlantic	53	191	38	51	6	25	.267	11	OF
1991	St. Lucie	Fla State	116	392	57	102	9	37	.260	24	OF
1992	Birmingham	Eastern	118	388	54	88	10	42	.227	14	OF
1993	Harrisburg	Eastern	50	180	51	64	15	39	.356	21	OF
	Ottawa	Internat'l	69	262	55	79	6	22	.302	29	OF
	MONTREAL	NL	10	9	3	4	1	5	.444	1	OF
1994	W Palm Beach	Fla State	3	8	5	6	1	3	.750	2	OF
	Ottawa	Internat'l	82	300	56	77	9	32	.257	22	OF
1995	Ottawa	Internat'l	42	154	25	43	4	24	.279	8	OF
	MONTREAL	NL	48	63	10	11	0	2	.175	3	OF
1996	Toledo	Internat'l	9	26	4	6	1	2	.231	4	OF
	DETROIT	AL	95	267	52	80	10	31	.300	11	OF
1997	DET-BOSTON	AL	81	164	22	35	3	20	.213	6	OF
	Pawtucket	Internat'l	1	3	0	0	0	0	.000	0	OF
1998	ATLANTA	NL	70	107	19	27	3	9	.252	4	OF
	Richmond	Internat'l	21	78	11	19	2	6	.244	8	OF
1999	Nashua	Atlantic	14	32	0	2	0	2	.063	0	OF
2000	Norfolk	Internat'l	15	31	9	9	1	4	.290	3	OF
	Pawtucket	Internat'l	48	154	44	47	9	31	.305	12	OF
	BOSTON	AL	9	20	4	5	0	0	.250	0	OF
	Albuquerque	Pac Coast	38	133	30	39	6	17	.293	7	OF
2001	Ottawa	Internat'l	22	81	14	27	5	15	.333	6	OF
	MONTREAL	NL	36	76	8	19	1	9	.250	3	OF
	Jupiter	Fla State	6	21	3	4	0	0	.190	0	OF
2002	Nashville	Pac Coast	110	385	71	114	10	46	.296	22	OF
MAJOR LEAGUE TOTALS			349	706	118	181	18	76	.256	28	

GEORGE "SPECS" TOPORCER

"Hey, Four Eyes!"

To this day what bespectacled kid doesn't shudder a little every time he hears that familiar jeer. Today glasses have become commonplace and sometimes even stylish, at least for adults. But that was not the case 80 years ago, especially for a serious athlete.

George Toporcer was the first non-pitcher to break the ice and wear eyeglasses in the major leagues. Wearing glasses doesn't seem like much of a hindrance now, but when the nearsighted Toporcer was active the only eyeglasses available were ordinary wire-framed reading glasses with heavy breakable lenses.

But the biggest obstacle young Toporcer had to overcome was not performing with glasses. It was the attitude of an era which dictated that nobody played ball with eyeglasses because it was dangerous and because a bespectacled player couldn't possibly expect to see well enough. In fact, a popular old baseball axiom of the time was, "Baseball doesn't make passes at players who wear glasses." Nevertheless, Toporcer made the St. Louis Cardinals squad in 1921 without the benefit of any high school, college, or professional baseball experience. He stayed with them until early in the 1928 season and compiled a solid .279 lifetime batting average as one of the best utility players in the game. He then moved down to the minor leagues and became one of the top performers in International League history.

"Specs" Toporcer's reading (and playing) glasses

The first professional baseball player to wear eyeglasses was Will White, a pitcher who won 229 games from 1878 through 1886, mostly with Cincinnati. The first 20th century player to wear corrective lenses was Lee Meadows, another pitcher, who made the big leagues in 1915 and lasted 15 seasons with three different National League teams and won 20 games for the Pittsburgh Pirates in 1926. Pitcher Carmen Hill, who also debuted in 1915 and also later enjoyed a 20-win season, was the second 20th century player to wear glasses. However, all of the bespectacled players who preceded Toporcer were pitchers who were not expected to carry their weight at the plate and did not face the rigors of playing the field every day.

George "Specs" Toporcer was born in New York City in 1899 and grew up in the Big Apple. Actor Jimmy Cagney grew up a few blocks away and was a grade school buddy who remained a lifelong friend. George's father was a cobbler and the family, which included two older brothers, lived in an apartment above the shoemaking shop. As a boy, baseball was the all-consuming passion of George's life, but for a skinny kid with eyeglasses, actually playing professional baseball seemed like a pipe dream. He was the Giants' biggest fan and cried himself to sleep the night they lost the 1908 National League pennant because rookie Fred Merkle neglected to touch second base on what should have been a game-winning hit. By the age of ten, George was hiking five miles each way to the Polo Grounds to watch the Giants in action. He didn't have the price of admission but was able to watch the games from Coogan's Bluff, a rocky hill behind the home plate area. Occasionally, when the Giants were out of town, he went to see the Yankees, who were then playing at Hilltop Park. But he had no real interest in the Highlanders, as the Yankees were called back then. He just wanted to see some of the American League stars of the period.

George was almost blind without corrective lenses. He'd worn eyeglasses since he started school because he was so nearsighted that he couldn't see the blackboard without them. When he was in the seventh grade, his school organized a baseball team, but he wasn't even allowed to try out because he wore eyeglasses and was thought to be too frail. Despite not being allowed to play, George followed the school team around to all its games. He got his big break when the team found itself a player short and he was the only alternative. He made the most of his opportunity, rapping out two hits and making a sensational catch in center field. From then on he was in the regular lineup.

In 1913 George's father died and his older brother Rudy took over the family business, which had evolved into producing arch-supports. George, who was a good student and an avid reader, had just graduated from grade school, but he had to give up his educational plans to help his brother in the shop. Fortunately, Rudy Toporcer understood his younger brother's love for baseball and set up a work schedule that allowed him time to play baseball in the afternoons.

George practiced religiously. The natural righthander taught himself to hit from the left side of the plate and developed into a good enough infielder to play for some of the best semipro teams in the New York area. Despite the eyeglasses, Toporcer's skills were starting to attract the attention of organized baseball. In 1920, while playing for a top semipro club from Orange, New Jersey, he finally got some professional coaching from former Red Sox infielder Billy Swanson and after the season, the young infielder signed with the Syracuse Stars.

Toporcer was eagerly looking forward to spending the 1921 season with Syracuse in the International League, but a couple of months after he signed the team became a St. Louis Cardinals' farm club. Toporcer, along with some other Syracuse prospects, was invited to spring training with the parent club and impressed manager Branch Rickey so much with his speed and all around sterling play that he made the team.

To reach the major leagues, Specs Toporcer had to overcome several obstacles. First there was the issue of his eyesight, which scared most organizations away. In fact, the first time Rickey saw Toporcer off the baseball field he watched in horror as his new infield prospect took off his glasses and groped his way to the showers with hands outstretched. Then there was his slight build, which made his durability questionable. Finally, the fact that George was Jewish didn't count in his favor in the 1920s. With the Cardinals, however, Toporcer finally ran up against a barrier that he couldn't hurdle—the immense talent of Rogers Hornsby.

George's best position was second base. The lithe 5'10", 165-pounder had a good glove, but he didn't have the strongest arm in the world. Unfortunately, Hornsby's best position was also second base and there was no question of beating out Rogers Hornsby. In 1920 Hornsby had settled in at second base after four seasons of bouncing between third base and shortstop. The change did wonders for the 24-year-old slugger as he won his first of six consecutive National League batting titles with a robust .370 average.

Rickey was so enamored with Toporcer, however, that he began the 1921 season with the speedy 22-year-old rookie at second and shifted Hornsby to left field. The new alignment didn't last long, but it wasn't George's fault. Hornsby just wasn't an outfielder. He'd always had problems with flyballs, which is bad enough for a second baseman, but disastrous for an outfielder. After a week, Hornsby was reinstalled at second base with Toporcer backing him up.

George enjoyed an excellent 1922 sophomore season, which would end up as his finest in the major leagues. He shared the shortstop job with fading veteran Doc Lavan and hit .324 in 116 games, 91 of them at short. He also demonstrated an aptitude for pinch-hitting, belting out six hits in fifteen trips to the plate for a .400 average. His defense at shortstop, however, was only mediocre at best. The versatile Toporcer spent the next four seasons as a supersub. In 1923 he got his only extended big league playing time at second base when he filled in for Hornsby, who missed about a third of the season with various ailments. In 1924 he hit .313 in a utility role and in 1925 he was back platooning at shortstop and hitting a solid .284. For the Cardinals' 1926 World Championship squad, Toporcer hit only .250 overall but had a fancy .391 average as a pinch hitter. He also made his only World Series appearance that fall, sacrificing in a run in his one time at bat.

Before the 1927 season, St. Louis traded Hornsby to the Giants, but the transaction didn't exactly clear the way for Toporcer to take over the Cardinals' second base job. The Cards obtained another Hall of Fame quality second baseman, Frankie Frisch, in exchange for Hornsby. While Frisch had one of the best years of his illustrious career year in 1927, Toporcer platooned with Lester Bell at third base and also saw duty at shortstop. His average fell to .248, but he played in 86 games, which was the most action he'd seen since the 1923 season.

In 1928 Rabbit Maranville, another future Hall of Famer, took over as the Cardinals' shortstop. With Frisch and Maranville, backed up by returned veteran Tommy Thevenow, in the middle of the infield and a new lefty-hitting third baseman named Andy High, there was little room for Toporcer on the roster. After going hitless in 14 at-bats, the 29-year-old infielder was sent down to the Cardinals' Rochester Red Wings farm team in the International League.

The demotion to Rochester ended Toporcer's major league career after only 546 games. The versatile utility man saw action in 249 games at shortstop, 105 at second base, and 95 at third, and also had 84 pinch-hit at-bats. His lifetime average of .298 as a pinch hitter was almost 20 points higher than his .279 overall career mark.

Although his big league career was over, Specs was just starting a rewarding second career. Finally, he got a chance to play second base every day, even if it was in the minor leagues. With Toporcer at the keystone sack, Rochester won four straight International League pennants from 1928 through 1931. In 1929 he was named the International League Most Valuable Player despite a .262 batting mark. That year he accepted a record 1,064 chances at second base and was part of an infield that completed 223 double plays, thought to be the highest total in the history of organized baseball. At the plate he was the consummate leadoff man, more than making up for a mediocre average by drawing 128 walks, stealing 31 bases, and scoring 142 runs. The next year he repeated as the league MVP as he improved his batting average to .307 and his on-base-percentage to .426.

He also hit a league-leading 49 doubles, stole 21 bases, and walked 125 times.

From 1932 through 1934 Toporcer managed the Red Wings in addition to handling second base chores and hitting over .290 each year. In five full seasons and parts of two others he played 880 games and established club records with 113 stolen bases and 628 runs scored for Rochester.

Like many former Cardinals, George left the St. Louis organization after the 1934 season due to a dispute with Rickey over financial matters. He finally got his chance to play for Syracuse in 1935 when he served as player-manager for the club. He continued managing in the minor leagues and making occasional appearances in the field through the early 1940s before becoming director of the Boston Red Sox farm system in 1943.

In 1948, while still the Red Sox farm director, Toporcer encountered serious eye problems aside from his normal poor vision. The retina in his left eye became detached and he underwent surgery that promised only a 50–50 chance of saving his sight in the eye. The operation was unsuccessful, as was a second attempt, and George resigned himself to being blind in one eye. He even returned to the dugout as manager of the International League Buffalo Bisons in 1951 but was forced to retire when the same condition that had cost him his sight in his left eye developed in the right one.

George endured three more operations in an effort to save his eyesight, but to no avail. Ironically, the procedures were performed at Columbia Presbyterian Medical Center, which was built on the site of Hilltop Park where a youthful George Toporcer spent many idyllic childhood afternoons watching the old Highlanders. After each operation, George had to spend months lying on his back with his head perfectly still. He occupied his mind recalling vivid images of Ty Cobb, Tris Speaker, Walter Johnson, Smoky Joe Wood, Hal Chase, and other American League stars cavorting around the old Hilltop Park of his boyhood.

But blindness was just another challenge to George Toporcer. He'd never believed in feeling sorry for himself, so after losing his sight he became a successful writer and public speaker. With the help of his longtime wife, Mabel, he wrote two books and many magazine articles about baseball and made hundreds of speeches, mostly to youth groups. He died in a fall at the age of 90 in Huntington Station, New York.

GEORGE "SPECS" TOPORCER
B. February 9, 1899 D. May 17, 1989

YEAR	TEAM	LEAGUE	G	AB	R	H	HR	RBI	AVE	BB	POS
1921	ST. LOUIS	NL	22	53	4	14	0	2	.264	3	2B
1922	ST. LOUIS	NL	116	352	56	114	3	36	.324	24	SS
1923	ST. LOUIS	NL	97	303	45	77	3	35	.254	41	2B-SS
1924	ST. LOUIS	NL	70	198	30	62	1	24	.313	11	3B-SS
1925	ST. LOUIS	NL	83	268	38	76	2	26	.284	36	SS
1926	ST. LOUIS	NL	64	88	13	22	0	9	.250	8	2B-PH
1927	ST. LOUIS	NL	86	290	37	72	0	19	.248	27	3B-SS
1928	ST. LOUIS	NL	8	14	0	0	0	0	0	0	PH-INF
	Rochester	Internat'l	88	322	59	96	0	30	.298	34	2B
1929	Rochester	Internat'l	169	615	142	161	2	46	.262	128	2B
1930	Rochester	Internat'l	167	622	134	191	1	61	.307	125	2B
1931	Jers Cty-Roch	Internat'l	136	498	81	138	2	52	.277	63	2B
1932	Rochester	Internat'l	167	655	103	195	1	77	.298	84	2B
1933	Rochester	Internat'l	131	471	93	140	1	40	.297	71	2B
1934	Rochester	Internat'l	105	364	59	106	1	30	.291	36	2B
1935	Syracuse	Internat'l	125	454	70	121	3	43	.267	67	2B
1936	Rocky Mount	Piedmont	79	253	46	70	1	26	.277	30	2B
1937	Hazleton	NY-Penn	20	37	8	14	0	7	.378	3	INF
MAJOR LEAGUE TOTALS			546	1566	223	437	9	151	.279	150	

CHICK HAFEY

The St. Louis Cardinals were baseball trailblazers in the development of the first farm system and they were also the first organization to embrace bespectacled ballplayers. They were the team that gave pitcher Lee "Specs" Meadows his first chance. Meadows broke in with the Cardinals in 1915 and pitched for them until he was traded to the Philadelphia Phillies in 1919, so the Cards were already accustomed to bespectacled players when Toporcer arrived in 1921.

Several years after Toporcer's breakthrough, hard-hitting outfielder Chick Hafey donned eyeglasses at the urging of the Cardinals' brain trust and eventually went on to become the first league batting leader to wear glasses.

Hafey joined the Cardinals during the 1924 season but didn't crack the regular lineup until 1927. While still a part-timer in 1926 he was beaned by an errant pitch. During the examination, the team physician noticed

Chapter 4—Impaired Organ Function or Chronic Illness 129

that Hafey couldn't see the doctor's hand when he held it above the lockers. For some reason, the young outfielder was immediately put on a seafood diet, but when that failed to improve his vision the Cardinals suggested that he wear glasses like teammate Toporcer. Chick resisted the advice at first, but eventually he started experimenting with corrective lenses and gradually got accustomed to the idea. In fact, he eventually required three pairs of glasses with difference prescriptions to adjust for constant changes in his vision.

Chick was a strapping six footer, who weighed in at about 185 pounds when healthy, but he suffered from chronic sinus problems that affected his eyesight and he would eventually undergo five operations on his sinuses. The severity of his sinus condition caused Hafey's sight to vary from day to day, which is why he required three different pairs of glasses. He also had ulcers and had to endure persistent stomach miseries.

Charles "Chick" Hafey was born February 12, 1903, in Berkley, California, one of eight children. It was an athletic family. An older brother pitched in the Pacific Coast League and two nephews later had brief big league careers. He originally signed with the Cardinals as a pitcher but was moved to the outfield in 1922 to take advantage of his bat. When Chick entered pro ball, he added a year to his age because he thought it would make him appear more mature, and the extra year stuck with him throughout his career.

After winning the Cardinals regular left field job in 1927, Hafey raised his batting average 58 points to .329 while leading the National League in slugging. He then hit .337 in 1928, .338 in 1929, and .336 in 1930, amazingly consistent production. His homer run totals for those three years were 27, 29, and 26—again incredible consistency. In 1931 Chick broke out of his rut to capture the league batting championship with a .3489 average that bested the Giants Bill Terry's .3486 mark and roommate Jim Bottomley's .3482 figure in the closest batting title contest in history.

After his batting championship season, Hafey was swapped to the lowly Cincinnati Reds when he held out for more money. He was only 29 years old, but his career went into a decline in Cincinnati as his troublesome sinus condition worsened. He batted .344 in 1932, but illness and two operations on his sinuses limited him to only 83 games. He played regularly in 1933 and 1934, but his batting averages sagged to .303 and .293 respectively and his old power was missing. Nevertheless, he was selected to start the first Major League All-Star Game in 1933 and in the second inning he laced out the first base hit in all-star competition.

In 1935 Hafey witnessed another historic event, the first night game in big league history, between the Reds and the Phillies on May 24, 1935.

Unfortunately, that first game under the lights signaled the end of Hafey's baseball career. He'd been sidelined most of the year with a shoulder injury and had only recently returned to the lineup. But the evening dampness aggravated Chick's sinuses and he sat out the game. He recognized, however, that night games were the future and saw the handwriting on the wall. A few days later, the 32-year-old slugger left the team after playing in only 15 games for the season.

After almost two full years away from the game, Hafey attempted a comeback in 1937. He hit only .261 in 89 games for the Reds and decided that retirement wasn't such a bad idea after all. He returned home to tend to his ranch in Walnut Creek, California. He raised sheep and cattle but continued to suffer from poor health. He died on July 2, 1973 in Calistiga, California, two years after his 1971 selection to the Baseball Hall of Fame.

Chick, who got his nickname because he lived on a chicken ranch, was a quiet, introverted personality, who was regularly taken advantage of by the Cardinals in salary negotiations. As a player he had all the tools. In the field he was fast and possessed a rifle arm. At the plate he was a deadly pull hitter with good power and speed on the bases. He won the batting championship in 1931 after missing all of spring training and the first few weeks of the regular season. Injuries, poor health, and contract hassles limited him to a high of 138 games in his eight years with St. Louis and he made the Hall of Fame despite the fact that he only appeared in 100 or more games seven times in a career that only consisted of 11 full seasons.

When Hafey was still playing, John McGraw the manager of the rival Giants remarked, "If Chick Hafey had two good eyes, he'd be the best ballplayer anybody ever saw." Rogers Hornsby, no slouch himself from the right side of the plate, called Hafey the best right-handed hitter he ever saw. And Cardinals general manager Branch Rickey, who's penurious ways eventually drove Chick out of St. Louis, later said, "If Hafey had had good eyesight and good health he might have been the finest right-handed hitter baseball has ever known."

Despite the success of Hafey and Toporcer, bespectacled baseball players continued to be a rarity until lighter, shatterproof lenses became available after World War II. Of course, pitchers with eyeglasses were more readily accepted. Mel Harder won 223 games in a 20-year career with the Cleveland Indians from 1928 to 1947, and Danny MacFayden came up in 1926 and pitched 17 seasons for several different teams. But eyeglasses were still such a novelty in baseball through the early 1940s that fellow players were compelled to provide bespectacled players with commemorative nicknames. At first they were invariably called "Specs," but gradually the monikers became more imaginative. Harder was called "Wimpy" and MacFayden was known as "Deacon Danny." Dom DiMaggio, who became the next great non-pitcher after Hafey to wear glasses, was christened "The Little Professor" due to his bookish appearance. It's suspected that pitcher Steve Larkin, whose entire big league career consisted of two appearances with the 1934 Detroit Tigers, was included in the 1934 Goudey baseball card set solely because the artists loved portraying baseball players in ridiculous looking glasses.

The use of eyeglasses in baseball suffered a brief setback in the late thirties when colorful veteran Lefty Gomez of the Yankees attempted to rejuvenate his fading fastball with corrective lenses. According to Gomez, the first time he peered in at Jimmie "The Beast" Foxx in the batter's box through his new specs, the clearer view of the muscular slugger terrified him so that he discarded them forever.

Despite this incident, eyeglasses became more accepted in baseball after World War II with the advent of shatterproof and plastic lenses. Through 1950 at least 50 players reportedly wore glasses sometime in their career. In 1950 Phillies pitcher Jim Konstanty became the first bespectacled player to win the Most Valuable Player Award, and in 1951 catcher Clint Courtney of the Yankees broke down the last barrier when he appeared behind the plate sporting a pair of wire rim glasses. Later in the decade another milestone was reached when relief pitcher Ryne Duren developed a Darth-Vader-like persona with an explosive fastball and thick, dark, bottle-bottom lenses. Few hitters were eager to take a toe hold against Duren's shaky control and daunting 20/200 vision.

By the 1970s corrective lenses were commonplace in baseball. Third baseman Darrell Evans, with the Atlanta Braves in 1971, is thought to be the first player to wear contact lenses. By 1973 a survey indicated that one in seven players wore either glasses or contact lenses and by the end of the decade it was estimated that more than one in five wore glasses and another 50 wore contacts.

When speaking about baseball in his later years, Specs Toporcer used to argue that modern day players were better than the players of his era. His contention was that contemporary ballplayers were bigger, stronger, faster, and smarter. Old Specs could have added that modern players can also see better.

CHARLES JAMES "CHICK" HAFEY
B. February 12, 1903 D. July 2, 1973

YEAR	TEAM	LEAGUE	G	AB	R	H	HR	RBI	AVE	SB	POS
1923	Ft. Smith	W Assn	144	573	83	163	*	*	.284	20	OF
1924	Houston	Texas	126	481	82	173	*	*	.360	3	OF
	ST. LOUIS	NL	24	91	10	23	2	22	.253	1	OF
1925	Syracuse	Internat'l	21	84	17	24	*	*	.286	3	OF
	ST. LOUIS	NL	93	358	36	108	5	57	.302	3	OF
1926	ST. LOUIS	NL	78	225	30	61	4	38	.271	2	OF
1927	ST. LOUIS	NL	103	346	62	114	18	63	.329	12	OF
1928	ST. LOUIS	NL	138	520	101	175	27	111	.337	8	OF
1929	ST. LOUIS	NL	134	517	101	175	29	125	.338	7	OF
1930	ST. LOUIS	NL	120	446	108	150	26	107	.336	12	OF
1931	ST. LOUIS	NL	122	450	94	157	16	95	.349	11	OF
1932	CINCINNATI	NL	83	253	34	87	2	36	.344	4	OF
1933	CINCINNATI	NL	144	568	77	172	7	62	.303	3	OF
1934	CINCINNATI	NL	140	535	75	157	18	67	.293	4	OF
1935	CINCINNATI	NL	15	59	10	20	1	9	.339	1	OF
1936	CINCINNATI	NL			(Voluntarily Retired)						
1937	CINCINNATI	NL	89	257	39	67	9	41	.261	2	OF
MAJOR LEAGUE TOTALS			1283	4625	777	1466	164	833	.317	70	

RON SANTO

Ron Santo debuted at third base for the Chicago Cubs on June 26, 1960, and through the end of the decade he missed only 13 of the Cubs 1,549 games. While impressive, this accomplishment seems to pale in comparison to Cal Ripken's record 2,502-game consecutive game streak, or Lou Gehrig's accomplishment of playing in 2,130 straight games, or even longtime teammate Billy Williams' National League-record-setting 1,117 consecutive appearances from September 22, 1963, through September 2, 1970.

However, when the fact that Santo was afflicted with type one juvenile diabetes during this period is taken into account, his achievement looms as one of the great iron man feats of all time. Santo not only went to his post every day despite his disability, he performed at a level that makes him a candidate for the Hall of Fame and with such energy and enthusiasm that he became one of Chicago's most popular sports figures.

Chapter 4—Impaired Organ Function or Chronic Illness 133

Ron Santo (left)— diabetic ironman

Ron Santo was born February 24, 1940, in Seattle, Washington. His childhood was far from idyllic. He grew up in a tough Italian neighborhood called "Garlic Gulch." His dad was a bartender with a drinking problem who left the family when Ron was six or seven. For a little while afterward he visited young Ron and his sister on weekends, but one day he just didn't show up and Ron didn't see him again for twelve years. His father did, however, get him interested in sports at an early age. Santo is though to be only the second Little Leaguer, after pitcher Joey Jay, to make it to the major leagues.

As a kid, Ron ran with a gang of neighborhood toughs and became involved in mischief like vandalism and minor theft. At age eleven, he got in trouble with the law for stealing cigarettes and was sent to parochial school to complete his education. Santo always felt that sports saved him from becoming just another punk. As a teenager, soccer and football, as well as baseball, kept him off the streets. In high school, he made All-City for three years in both football as a quarterback and baseball as a third baseman. As senior in 1958 he was selected to play in the Hearst All-Star Game at the Polo Grounds in New York. He caught for the United States

Team while a youngster named Joe Torre caught for the New York All-Stars. Although his team lost, Santo's bat caught the attention of scouts nationwide. Despite better offers, he signed with the Cubs for $20,000 because he felt that they offered the best opportunity for him to reach the majors quickly.

Before leaving for his first Cubs minor league camp, however, a routine physical by his personal physician revealed Santo's diabetes. Ron was shocked. He felt great and had never experienced the common symptoms such as fatigue, frequent urination, weight loss, or excessive thirst. The 18-year-old youngster got another jolt when he read that the life expectancy of a juvenile diabetic was 25 years and that diabetes was the number one cause of blindness, the number two cause of kidney failure, and the number three cause of hardened arteries. He also learned that traumatic events were believed to trigger the disease and always suspected that his father leaving the family may have started it.

Despite attending a special educational program for diabetics in a Seattle clinic and seeing a 35-year-old woman sitting next to him keel over in class and go into a coma, Ron decided to forgo professional medical advice in favor of his own program. Exhibiting the stubborn belief in his own immortality that is characteristic of youth, he felt that he could control the disease with diet and exercise. He was determined not to take insulin, the hormone that enables the body to produce energy by metabolizing sugar from the blood, and equally determined not to let his new employer find out about his condition. He even discovered how to mask signs of the disease by rigorously exercising to drive his blood sugar level down before physical examinations.

Santo reported to the Cubs' minor league camp in Mesa, Arizona, and quickly impressed the Chicago brass with his bat. The Cubs had signed him as a catcher but soon shifted him back to third base, which was a weak spot in the organization. He spent the 1959 season with the Cubs' San Antonio farm team in Class AA and hit for a .327 batting average. On defense, however, he committed 53 errors and registered a horrid .884 fielding percentage.

After marrying his high school sweetheart in the off-season, Santo almost won the Cubs' starting third base job in spring training. But the club was afraid to start the season with a 20-year-old recruit at third and acquired veteran Don Zimmer from the Dodgers just before the start of the season to man the hot corner. Ron began the 1960 campaign with Houston in the Class AAA American Association. However, Lou Boudreau took over as Cubs manager from Charlie Grimm early in the season and pressed for Santo's recall, even though he wasn't exactly tearing up the American

Association. Ron was summoned to the big leagues and installed at third, where he enjoyed a moderately successful freshman season, batting .251 in 95 games and making the Rookie All-Star Team.

Santo followed up with a solid 1961 sophomore season. Playing in every game he hit .284 and slammed 23 homers with 83 runs batted in. He still wasn't taking insulin, but the club doctors apparently weren't screening for the disease, so his condition wasn't showing up in routine team physical exams. After the season, however, the first symptoms began to surface. Ron began having pain in right leg, losing weight, and urinating excessively. He lost 22 pounds before he finally went to see a doctor who immediately put him on insulin.

Of course, Santo had to tell the Cubs' team physician, but he insisted that as few people as possible know about it. He wanted to make the allstar team before his condition became widely known so that there would be no question about his ability to perform with the disease.

But the challenge was monumental. The toughest opponent a diabetic athlete has to face is his own metabolism. Competition makes unpredictable demands on the body. Exercise lowers sugar levels, especially prolonged or vigorous activity. The nemesis of diabetic athletes is a sudden plunge in the blood sugar level that cripples their ability to react and think. Furthermore everybody's metabolism is different and each diabetic has to learn to cope with his own individual symptoms and learn the warning signs of an oncoming diabetic event. Complicating the situation is that the job of major league baseball player is not a nine-to-five occupation. With constant travel, doubleheaders, night games, and other demands on his time, it's extremely difficult for a professional athlete to maintain the strict diet and consistent eating schedule necessary to properly control his blood sugar level, especially when he's trying to keep his condition a secret.

The 22-year-old Santo had a terrible year in 1962 as he struggled to regulate his body chemistry and adjust to daily insulin injections. His batting average dropped to .227 and he led the league's third basemen in errors. The Cubs ended up in ninth place in the first year of National League expansion to ten teams. Somehow they managed to finish behind the newly formed Houston Colts expansion outfit, despite a regular lineup that included three future Hall of Famers (Ernie Banks, Billy Williams, and Lou Brock), the 1962 National League Rookie of the Year (Ken Hubbs), an all-star outfielder who hit .318 that year (George Altman), and Ron Santo.

In 1963 the Cubs posted their first winning record since 1946 and moved up to seventh place largely due to the hitting of Santo and Billy Williams and improved pitching led by lefty Dick Ellsworth, who won 22 games. Ron batted .297 with 25 homers and 99 runs batted in and led the league in putouts and assists at third base. More importantly he cut down on his errors and got rid of the unwanted league leadership in that category.

Over the next decade Santo established himself as one of the top third baseman in baseball. In the National League he was generally acknowledged as the best after veteran St. Louis third sacker Ken Boyer began to tail off in 1965. In the American League he was overshadowed by Baltimore's Brooks Robinson, a future Hall of Famer who was a superior gloveman, but a lesser hitter than Santo. From 1963 through 1973 Ron hit .286 and averaged 26 homers and 98 runs batted in a year, even though pitching dominated most of the era.

The 1964 campaign was marred by the death of Santo's roommate and close friend, Kenny Hubbs, when the small plane Hubbs was piloting crashed in Provo Utah before the season. Although Hubbs was only 22 years old, he'd already established National League fielding records for a second baseman. Ron was distraught for some time but rebounded to record his first 30-homer, 100-runs-batted-in year and lead the league in walks for the first time. Surprisingly, given his lack of speed, he also led the league with 13 triples that season. In 1965 Santo blasted a career high 33 homers while again driving in more than 100 runs.

The 1966 season marked the hiring of Leo Durocher as manager of the Cubs. Since the early 1960s, the club had been managed by a "college of coaches." Membership and rank in the college varied, but confusion remained constant. Durocher's hiring put an end to the novel experiment and started the promising young Cubs on the right track. Santo hit in a club-record 28 straight games that season, despite being hit in the face by Jack Fisher of the New York Mets in the midst of the streak and missing a week with a broken cheekbone.

Although the Cubs dropped 103 games under Durocher in 1966, they improved to third place in 1967, buoyed by the maturation of young stars like pitchers Ferguson Jenkins and Bill Hands, catcher Randy Hundley, second baseman Glenn Beckert, and shortstop Don Kessinger, who joined old stand-bys Santo, Williams, and Banks to form a solid nucleus.

After another third place finish in 1968, Chicago jumped out of the box in 1969 and looked like a sure bet to win their first National League pennant since 1945. But after topping the standings all season they fell out of first place on September 11. A seemingly insurmountable eight game lead seemed to evaporate overnight as the "Miracle" New York Mets won 35 of their last 49 games to overtake the Cubbies and open up and an eight game margin of their own.

Chapter 4—Impaired Organ Function or Chronic Illness

It was a bitter pill for the emotional Santo to swallow. Enjoying a banner year, he drove in a career best 123 runs and appeared to have clinched the league's Most Valuable Player Award until the Cubs' collapse. During the season, he drew criticism for unnecessarily inciting the opposition when, in a burst of enthusiasm over a Cub victory, he jumped up and clicked his heels. The stunt delighted the hometown fans and became a regular routine, which opposing teams deeply resented in the days before "taunting" became an accepted part of the sports scene.

Although Chicago remained a contender for several years after their heartbreaking collapse, the Pittsburgh Pirates took control of the National League Eastern Division, and it became evident that 1969 had been the Cubbies big chance. Durocher left the team during the 1972 season, and when the club sagged to fifth place in 1973, a major changing of the guard was in order. Shortly after the World Series, six-time 20 game winner Ferguson Jenkins was swapped to the Texas Rangers for a promising young third baseman named Bill Madlock. Subsequently, a trade of Santo to the California Angels was arranged, but the veteran wanted to remain in Chicago and became the first major leaguer to exercise the newly gained right of a 10-year man to reject a transfer to another team.

Despite talk of shifting Santo to the outfield to make room for Madlock, it was obvious that his days with the Cubs were numbered. In December a trade was worked out with the crosstown White Sox that would allow him to remain in the windy city.

But the 1974 season was a disaster. The White Sox really didn't need Santo. They already had a slugging third baseman named Bill Melton, who'd led the American League in homers two years earlier. Ron, of course, tried to make the best of the situation. He served as designated hitter (although he hated it), backed up Melton at third, played 39 games at second base, and also filled in at first base and shortstop. He hit a meager .221 with only five homers and feuded with enigmatic Sox superstar Dick Allen over his lackadaisical attitude toward the game. At the end of the season Santo retired, despite having another year to go on the lucrative two-year deal he signed before the season.

Santo ended his 15-year major league career with a .277 batting average in 2,243 games. The righthanded slugger belted 342 home runs, drove in 1,331 runs, and scored 1,138 times. He drew 1,108 walks, leading the league four times in that department, and twice led the league in on-base percentage. He was a nine-time National League All-Star and belted over 30 homers four years in a row and knocked in more than 90 runs for eight straight seasons. In the field, the one-time scatter-arm won five consecutive Gold Glove awards from 1964 to 1968 and set a record by leading the league in total chances eight times.

But his most lasting accomplishment was when he went public with his diabetic condition after the 1971 season. Because Ron was already an established star the press and the public took the announcement in stride, but it certainly did a lot to change the public perception of diabetics. Santo was a fiery, energetic, 6 foot, 190-pound block of muscle with a track record of durability and dependability — hardly the image of diabetes sufferers in most people's mind up until that time.

Unfortunately this unselfish contribution is not considered in Hall of Fame voting. Although support for Santo's election to the Hall has grown since he first became eligible in 1980, he never garnered the required number of votes. He peeked with 204 of the required 355 in 1998, his last year of eligibility for selection by the writers, and his fate now rests with the Veterans Committee. Beginning in 2003 a new format was established where the balloting is now done by living members plus certain executives. The new system failed to anoint a new member in 2003, but Santo finished a strong third among the candidates.

During his playing career, Ron had become a businessman. He got into the pizza business where he occasionally surprised customers with personal deliveries and eventually even had part of the concession business at Wrigley while he was with the Cubs. After his career ended, he spent time in the crude oil business, was successful in real estate, and owned four Kentucky Fried Chicken franchises. He also became an owner of Unipoint Corporation, which operates Union 76 truck stops. He returned to the public eye in 1990 when he joined the Cubs' media team as color commentator for WGN radio.

Though insulin may be necessary to keep a diabetic alive, it's not a cure and will not stop the threat of complications from the disease. Healthwise, Santo has suffered greatly from the side effects of diabetes in recent years. Retinopathy has impaired his vision and he has to undergo laser treatments three times a week to slow the deterioration of his vision. He suffered a heart attack in 1999 and two years later had his right leg amputated below the knee.

But, just like in his playing days, Santo shook off these setbacks and returned to his post. He's still in the Cubs' broadcast booth and continues to work tirelessly as a volunteer and member of the board of directors for the Juvenile Diabetes Foundation. In fact, the Chicago chapter recently raised more than $4.3 million for its 24th annual Ron Santo Walk to Cure Diabetes.

Thinking back on his career, Santo wonders what it would be like to play with diabetes now. In the 1960s the press still afforded players some privacy. The media, fans, and most of his teammates didn't even know he had the disease for more than a decade. By the time he went public with his condition in 1971 he was an established star, so there couldn't be any doubt about his ability to play with the disease. With today's medical and dietary advancements the disease would be much easier to live with. Diabetics can now closely monitor their metabolism with hand held meters that analyze a drop of blood on chemically treated strips. Portable insulin pumps are also available for a needed adjustment. But there would be no way to keep the media from finding out and wildly speculating with every injury or slump.

After he retired Santo said, "[Diabetes was] one reason I played so hard. I kept thinking that my career would end any day. I never really wanted out of the lineup. The diabetes thing was hanging over my head."

Since Ron Santo retired there have been other big leaguers with diabetes, though their conditions have generally not been as serious as Ron's. The most notable is pitcher Bill Gullickson, who pitched for 13 years in the major leagues and two years in Japan from 1980 through 1994. Gullickson won 162 games in his major league career including a 20-win season with the Detroit Tigers in 1991. Like Santo, he suffers from the most severe form of diabetes where the body produces virtually no insulin. It's probably a sign of public acceptance of the condition that Gullickson's baseball biographies generally don't even mention diabetes, although there was some publicity about his condition early in his career.

Recently, 29-year-old, veteran right-handed pitcher Jason Johnson was rushed off a Baltimore Orioles spring training practice field in Fort Lauderdale, Florida after a diabetic episode. Johnson, who wears an insulin pump, was treated by Orioles medical staff and emergency paramedics and walked to the clubhouse with minimal assistance a few minutes later. In another indication of the public's general acceptance of the disease, the event warranted only a few lines in the sports pages.

Although Santo was the first major leaguer known to suffer from severe diabetes while an active player, there's some evidence that he may not have been the first or even the most famous.

Jackie Robinson, the first black man to play modern major league baseball, may also have been the first insulin-dependent diabetic in the big leagues. Robinson, who acknowledged his condition a few years after retiring from the game after the 1956 season, died at the age of 53 in 1972 from complications related to diabetes.

Although Robinson and his family always maintained that he had not been diagnosed with diabetes until after his retirement, Jackie allegedly told roommate Roy Campanella he had the disease late in his career. Tennis star Bill Talbert, who was the first famous athlete known to be diabetic and knew Robinson well, believed that Jackie developed insulin-dependent diabetes when he was about 30 years old.

"I think Jackie felt it was a weakness. With all the publicity about blacks in baseball, he didn't want another thing to talk about," Talbert is quoted as saying.

If Jackie Robinson was indeed suffering from diabetes while an active player, it makes his tremendous achievements even more remarkable. He may have been a trailblazer in yet another way.

RONALD EDWARD SANTO
B. February 25, 1940

YEAR	TEAM	LEAGUE	G	AB	R	H	HR	RBI	AVE	BB	POS
1959	San Antonio	Texas	136	505	82	165	11	87	.327	*	3B
1960	Houston	Am Ass'n	71	272	40	73	7	32	.268	8	3B
	CHICAGO	NL	95	347	44	87	9	44	.251	31	3B
1961	CHICAGO	NL	154	578	84	164	23	83	.284	73	3B
1962	CHICAGO	NL	162	604	44	137	17	83	.227	65	3B
1963	CHICAGO	NL	162	630	79	187	25	99	.297	42	3B
1964	CHICAGO	NL	161	592	94	185	30	114	.313	86	3B
1965	CHICAGO	NL	164	608	88	173	33	101	.285	88	3B
1966	CHICAGO	NL	155	561	93	175	30	94	.312	95	3B
1967	CHICAGO	NL	161	586	107	176	31	98	.300	96	3B
1968	CHICAGO	NL	162	577	86	142	26	98	.246	96	3B
1969	CHICAGO	NL	160	575	97	166	29	123	.289	96	3B
1970	CHICAGO	NL	154	555	83	148	26	114	.267	92	3B
1971	CHICAGO	NL	154	555	77	148	21	88	.267	79	3B
1972	CHICAGO	NL	133	464	68	140	17	74	.302	69	3B
1973	CHICAGO	NL	149	536	65	143	20	77	.267	63	3B
1974	CHICAGO	AL	117	375	29	83	5	41	.221	37	DH-2B-3B
MAJOR LEAGUE TOTALS			2243	8143	1138	2254	342	1331	.277	1108	

RUSS CHRISTOPHER

Many professional baseball players have risked their health to continue their careers, but pitcher Russ Christopher actually put his life on the line every time he stepped on the field.

Chapter 4—Impaired Organ Function or Chronic Illness

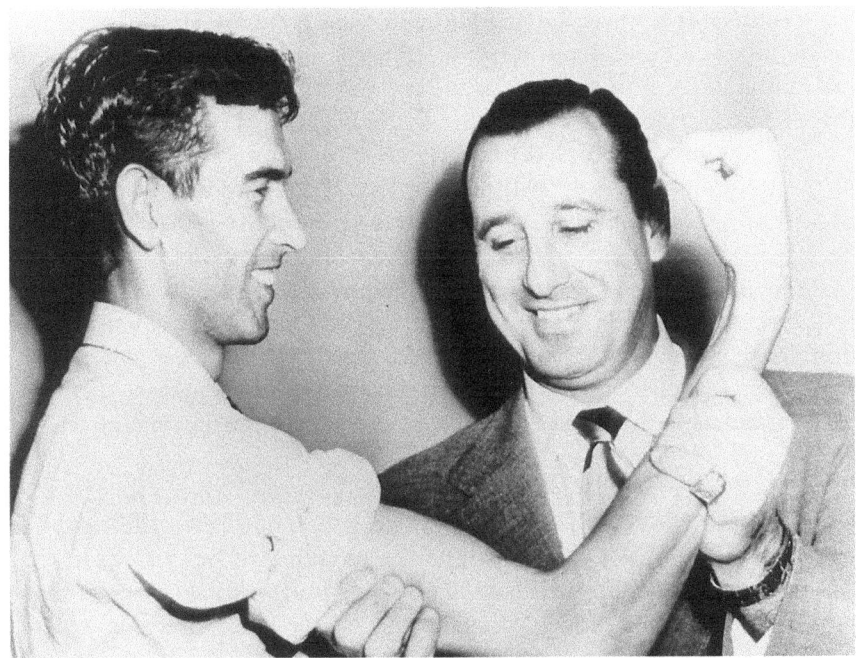

Russ Christopher talks comeback with Indians GM Hank Greenberg

Christopher suffered from a weak heart that resulted from a childhood case of rheumatic fever. He had a hole in his heart which leaked circulated blood back into the bloodstream instead of sending it through the lungs to be re-oxygenated. He was described as a "blue baby" who had somehow survived to adulthood. From the start he'd been advised by doctors not to play baseball, but he played seven seasons in the American League with the Philadelphia Athletics and Cleveland Indians, first as a top notch starting pitcher and later as an ace reliever.

Russ' last season was 1948 when he helped the Indians capture the American League pennant and the World Championship. He battled pneumonia in the spring and was so weak that he had to refrain from strenuous exercise and couldn't practice throughout the season. In fact, he wasn't able to throw more than a couple of warm-up tosses in the bullpen without having trouble breathing, so Cleveland manager Lou Boudreau had to use him very judiciously. In 45 appearances he pitched only 59 innings, but he saved a league-high 17 games and was critical to the Indians' success.

Russ Christopher was born September 12, 1917, in Richmond, California. He had a younger brother, Loyd, who enjoyed a lengthy minor league career as a power-hitting outfielder and played a handful of games in the big leagues. A nephew, Loyd Jr., was also a professional player in the minor leagues for a short time. Russ started as an outfielder too, but shifted to the mound to ease the strain on his bad heart.

At the age of 20 in 1938 Christopher entered organized baseball as a pitcher and outfielder. By 1941 he'd turned to pitching full time and had moved up to the Newark Bears, the top farm team in the New York Yankees chain and the International League Champions that season. Russ posted a 16–7 won-lost mark on a staff that was led by Johnny Lindell and included Hank Borowy, Tommy Byrne, and Al Gettel in the starting rotation. Lindell would be converted to the outfield the next year and enjoy a fine career with the Yankees, while Borowy, Byrne, and Gettel would eventually graduate to the Yankees and establish themselves as fine major league hurlers.

The Yankees were apparently concerned about Christopher's health, however, and allowed him to be drafted by Connie Mack's Philadelphia Athletics prior to the 1942 campaign. After a couple of lackluster seasons, Russ led the sixth place Athletics staff with 14 victories against the same number of losses and recorded a sparkling 2.97 earned run average in 1944. He enjoyed another strong season in 1945 with a 13–13 won-lost record, completing 17 starts and compiling a 3.17 earned run average. He was considered one of the top starting pitchers in the game at the time.

Christopher's health started to fail in 1946 and he began the transition to the bullpen. In 1947 he relieved full-time and had an excellent season, winning 10 games while saving 12 others, and posted a 2.90 earned run average. But in the spring of 1948 Christopher came down with a serious case of pneumonia while the Athletics were playing the Washington Senators in Orlando. He was left behind to recuperate in an Orlando hospital.

Russ appeared to be through. When Cleveland Indians owner Bill Veeck approached Athletics owner-manager Connie Mack about acquiring Christopher, Mack was hesitant to sell him an unhealthy player. "I'm afraid this might be the final blow for the poor boy," Connie warned. But Veeck was in desperate need of another dependable relief pitcher and was willing to take a chance on Christopher. Veeck offered to purchase his contract for $25,000, with the caveat that he would talk to Christopher first, and the Mack reluctantly accepted the offer.

When he visited him in the Orlando hospital, Veeck almost backed out of the deal because of Christopher's cadaverous appearance. Russ was so weak that he could barely talk. When Veeck asked if he thought he could still pitch, he honestly admitted that he didn't know, but promised to do his the best if Veeck acquired him. The deal was made to the Indians' lasting gratification.

With Cleveland, Christopher became one the first classic closers, rarely pitching to more than a few batters in any appearance. If he had to throw more than a dozen or so pitches after entering a game his lips would turn purple from the exertion. The first half of the season, Christopher's efforts kept the Indians in the race. But despite Boudreau's careful handling, he grew progressively weaker as the season went on and was scarcely used at all in the final month. After pitching he would have to take a steaming shower to stimulate his circulation and then wrap himself in warm blankets. Late in the season, the concerned management of the club suggested that he go home, but Russ demurred. "The doctors know what's wrong with me and they say it doesn't matter…. I'm a pitcher. If I die, I might as well die pitching," he bravely declared.

Christopher's greatest disappointment in 1948 was his performance in his first and only World Series action against the Boston Braves. Called in with the Indians behind 8 to 5, he promptly gave up run scoring hits to the only two hitters he faced. He was relieved by Satchel Paige, who made history that day by becoming the first black man to pitch in the World Series. The Indians lost 11 to 5 but prevailed the next day to capture the championship.

Russ didn't really want to leave baseball after the 1948 season, but his wife ultimately convinced him to quit for his health. In March 1949 he officially retired to take a less strenuous job with an aircraft manufacturer in San Diego. Russ finished his major league career with 54 wins against 64 losses and a fine 3.37 lifetime earned run average. He appeared in relief 144 times and started 97 games, completing 46 of them.

In 1951 Russ underwent heart surgery and was so encouraged that for a while he even thought about attempting a comeback. But his heart problems worsened and he died in Richmond at the age of 37 on December 5, 1954.

Although Christopher was generally described as gentle, shy, and quiet, he could be a fearsome looking presence on the mound. He was tall and skinny, standing more than 6'3" in height and weighing only about 170 pounds. Protruding jug handle ears, a big nose, and a sallow complexion added up to appearance that made hitters feel like they were facing Count Dracula. A sore arm early in his career had forced the righthander to adopt a submarine style underhand delivery which resulted in a nasty sinking fastball. Revered journalist Red Smith called the pitch "malevolent." John Berardino, a teammate on the 1948 Indians who later dropped the second "r" from his name and went on to soap opera fame as

Dr. Steve Hardy of *General Hospital*, described the pitch as "... a true sinker ball.... It just did a lot of sinking."

Despite his physical disability, Russ never complained about his condition and was considered a great teammate who truly loved the game. When doctors advised him to quit baseball and limit his exertions, his response was invariably if he was going to die it might as well be doing the thing he loved most, playing baseball.

RUSSELL ORMAND CHRISTOPHER
B. September 12, 1917 D. December 5, 1954

YEAR	TEAM	LEAGUE	G	IP	SO	BB	W	L	ERA	CG	SV
1938	El Paso	Ariz-Texas	(Played Outfield — Batted .160)								
	Clovis	W Tex-NM	13	106	75	52	7	5	4.50	*	*
1939	El Paso	Ariz-Texas	32	225	163	78	18	7	3.68	*	*
1940	Wenatchee	Wisc-Ill'ois	20	141	87	52	8	8	4.72	*	*
1941	Newark	Internat'l	31	185	69	77	16	7	2.82	*	*
1942	PHILADELPHIA	AL	30	165	58	99	4	13	3.82	10	1
1943	PHILADELPHIA	AL	24	133	56	58	5	8	3.45	5	2
1944	PHILADELPHIA	AL	35	215	84	63	14	14	2.97	13	1
1945	PHILADELPHIA	AL	33	227	100	75	13	13	3.17	17	2
1946	PHILADELPHIA	AL	30	119	79	44	5	7	4.30	1	0
1947	PHILADELPHIA	AL	44	81	33	33	10	7	2.90	0	12
1948	CLEVELAND	AL	45	59	14	27	3	2	2.90	0	17
MAJOR LEAGUE TOTALS			241	1000	424	399	54	64	3.37	46	35

JOE HOERNER

Almost 20 years after Russ Christopher left the big leagues another relief pitcher with a heart problem managed to establish himself in the majors.

Early in his career, Joe Hoerner was forced to change his pitching motion from overhand to sidearm to ease the strain on damaged heart muscles. Although he didn't reach the big leagues to stay until he was almost 30 years old, his damaged heart didn't prevent him from becoming the ace reliever for the St. Louis Cardinals in their pennant-winning 1967 and 1968 campaigns.

Joe Hoerner was born in Dubuque, Iowa, on November 12, 1936, and raised in the rural community. He suffered broken ribs and a separated shoulder in an automobile accident in his junior year of high school. But the most serious injury he sustained in the wreck was damage to muscles and tendons in the chest cavity, although symptoms didn't show up for several years.

After high school, Hoerner decided to put off going to college and give professional baseball a try. An older brother had played minor league baseball as would a younger one, so the bloodlines were there. He got a tryout and signed with the Chicago White Sox organization and began his career as a starting pitcher with Duluth-Superior in the Northern League in 1957.

In 1958 Joe was pitching for Davenport in the Three I League when he suddenly passed out and dropped to the ground. He was rushed to a hospital where he almost died before normal breathing was restored. Despite receiving medication for the muscle condition around his heart, he continued to experience problems the next year and bounced around to different teams and different hospitals. He was afraid he was in danger of being released because of his health problems.

Finally, Joe decided to drop down to a sidearm delivery in hopes that it would help his condition by cutting down on the stress his left-handed, overhand motion put on the muscles on the left side of his chest. The change not only alleviated his physical problem, it also seemed to improve his effectiveness. But he still didn't make much progress toward the major leagues, until 1964. That year, the 27-year-old lefty, who had drifted into the Houston organization, was converted into a relief pitcher. The move was an immediate success. He had two successful years in the bullpen with Oklahoma City before being selected by the Cardinals in the minor league draft.

In St. Louis, Hoerner became the club's stopper until he was traded to the Philadelphia Phillies along with catcher Tim McCarver and center fielder Curt Flood for super slugger Dick Allen and infielder Cookie Rojas after the 1969 campaign. The deal, of course, was the historic transaction that started organized baseball on the road toward free agency when Flood challenged the reserve clause all the way to the Supreme Court.

Hoerner had two good years with the Phillies, but in May 1971 he suffered a recurrence of the heart problems that had plagued him earlier in his career. Despite his brilliant 1.97 earned run average for the 1971 season, the Phillies evidently didn't feel they could rely on his health and installed starter Chris Short in the main left-handed relief role for the 1972 campaign. A swap to the Atlanta Braves in June 1972 started Joe on a nomadic trek that would land him with six teams in the next six years before he finally retired in 1977 at the age of 40.

Like many lefties, Hoerner was considered something of a flake. His most memorable stunt occurred in 1967 when he commandeered the team bus and drove the future World Champions from Atlanta Stadium to the team's hotel, demolishing a large neon sign in the Marriott parking lot before delivering his frightened passengers home safely. Apparently Joe enjoyed his brief foray into the travel business. When he retired as an active player, he opened up a successful travel agency with former teammate (and passenger) Dal Maxvill.

For his major league career Hoerner pitched in 493 games without making a single start. The 6'1" 200-pound reliever recorded a 2.99 lifetime earned run average which included marks below 2.00 in three different seasons. His best year was 1968 when he posted an 8–2 won-lost record and a sensational 1.47 earned run average for the pennant-winning Cards.

Quite impressive credentials for a fainthearted pitcher!

JOSEPH WALTER HOERNER
B. November 12, 1936 D. October 4, 1996

YEAR	TEAM	LEAGUE	G	IP	SO	BB	W	L	ERA	H	S
1957	Duluth-Superior	Northern	28	185	86	71	16	5	2.58	166	*
1958	Davenport	Three I	29	157	85	52	8	8	4.41	176	*
1959	Charleston	Sally	15	28	19	20	1	1	3.21	33	*
	Duluth-Superior	Northern	4	17	14	17	1	3	5.29	23	*
	Lincoln	Three I	9	32	21	10	2	1	3.09	29	*
1960	Charleston	Sally	46	157	132	51	11	9	2.97	135	*
1961	San Diego	Pac Coast	4	9	6	3	0	0	3.00	11	*
	Charleston	Sally	25	130	86	31	6	13	3.11	141	*
1962	Oklahoma City	Am Ass'n	7	10	9	2	0	0	5.40	22	*
	Savannah	Sally	27	94	60	26	9	1	2.49	81	*
1963	San Antonio	Texas	33	156	126	31	11	7	3.29	153	*
	HOUSTON	NL	1	3	2	0	0	0	0.00	2	0
1964	Oklahoma City	Pac Coast	51	62	71	20	3	3	1.31	34	*
	HOUSTON	NL	7	11	4	6	0	0	4.91	13	0
1965	Oklahoma City	Pac Coast	53	65	55	14	8	3	1.94	59	*
1966	ST. LOUIS	NL	57	76	63	21	5	1	1.54	57	13
1967	ST. LOUIS	NL	57	66	50	20	4	4	2.59	52	15
1968	ST. LOUIS	NL	47	49	42	12	8	2	1.47	34	17
1969	ST. LOUIS	NL	45	53	35	9	2	3	2.89	44	15
1970	PHILADELPHIA	NL	44	58	39	20	9	5	2.64	53	9
1971	PHILADELPHIA	NL	49	73	57	21	4	5	1.97	57	9
1972	PHIL-ATL	NL	40	45	31	13	1	5	4.40	55	5
1973	ATLANTA	NL	20	13	10	4	2	2	6.23	17	2
	KANSAS CITY	AL	22	19	15	13	2	0	5.21	28	4
1974	KANSAS CITY	AL	30	35	24	12	2	3	3.86	32	2

YEAR	TEAM	LEAGUE	G	IP	SO	BB	W	L	ERA	H	S
1975	PHILADELPHIA	NL	25	21	20	8	0	0	2.57	25	0
1976	TEXAS	AL	41	35	15	19	0	4	5.14	41	8
1977	CINCINNATI	NL	8	6	5	3	0	0	12.00	9	0
MAJOR LEAGUE TOTALS			493	563	412	181	39	34	2.99	519	99

JOHN HILLER

A contemporary of Joe Hoerner, John Hiller, pitched in 15 major league seasons, all with the Detroit Tigers. For the first part of his career he was an underachieving reliever and spot starter. For the second part he was one of the top firemen in the American League. In between he suffered a heart attack which could have ended his baseball career, but instead allowed him to finally reach his full potential.

The Canadian born lefthander was discovered pitching sandlot ball in Toronto and signed with the Tigers in 1962. After a couple of late-season trials in the majors he came up to stay in 1967. In 1968 the versatile 25-year-old registered a 2.39 earned run average and a 9–6 won-lost mark as a starter and reliever. The Tigers were the World Champions of baseball, with Denny McLain winning 31 games in the regular season and number two starter Mickey Lolich capturing three victories in the World Series against the St. Louis Cardinals.

Great things were expected of Hiller after his promising 1968 campaign, but somehow he had difficulty living up to expectations. The next two years, pitching primarily in relief, he posted a mediocre record of 10 wins against 10 losses. His weight, as well as his attitude, was a problem. The six-footer ballooned to a beefy 220 pounds and didn't seem to have enough desire to stay in shape. He was generally regarded as lazy and lacking ambition.

But in January 1971 everything in John Hiller's life changed. He was enjoying his first smoke of the day at the breakfast table in his Duluth, Minnesota, home when he experienced a strange heaviness in his chest. Thinking it was only his tobacco-abused lungs acting up on him, he snuffed the cigarette out and waited another two hours before firing another one up — with the same result. He'd had pneumonia in 1966 and was afraid it might be another attack. When his symptoms worsened he went to the emergency room where the doctor reported, "I don't want you to worry, but you've had a heart attack." His first reaction was, "I'm a baseball player ... will I be able to go back and play ball?"

Hiller sat out the entire 1971 season when he should have been in the prime of his career at age 28. His doctors were not overly optimistic that he would ever be able to pitch again, often asking him what kind of education he had or what else he could do besides pitch. It seems that his physicians were among those who didn't feel that pitching in the pressure-packed world of professional baseball was the ideal occupation for a recovering coronary patient.

John, however, religiously obeyed doctors' orders to quit smoking, watch his diet, and get plenty of exercise. By the spring of 1972 the once flabby, big-bellied hurler had reduced his weight by about fifty pounds and felt ready to return to the mound. The Detroit front office, however, was fearful of letting him suit up, although they did offer him a job as special coach working with young players at the organization's minor league spring training complex in Lakeland, Florida.

But John was chafing at the bit to return to the mound. After the season got underway, he got his heart specialist to give him the go-ahead to pitch again and he returned to the active roster in July of 1972. He posted a sparking 2.05 earned run average in 24 appearances to help the Tigers capture the 1972 Eastern Division Championship. In the League Championship Series, he pitched three scoreless innings to win the fourth contest, although the Tigers ultimately lost to Oakland in five games.

The 1973 season was a dream come true for the 30-year-old Hiller. It was one of the best seasons ever enjoyed by a relief pitcher in the history of major league baseball. He established a since-broken major league record with 38 saves and won 10 games (against 5 losses) to give him a stake in 56% of the Tigers' victories that year. His earned run average was a microscopic 1.44 for 125 innings of relief and he struck out almost a batter per inning while surrendering only 89 hits. His 65 appearances also led the league and his combined wins/saves total of 48 stood as the major league record for 10 years. For his efforts he won the Fireman of the Year Award, the Comeback Player of the Year Award, the Tiger of the Year Award, and the Hutch Award — given for courage and sportsmanship.

Unlike today's closers, relief aces of Hiller's era were workhorses, and John was one of the most durable. In 1974 he pitched 150 innings in 59 relief appearances and accomplished the remarkable feat of establishing an American League season record for relief wins with 17 while also tying the league record for relief losses with 14 in the same campaign. Both league records still endure, although the victory record was later equaled by Bill Campbell of the Minnesota Twins. National Leaguer Roy Face holds the Major League mark for relief victories with 18 for the Pittsburgh Pirates in 1959, while Gene Garber lost a record 16 games out of the Atlanta bullpen in 1979. Hiller is still tied for second place in major league history in both categories.

Hiller continued as the ace of the Detroit bullpen through 1979 before retiring early in the 1980 season at the age of 37. His lifetime won-lost record was 87 and 76 and he held the club record for career saves with 125 until it was broken by Todd Jones during the 2000 season.

John often joked that he wished he'd had the heart attack ten years earlier because it might have made a better pitcher out of him. He also claimed that it made him a better human being. By his own admission, John was something of a pain-in-the-butt before his heart attack. He hated to deal with autograph seekers and was one of those players who blew by waiting admirers after the game without a word. He later conceded that he was usually in too much of a hurry to find a cold beer to sign for the fans. His fan mail went unanswered, often tossed in the garbage without a glance. He wasn't philosophically or morally opposed to the adulation, he just didn't give a damn. But after his illness, Hiller acquired new insight and gained an appreciation for life. He realized that while baseball was just a job, it was a great job that would be over all too soon. He started to enjoy and oblige the fans. He answered mail from heart patients and their relatives from all over the country, sometimes telephoning them directly at his own expense.

Apparently it took a heart attack for John Hiller to find that he had one.

JOHN FREDERICK HILLER
B. April 8, 1943

YEAR	TEAM	LEAGUE	G	IP	SO	BB	W	L	ERA	GS	S
1963	Jamestown	NY-Penn	29	181	172	78	14	9	4.03	*	*
1964	Duluth-Superior	Northern	30	167	137	66	10	13	3.45	*	*
1964	Knoxville	Southern	3	15	15	4	0	3	3.60	*	*
1965	Montgomery	Southern	47	103	84	32	5	7	2.53	*	*
	DETROIT	AL	5	6	4	1	0	0	0.00	0	1
1966	DETROIT	AL	1	2	1	2	0	0	9.00	0	0
	Syracuse	Internat'l	54	87	69	33	3	7	4.45	*	*
1967	Toledo	Internat'l	13	45	39	21	5	1	3.00	*	*
	DETROIT	AL	23	65	49	9	4	3	2.63	6	3
1968	DETROIT	AL	39	128	78	51	9	6	2.39	12	2
1969	DETROIT	AL	40	99	74	44	4	4	3.99	8	4
1970	DETROIT	AL	47	104	89	46	6	6	3.03	5	3
1971	DETROIT	AL	(Did Not Play — On Disabled List)								

YEAR	TEAM	LEAGUE	G	IP	SO	BB	W	L	ERA	GS	S
1972	DETROIT	AL	24	44	26	13	1	2	2.05	3	3
1973	DETROIT	AL	65	125	124	39	10	5	1.44	0	38
1974	DETROIT	AL	59	150	134	62	17	14	2.64	0	13
1975	DETROIT	AL	36	71	87	36	2	3	2.17	0	14
1976	DETROIT	AL	56	121	117	67	12	8	2.38	1	13
1977	DETROIT	AL	45	124	115	61	8	14	3.56	8	7
1978	DETROIT	AL	51	92	74	35	9	4	2.34	0	15
1979	DETROIT	AL	43	79	46	55	4	7	5.24	0	9
1980	DETROIT	AL	11	31	18	14	1	0	4.35	0	0
MAJOR LEAGUE TOTALS			545	1241	1036	535	87	76	2.83	43	125

DANNY THOMPSON

For a ballplayer, it's difficult enough to perform with an ailment that hinders him physically, but imagine the psychological burden of playing with the specter of death looming in the near future.

Danny Thompson faced that challenge. An infielder for the Minnesota Twins and Texas Rangers, Thompson played at the major league level for four years after being diagnosed with leukemia. The mental pressure of dealing with his condition caused him to lose his spot in the lineup, but he courageously pulled himself together and reclaimed his regular shortstop job. He finished his seventh season in the big leagues only a few months before the deadly disease claimed his life at the age of 29.

The 1972 season had been a breakout year for Thompson. It was his first year as the Twins regular shortstop and he played 144 games and led all full-time major league shortstops with a .276 batting average. But in early February 1973, as he was gearing up for spring training, a bombshell was dropped on him. In a preseason team physical a few days earlier,

Danny Thompson — played four years with deadly leukemia

Chapter 4—Impaired Organ Function or Chronic Illness   151

routine blood work had disclosed an abnormally high white blood cell count and additional tests were ordered. Now the results were in and the doctor's suspicion had been confirmed. Danny was suffering from leukemia.

Leukemia is a malignant proliferation of immature white cells in blood (granulocytes) or bone marrow (lymphocytes). Both strains of the disease can be either acute or chronic, with the chronic forms being more advanced. Symptoms include fatigue, weakness, weight loss, fevers, bone and joint aches, a tendency to bruise easily, and enlarged lymph nodes. Common complications are anemia and susceptibility to infections. Today chemotherapy, antibiotics, and bone marrow transplants have improved life expectancy rates for victims, but the disease is still deadly. It was even more so 30 years ago when Thompson was diagnosed with it.

Danny and his wife Jo traveled to the famed Mayo Clinic in Rochester, Minnesota, where he was diagnosed with acute granulocytic leukemia, the slowest spreading and most controllable strain. Thompson's illness was in a dormant stage and he was not exhibiting symptoms. Doctors at the Clinic told him that the disease could be controlled as long as it didn't become acute or active and it might not become acute for some time. There was even hope that a cure might be discovered before his condition reached that point. So Danny resumed the job he loved—playing baseball.

Danny Thompson was born on February 1, 1947, in Wichita, Kansas, the second of five children. The three eldest kids were boys and the two youngest were girls. Shortly after he was born, Danny's family moved to Capron, Oklahoma, a small farming community of about 60 folks in the northwest part of the state. In Capron, the Thompsons owned and operated a combination restaurant, grocery, and hardware store that also served as the family home. The Thompson family was athletically oriented. Danny's father Jim had been an outstanding high school athlete. He won 14 letters and received an offer to play professional baseball which he had to turn down for financial reasons. Every weekend the clan would head to nearby Alva so the boys could play Little League ball. Both Danny and Monty, the youngest boy, would end up getting a baseball scholarships to Oklahoma State University, but young Danny was the one who was really hooked on the sport. While Danny was still a child, Jim Thompson developed some health problems that forced them to sell the store and move back to Kansas for a while. The family soon returned to Capron, but Jim had to stay and work in Wichita for several years before obtaining a job closer to home as a petroleum salesman.

In high school, Danny compiled a record of 37 wins against 7 losses as a pitcher. This record is particularly remarkable considering that there were only 13 boys at tiny Capron High and they all played on the baseball team. He once struck out 33 batters in an 11-inning game and lost on a passed ball. Danny also played for an American Legion team in Enid, Oklahoma, from the time he was 15 years old.

After graduation, Thompson was drafted by the New York Yankees but accepted the scholarship to Oklahoma State instead. "He was the best kid I ever worked with," said OSU baseball coach Chet Bryan. "He was just a little special and he played that way. He was dedicated and that's the type of boy a coach enjoys working with. He was a winner." Although Thompson became an All-American shortstop at OSU, Bryan secretly doubted his chances of making it in the pros because of a lack of speed. In fact, Danny didn't really have that much natural talent. Other kids could outrun, out-throw, and outhit him, but he made up for it with determination and hard work.

Drafted by the Twins after his junior year, Danny signed for a modest bonus and traveled to St. Cloud, Minnesota, with his new bride to begin his professional baseball career in the rookie Northern League. The following season, the solid 6-foot, 180-pound right-handed hitter was promoted to Charleston in the Southern League. By 1970, his third campaign as a professional, he had advanced to the Twins Class AAA American Association franchise in Evansville, Indiana.

Thompson had made a good impression on the Twins brass at the club's 1970 spring training camp, so when batting champion Rod Carew tore ligaments in his knee, Danny was called up to fill in at second base — a new position for him. He did a workmanlike job in 96 games and helped the Twins repeat as the American League Western Division Champions. He played all three games of the League Championship Series at second base as the Twins were swept by the Baltimore Orioles.

A mysterious arm injury, which may have been the first sign of his illness, limited Thompson's sophomore season to only 48 games. His back foot slipped while he was making a routine throw and he woke up the next day with a sore arm, a lump under his armpit, and a bruised rib cage. The soreness lingered through much of the season. Early in his career Danny was called "Shotgun" because of his powerful throwing arm, but his new nickname became "Chicken Wing," in recognition of the lame appendage.

But gradually the arm came around. In the off-season the Twins, who'd tumbled to fifth place in the American League West, traded veteran shortstop Leo Cardenas to the California Angels for relief pitcher Dave LaRoche and installed the 25-year-old Thompson at the critical shortstop position. Although Danny led the league's shortstops in errors in 1972, he hit well and provided stability in the middle of the infield. The Twins moved up to third place in the American League West and Thompson was eagerly looking forward to a promising career when he found out that he had an incurable and ultimately fatal disease.

Initially, Danny tried to keep his illness confidential. The last thing he wanted was for people to feel sorry for him, but somehow the press managed to find out and published the news. Soon everyone was talking about "the baseball player with leukemia." In every city he visited during the exhibition season reporters badgered him about his condition, and letters from leukemia victims and their families began pouring in.

Early in the 1973 season, Danny suffered from assorted muscle aches and pulls. Despite assurances to the contrary from his doctors, he began to worry that the disease was causing these minor injuries. Although he succeeded in hiding his insecurities from teammates, he was having a tough time adjusting to his condition. He began to obsess about what would happen to his family if he died. Eventually he lost his firm grip on the regular shortstop job. He fielded poorly and finished the season with a lowly .225 batting average in 99 games.

A couple of things helped Thompson get over this rough period in his life. His wife Jo refused to let him feel sorry for himself and encouraged him to forget about his illness and focus on playing baseball. In addition, he rediscovered religion and became active in the Fellowship of Christian Athletes. He began reading the Bible and attributed a new-found peace of mind to studying the scriptures. He was still determined to beat the leukemia but was no longer afraid of the thought that it might kill him.

After the 1973 season ended, Danny went back to the Mayo Clinic and found that his white blood cell count had increased alarmingly. Until then the disease was being monitored, but not treated. The decision was made to begin chemotherapy immediately. In addition to taking medication, Danny was ordered to consume several bottles of beer a day to flush out his system. Later he was started on an immunization program where live leukemia cells were injected in his body to try to shock his immune system into action — destroying white blood cells. The procedure was still in the experimental stage and Danny was one of the first patients to undergo the treatment. He was given regular injections that would make him violently ill for days. Then boils would form where he was injected and drain streams of pus almost constantly.

Despite the side effects, the injections seemed to help. Danny began the 1974 season as the third-string shortstop but succeeded in working himself back into the starting lineup. For the season, he cut his errors in half and hit a respectable .250 in 97 games despite missing more than a month of action with a pulled thigh muscle. Thompson was upbeat in discussing his baseball future after his successful campaign. "At the Mayo Clinic, they said playing ball was the best thing for me," he said. "There's no use crying or sitting around. I've got a lot of spunk in me and I'm going to use it up."

The Twins, however, appeared to have written him off. While he was on the disabled list with the thigh injury, manager Frank Quilici convinced team owner Calvin Griffith that Thompson was no longer a major league shortstop. In addition the Twins team physician told Griffith that Danny's leukemia was worsening. In turn, Griffin told the media that the club needed a shortstop to become a championship caliber team again.

But Danny prevailed despite the lack of confidence demonstrated by his bosses. He had to win back the shortstop job again in 1975, but ended up hitting a solid .270, with a career high five homers in 112 games. He committed 26 errors in the field, however, and after the season the ever-supportive Griffith suggested that he consider a coaching position at Oklahoma State. Danny wasn't about to quit playing, but in the off-season he did enroll at Northwestern Oklahoma State College to work toward completing a degree which would help if and when he decided to pursue a coaching career.

For the immediate future, however, Danny Thompson was concentrating on the Minnesota Twins shortstop job. In a contentious salary negotiation session before the 1976 season, Thompson threatened to play out his option, but Griffith told him that nobody would want a ballplayer who's going to break down overnight.

When the season started, new Twins manager Gene Mauch used Thompson sparingly, and on the first of June he was traded to the Texas Rangers. In the deal the Twins finally acquired a new shortstop in young Roy Smalley, although it cost them longtime ace hurler Bert Blyleven. Although many considered Danny to be little more than a throw-in, he was warmly welcomed by the Rangers, who immediately signed him to a new contract with a substantial raise. In his first game with Texas he got four hits, including a three run homer and a run scoring double and received a standing ovation from the hometown fans. He became a valuable sub for the Rangers, filling in around the infield for the rest of the year. He ended the season with a combined .222 average in 98 games for Minnesota and Texas.

Danny was happy with the Rangers and was finally becoming more comfortable discussing his condition with others. He'd begun visiting children with cancer in hospitals and encouraging others in their battle with leukemia. But early in the off-season, Danny's health took a sudden turn for the worse. His spleen became swollen and his white blood cell count skyrocketed. The first indication many of Danny's friends had of his deteriorating condition was in early November when he had to cancel out of a long-planned hunting trip to Silver Creek, Nebraska, with some former teammates. In early December, his spleen had to be removed and it was found to weigh about ten times more than normal. The operation was kept quiet, because Danny still stubbornly harbored hopes of playing in 1977.

On December 10, 1976, Danny Thompson died at the Mayo Clinic from complications caused by leukemia. He was two months shy of his 30th birthday and left behind a wife and two young daughters, ages three and seven. More than 500 mourners attended his funeral at the local high school gymnasium in Burlington, Oklahoma, where the family had moved the previous winter.

During his time with the Twins, Danny had become good friends with future Hall of Fame slugger Harmon Killebrew, who hailed from Idaho. After Thompson's death, Killebrew organized the annual Danny Thompson Memorial Golf Tournament in Sun Valley, Idaho, to remember Danny and commemorate his heroic struggle. Proceeds go to the University of Minnesota Leukemia Research Fund. The event still draws some big names in sports and politics and has generated more than $3 million for the fight against leukemia since its inception.

Thompson's major league career spanned seven years. He spent more of his time in the big leagues playing under the shadow of leukemia than without it. His lifetime batting average was .248 in 694 games, the majority of them played at the all-important shortstop position.

Danny Thompson was never a star. In fact, he struggled throughout his career to be recognized as a competent major league shortstop, but he was well liked and respected by his teammates and his dedication was never questioned. "Desire was the thing that was the most typical of him," former teammate Killebrew said after his death. "He was a man who loved the game, who loved to play ball."

In 1975 Danny had been honored with the prestigious Hutch Award, which was named after former pitcher and manager Fred Hutchinson who lost a mortal battle with cancer at the height of his managerial career. The award is presented annually to the player who best exemplifies Hutch's courageous spirit. Shortly after his death, Danny was memorialized with an award of his own — the Danny Thompson Award, which is presented by the Baseball Chapel for exemplary Christian spirit.

Danny Thompson's indomitable character is illustrated by a comment he made in 1974 after the home crowd got on him for making two errors in one inning. "That was super," he said. "I don't want people saying, 'Oh, he's got leukemia, he can make errors.' They booed the hell out of me and I loved it. I knew they were accepting me as a ballplayer."

DANNY LEON THOMPSON
B. February 1, 1947 D. December 10, 1976

YEAR	TEAM	LEAGUE	G	AB	R	H	HR	RBI	AVE	E	POS
1968	St. Cloud	Northern	63	241	36	68	7	38	.282	21	SS
1969	Charlotte	Southern	82	291	45	88	2	40	.302	15	SS
1970	Evansville	Am Ass'n	58	215	26	53	0	18	.247	5	SS
	MINNESOTA	AL	96	302	25	66	0	22	.219	6	2B-3B
1971	MINNESOTA	AL	48	57	10	15	0	7	.263	4	INF
1972	MINNESOTA	AL	144	573	54	158	4	48	.276	32	SS
1973	MINNESOTA	AL	99	347	29	78	1	36	.225	24	SS
1974	MINNESOTA	AL	97	264	25	66	4	25	.250	13	SS
1975	MINNESOTA	AL	112	355	25	96	5	37	.270	26	SS
1976	MINN-TEXAS	AL	98	320	21	71	1	19	.222	6	INF
			694	2218	189	550	15	194	.248	111	

WALT BOND

Ironically, another major leaguer who played while suffering from leukemia was also a member of the Minnesota Twins shortly before Danny Thompson joined the organization. Walt Bond, a huge 6'7", 228-pound first baseman-outfielder played for the Twins in 1967 until his affliction forced him into premature retirement. He died on September 14 of that year, only months before Danny Thompson signed his first Minnesota contract.

Walt Bond, who was born in Denmark, Tennessee, on October 19, 1937, began his professional career with the old Kansas City Monarchs. He was one of the last Negro League players to make the major leagues. The powerful left-handed hitter signed with the Cleveland Indians organization and compiled impressive stats in the Florida State, Carolina, and Eastern Leagues before opening the 1960 season with the Indians.

Cleveland considered Bond a topflight prospect. He'd been impressive in exhibition games, showing tremendous power and exceptional speed for a big man. In fact, his great promise persuaded the Indians to make the infamous trade of league home run king and fan idol Rocky Colavito to the Detroit Tigers for batting champion Harvey Kuenn just before the beginning of the regular season. Under incredible pressure to replace Colavito, Walt started the season in the regular lineup, but didn't hit and soon found himself warming the bench. A demotion to the minors seemed to help, and he returned for a late season stint with the Indians. For the season he batted only .221 in 40 games at the major league level but tore up the Pacific Coast League during his months with Vancouver. The next few years were basically repeats of that pattern — promising minor league performances, but failure at the big league level.

It was during this period that rumors and speculation about Bond's health began to surface. Unlike Danny Thompson, Bond's condition was never made public, and many in the baseball world suspected that the leukemia rumors were either an excuse or an effort to find an explanation for the failure of such a talented young player.

Interestingly, Bond's figures in three trials with the Indians from 1960 through 1962 weren't bad. His batting average was only .245, but he belted 13 homers and drove in 42 runs in only 233 at-bats, numbers which project to about 28 home runs and 90 runs batted in over a full season. It's possible that the Indians became aware of and concerned about Bond's illness and, like Calvin Griffin years later, they weren't willing to invest a lot in a player who might break down overnight.

After another fine minor league season in 1963 with Jacksonville in the International League, Bond was acquired by the Houston Colts and finally put together a full season in the big leagues. He began the season splitting time between the outfield and first base, but eventually won the regular first baseman's job outright. For the year he batted .254, slammed 20 homers, and drove in 85 runs in 148 games as the club's top slugger and cleanup man.

In 1965 the Colts moved into the Astrodome and became the Astros. The Astrodome was a power hitter's nightmare with its imposing dimensions and heavy air, and Bond's power numbers wilted accordingly. Despite raising his average to .263, he hit only seven home runs and lost his starting first base spot when the Astros acquired Jim Gentile from the Kansas City Athletics in June.

Cut lose by Houston after the season, Bond hooked up with the Twins organization and enjoyed a solid 1966 season with their Denver farm club in the Pacific Coast League. In the spring of 1967 he made the Minnesota roster as a spare outfielder and pinch hitter and was hitting a productive .313 in 10 games when failing health forced him to the sidelines.

A few months later, Walt Bond was dead. Like Danny Thompson, Bond was just short of his 30th birthday when he succumbed to leukemia in Houston.

WALTER FRANKLIN BOND
B. October 19, 1937 D. September 14, 1967

YEAR	TEAM	LEAGUE	G	AB	R	H	HR	RBI	AVE	SO	POS
1957	Cocoa	Fla State	111	415	74	136	11	80	.328	*	OF
1958	Burlington	Carolina	123	439	66	130	13	70	.296	*	OF
1959	Reading	Eastern	128	459	74	127	16	82	.277	*	OF
1960	CLEVELAND	AL	40	131	19	29	5	18	.221	14	OF
	Toronto	Internat'l	15	43	2	7	1	3	.163	*	OF
	Vancouver	Pac Coast	74	267	52	85	12	45	.318	*	OF
1961	CLEVELAND	AL	38	52	7	9	2	7	.173	10	OF
	Salt Lake City	Pac Coast	70	230	42	65	8	37	.283	*	OF
1962	Salt Lake City	Pac Coast	132	472	80	151	11	76	.320	*	OF
	CLEVELAND	AL	12	50	10	19	6	17	.380	9	OF
1963	Jacksonville	Internat'l	134	479	55	132	25	82	.276	*	OF
1964	HOUSTON	NL	148	543	63	138	20	85	.254	90	1B-OF
1965	HOUSTON	NL	117	407	46	107	7	47	.263	51	OF-1B
1966	Denver	Pac Coast	*	*	*	*	18	74	.316	*	OF
1967	MINNESOTA	AL	10	16	4	5	1	5	.313	1	OF
	Jacksonville	Internat'l	*	*	*	*	1	1	.100	*	OF
MAJOR LEAGUE TOTALS			365	1199	149	307	41	179	.256	175	

Five

Neurological and Psychological Disorders

GROVER CLEVELAND ALEXANDER

The Grover Cleveland Alexander story is one of the saddest in the history of baseball. Alex, as he was commonly known, pitched in the major leagues from 1911 through 1930 and was one of the greatest hurlers of all time. He attained that status despite suffering from epilepsy. But instead of receiving recognition and support for his heroic battle against the debilitating disease, he was a victim of the ignorance and prejudice of his times.

For centuries epilepsy, which is often characterized by violent seizures, was considered a demonic possession. Gradually it came to be considered a psychiatric disorder and eventually was identified as an electrochemical imbalance in the brain. In the early 20th century, however, it was a greatly misunderstood and feared condition. Epileptics were generally considered to be incompetent and even dangerous. The disorder was commonly treated with electro-shock therapy. In fact, a surgical procedure known as "trepanation," which involves boring holes in the skull in an attempt to free the demons inside, was still performed in those days, although it was no longer widely accepted. Jacksonian or focal epilepsy, which seems to be the form that plagued Alexander, is characterized by involuntary rhythmic movements that usually start in one limb and progress through the body. It may lead to classic "grand mal" convulsions which can result in violent jerking motions, foaming at the mouth, breathing difficulty, and loss of consciousness.

Epilepsy may be genetic or it can be brought on by trauma to the brain. Alex probably developed the disorder in 1909, his first season of professional baseball, when he was beaned by a double play relay while running the bases. He was unconscious for days and suffered vision problems for almost a year. His condition was probably aggravated when he served in an artillery brigade in France during World War I. Alexander spent seven weeks on the front lines, where he was constantly exposed to the firing of large artillery cannons. In addition to worsening his epilepsy the experience resulted in deafness in one ear and chronic headaches that would remain with Alex for the rest of his life.

After returning from the war, Alex began a long slide into alcoholism, which was probably directly related to his illness. He may have first begun drinking heavily in an attempt to ward off increasingly frequent seizures, but it's equally likely that Alex started drinking to excess in an attempt to mask his infirmity, since alcoholism was much more socially acceptable than epilepsy at the time.

In *The Glory of Their Times* by Lawrence S. Ritter, former teammate Hans Lobert recalls that Alexander didn't really start drinking heavily until after he returned from military service. Lobert also recounts how Alex would experience several epileptic episodes a year and his teammates would hold him down and pour brandy down his throat until he calmed down. Since the years 1911 through 1914 were the only years that he and Alexander were teammates, Lobert's account seems to confirm that Alex suffered from epilepsy prior to his tour of duty in the army.

In 1952, two years after his death, a Hollywood version of Alex's life was released. *The Winning Team* starred Doris Day as Alex's wife Aimee, while Ronald Reagan, in one of his better roles before being demoted to politics, drew second billing as Alexander. Predictably, many artistic liberties were taken, even though Aimee Alexander was a production consultant for the popular film. Although Alexander's convulsions are vividly portrayed, the terms *epilepsy* and *seizure* are never used in the movie. Instead, Alexander's affliction is delicately referred to as his "trouble" and the symptomatic episodes are called "blackouts," which indicates that midway through the 20th century epilepsy was still a distasteful subject.

Grover Cleveland Alexander was born into a large farming family in rural Elba, Nebraska, on February 26, 1887. He was the second youngest of thirteen children, twelve of them boys—including a brother, Ray, who pitched in the minor leagues. After so many prior male offspring, Alex's parents must have run out of fresh names so they christened him after Grover Cleveland, the President of the United States at the time. As a boy, Alex developed a strong, accurate throwing arm by firing stones at just about any target he laid eyes on. He really didn't care for farming, so after finishing high school in nearby St. Paul he got a job with the telephone company stringing the first lines across rural Nebraska. Fortunately, the phone company job left Alex with time to pitch in local semipro leagues,

Chapter 5—Neurological and Psychological Disorders 161

Grover Cleveland Alexander — a victim of epilepsy

where he caught the eye of Jap Martin, manager of the Galesburg, Illinois, team in the Class D Illinois-Missouri League.

The 22-year-old phenomenon performed brilliantly for Galesburg until July 27, 1909, when the errant throw knocked him unconscious and almost killed him on the spot. Ironically, Alex was taking a day off from his mound chores at the time and was in the lineup as an outfielder. He was finished for the season, and for a while it looked like his budding career was over. The blow to the head had damaged the optic nerve, leaving him with double vision.

Over the winter, Galesburg sold Alex to Indianapolis without bothering to mention his vision problem. He still couldn't see straight when he reported to Indianapolis, so they quickly shuffled him off to the unsuspecting Syracuse team in the New York State League. Syracuse ended up with a real bargain. Alexander's eyesight suddenly improved and he racked up 29 victories for the 1910 season, including 13 shutouts.

But big league teams were still wary because of Alex's vision problems and Syracuse was not exactly flooded with offers for the 24-year-old hurler. Finally, the Philadelphia Phillies obtained his services for $750. What an investment! As a raw rookie in 1911 Alex led the National League in wins with 28, innings pitched with 367, and shutouts with 7. His greatest years were from 1911 to 1917 when he won 190 games while losing only 88 for the Phillies, including 30 or more wins for three straight seasons. He led the league in every important pitching statistic at least once and won both ends of a doubleheader twice during the period. Despite pitching in Philadelphia's tiny Baker Bowl, with a short right field wall that was only 272 feet from home plate, he hurled 16 shutouts in 1916, which is still the Major League record.

At 6'1" and 185 pounds, Alexander was a big man for his time. He had an awkward, disheveled appearance and wore a comical looking cap that always seemed to be a few sizes too small. But the big righthander had a smooth, effortless pitching motion and a rubber arm. He took a short, economical windup and delivered the ball from a slightly sidearm angle with extraordinary control. Personally, Alex was a soft-spoken, likeable guy who was called "Dode" as a youngster. Early in his career he picked up the nickname "Pete" because teammates thought he resembled a cartoon character named Alkali Pete. He was also referred to as "Alexander the Great" by the press. As a point of interest, some scholars think that the original Alexander the Great may also have been an epileptic.

The Phillies were National League "also-rans" when Alex joined up, but he pitched them to the 1915 pennant with his first 30-win season. It would be the last pennant they'd capture for another 35 years. The Phils finished second to the New York Giants in 1916 and 1917 despite a pair of 30-win seasons from Alex, but before the 1918 campaign he was sold with catcher Bill Killefer to the Chicago Cubs for a record $65,000. Economics dictated Alexander's trade to the Cubs. The Phillies knew he was going to be drafted into the service and was demanding up-front money to sign a new contract — which the Cubs were willing to pay.

Alex entered the armed service after pitching just three games for the Cubs in 1918 and was discharged just before the 1919 season began. He'd gotten married along the way, to the former Aimee Marie Arrants. Although *The Winning Team* portrayed the couple as childhood sweethearts, they'd actually met in St. Paul the winter before Alex reported to Chicago.

When he got out of the army, Alexander was 32 years old and would never be the same pitcher he was before his military stint. Still, he won 128 games against 83 losses in seven full seasons and parts of two others for the Cubs before moving to the St. Louis Cardinals early in the 1926 campaign.

This portion of Alex's career is one of those points where Hollywood veers sharply from reality. In *The Winning Team*, Alex is released by the Cubs and becomes a down-and-out drunk. The movie chronicles how he's abandoned by organized baseball and bounces around with various semi-pro clubs, including the bearded House of David team. He finally hits rock-bottom working as a warm-up act for a flea circus before being dragged from the gutter by Aimee, who persuades the Cardinals to give him another chance.

The reality is that the Cardinals purchased the veteran hurler from the Cubs in June of 1926 for $6,000 — not a small sum in that era. Alex was 39 years old, but had won 15 games in 1925 and was still considered the ace of the Cubs staff. Joe McCarthy, who would later enjoy a Hall of Fame career as manager of the Yankees, had taken over as the Cubs manager in 1926 — his first major league assignment. He simply couldn't abide Alex's drinking or his casual approach to the game. McCarthy was a serious, no-nonsense manager who knew that he was considered an unproven busher by most of the veteran Cubs and had to gain their respect. Alex was making that task extremely difficult.

A run-in with McCarthy before an early season series with the Brooklyn Dodgers may have been the last straw for "Ole Pete." In the midst of an intense team strategy meeting, Alexander made a belated entrance and ambled unsteadily to the rear of the room. Finally locating a seat, he immediately dozed off to the ill-concealed amusement of the other players. McCarthy, studiously ignoring Alex, eventually got around to discussing signs. The Dodgers had acquired hard-partying, light-hitting infielder Rabbit Maranville from the Cubs in the off-season. "Rabbit's a smart baseball operator," Marse Joe intoned. "He knows our signs from last season so we'll have to change them today. Otherwise, the first time he gets to second base he'll steal every one of them."

Alex, apparently roused from his nap by the mention of his former drinking buddy, contemplated McCarthy's shrewd insight and unwisely elected to share his own strategy for dealing with the Maranville situation. In his characteristic soft, gravelly voice he broke up the meeting by advising a red-faced McCarthy, "Don't worry about Rabbit, Joe. He won't even reach second base."

In St. Louis, Alex gained his greatest artistic, if not statistical, success. He joined a hungry, star-studded, young team led by player-manager Rogers Hornsby and won nine important games down the stretch. His pitching was a major factor as the Cardinals captured the National League pennant by a slight two-game margin.

But the 1926 World Series was where Alexander would achieve his greatest fame. After the Cardinals had dropped the Series opener, Alex won the second game at Yankee Stadium. The Cards lost two of three in St. Louis and traveled back to New York for the last two contests. In game six, Alex again evened the Series up with another complete game victory.

In the Series finale, the Cardinals clung to a slim 3–2 lead going into the bottom of the seventh inning. Yankee leadoff hitter Earle Combs walked to start the inning and was sacrificed to second by Mark Koenig. The next hitter, Babe Ruth, who'd already slammed four homers in the series, was intentionally walked. Cleanup hitter Bob Meusel forced Ruth at second, sending Combs to third and bringing up young Lou Gehrig, who was playing in his first championship series. The Cards elected to walk Gehrig and take their chances with Tony Lazzeri, the sensational rookie second baseman and a future Hall of Famer, himself.

Cardinals starter Jesse Haines was tiring and had developed a blister on his finger from throwing his knuckleball. After a short conference on the mound, Hornsby signaled to the bullpen. A murmur of surprise raced through the crowd as Alexander, who hadn't even been warming up, sauntered to the mound to face Lazzeri.

On the first pitch, Alex slipped a called strike past the Yankee second baseman. The eager young slugger jumped on the next offering and smashed a drive down the third base line which would have cleared the bases if it hadn't curved foul at the last minute. On the next pitch, Alex fired a quick sidearm curve to send Lazzeri down swinging and retire the side. He then held the Bronx Bombers scoreless for the next two innings to preserve the victory.

The Lazzeri strikeout was to become the defining moment of Alexander's magnificent career and serve as the climax for *The Winning Team*. The confrontation eventually assumed mystical proportions and the surrounding circumstances became somewhat blurred by time and imagination. A popular myth is that Alex spent most of the previous night celebrating his sixth game victory and was still drunk, or at least suffering from a hangover, when called in to face Lazzeri. Some claim that the pat on the butt Hornsby gave the old-timer was really to see if he was carrying a flask rather than convey encouragement.

To his dying day, however, Alexander denied he'd been drinking before the decisive game. "I was cold sober the night before I relieved Haines in the seventh game," he said shortly before his death. "After Saturday's game, Hornsby came over to me in the clubhouse and asked me not to celebrate, telling me he might need me in the seventh game. So I stayed in my hotel room all night." Aimee, who was in New York for the Series, backed up Alex's story. She confirmed that they'd stayed in the hotel that night and just had a few highballs together.

After his 1926 heroics, Alex signed a new pact with St. Louis for $17,000, his best contract ever. Only the Babe and the Washington Senators great hurler, Walter Johnson, earned more. Alex responded with 21 wins in 1927. In 1928 he helped the Cardinals to another pennant with 16 victories, but this time he lost his only World Series start to the Yankees with Lazzeri reaching him for a key hit.

When the 1929 season began, the 42-year-old Alexander needed only nine more victories to surpass Christy Mathewson's National League record of 372 career wins. Mathewson's career was winding down when Alex broke in with the Phillies, but they'd faced each other on three occasions when Alex was a young man. Passing Matty had been Alexander's goal for many years.

Though Alex may have been sober when he retired Lazzeri, his growing alcohol problem was no secret in baseball circles. It was affecting his performance on the field more and more and was becoming an embarrassment to the team. Due to his excessive drinking, Alex and Aimee were having serious marital problems and she divorced him during the 1929 season. Despite drinking heavily all year, he'd still managed to win eight games by midsummer to tie Mathewson's record. After Aimee left him, however, his condition deteriorated to the point that he could no longer perform, and at the team's urging he agreed to enter a sanitarium — still stuck on eight wins.

Alex returned after a month's rehabilitation and promptly recorded win number 373 in Philadelphia on August 10 to break the tie with Mathewson. Sadly, it would be his last hurrah, as a postgame victory celebration with some old cronies from his early days with the Phillies turned into an extended binge. When he wasn't in shape to take his next turn on the mound, he was shipped back to St. Louis. The Cardinals had sent Alex home hoping he would dry out and rejoin the rotation, but he couldn't stay sober and was eventually suspended for the rest of the season.

However, Alex would be afforded another chance to add to his final victory total. In the off-season, the 43-year-old hurler was traded back to Philadelphia where he'd begun his fabulous career 19 years earlier. In 1930 the Phillies would finish last in the standings while setting major league records for both highest team batting average (.315) and highest team earned run average (6.71). But Alex couldn't even hold a spot on that most horrendous of pitching staffs and was released early in the year after losing three games without a victory. When packing to leave Philadelphia and major league baseball for the last time, Alexander muttered to a veteran sportswriter, "I'm leaving the same way I came — with nothing."

After being cut by the Phils, Alex caught on with Dallas in the Texas League but was soon released. Finally through with organized baseball, he went on to pitch for various touring teams until he was more than 50 years old. This time his service really did include several years with The House of David team.

Aimee had come back to Alex in 1931. They were remarried and she traveled with him for five years before giving up and divorcing him again. As times worsened, Alex began picking up a few bucks demonstrating his pitching technique as a carnival sideshow act and for a time he really did share the bill with performing fleas, as well as the Fat Lady and The Tattooed Man, for the Hubert Brothers Flea Circus and Museum in New York. He also found occasional employment as an instructor at former manager Rogers Hornsby's baseball school in Texas. Alex was always hoping to land a job as pitching coach at the major league level, but his reputation was so bad that he never received an offer.

Except for pitching, poor Alex had difficulty with everything in life. He was inducted into the newly established Hall of Fame in 1938 and came away from the ceremony with a replica of the tablet that had been placed there in his honor. "You know, I can't eat tablets or nicely framed awards," he grumbled to renowned sportswriter Fred Lieb. Alex ended up living off the proceeds from a small pension fund that Cardinal owner Sam Breadon had the foresight to establish for him during his time with the Cards. When he ran out of money, he would hock his World Series ring, and Breadon would always redeem it for him.

The fact that he'd finished ahead of Mathewson for the National League career wins record was something that Alex took tremendous pride in. But that distinction, like everything else Alex valued, slipped away from him when statistical researchers in the 1940s added another victory to Matty's career total.

On November 4, 1950, Alexander was found dead in a rented room in St. Paul, Nebraska, pennyless and alone—an unfinished letter to his beloved Aimee on the table. He'd been in poor health for some time and the coroner put "heart attack" on the death certificate, but Aimee always believed that his death had been caused by a fall during a final seizure.

With a total of 373 career victories, Alexander still shares the record for the most wins in National League history with Matty, and it's still the third highest total in major league history behind Cy Young and Walter Johnson. Alex lost only 208 decisions in his career and never turned in a losing record in either the majors or the minors until his final season. He also threw 90 shutouts in his career, a National League record that still stands, and he compiled a marvelous 2.56 lifetime earned run average.

It's impossible to know for certain if Alex began drinking heavily because of his affliction, but it's fairly certain that the two were closely connected. In *The Winning Team*, Alexander's days with the Cubs are numbered when one of his "blackouts" is mistaken for drunkenness. It's very likely that many incidents in Alex's life that were attributed to excessive drinking were actually epileptic seizures. Aimee Alexander always claimed that a great deal of Alex's erratic behavior, such as disappearing for several days, which was blamed on his drinking, was actually caused by epileptic episodes.

Given Grover Cleveland Alexander's tremendous accomplishments while suffering from epilepsy, it boggles the mind to imagine what he might have accomplished if modern anti-convulsant drugs were available to him, or if he'd lived in more enlightened times and been able to better handle his disability.

GROVER CLEVELAND ALEXANDER
B. February 26, 1887 D. November 4, 1950

YEAR	TEAM	LEAGUE	G	IP	SO	BB	W	L	ERA	CG	SHO
1909	Galesburg	Ill'ois-Mo.	24	219	198	42	15	8	*	*	*
1910	Syracuse	NY State	43	245	204	67	29	14	*	*	13

YEAR	TEAM	LEAGUE	G	IP	SO	BB	W	L	ERA	CG	SHO
1911	PHILADELPHIA	NL	48	367	227	129	28	13	2.57	31	7
1912	PHILADELPHIA	NL	46	310	195	105	19	17	2.81	25	3
1913	PHILADELPHIA	NL	47	306	159	75	22	8	2.79	23	9
1914	PHILADELPHIA	NL	46	355	214	76	27	15	2.38	32	6
1915	PHILADELPHIA	NL	49	376	241	64	31	10	1.22	36	12
1916	PHILADELPHIA	NL	48	389	167	50	33	12	1.55	38	16
1917	PHILADELPHIA	NL	45	388	201	58	30	13	1.86	35	8
1918	CHICAGO	NL	3	26	15	3	2	1	1.73	3	0
1919	CHICAGO	NL	30	235	121	38	16	11	1.72	20	9
1920	CHICAGO	NL	46	363	173	69	27	14	1.91	33	7
1921	CHICAGO	NL	31	252	77	33	15	13	3.39	21	3
1922	CHICAGO	NL	33	246	48	34	16	13	3.63	20	1
1923	CHICAGO	NL	39	305	72	30	22	12	3.19	26	3
1924	CHICAGO	NL	21	169	33	25	12	5	3.03	12	0
1925	CHICAGO	NL	32	236	63	29	15	11	3.39	20	1
1926	CHIC-ST LOUIS	NL	30	200	47	31	12	10	3.05	15	2
1927	ST. LOUIS	NL	37	268	48	38	21	10	2.52	22	2
1928	ST. LOUIS	NL	34	244	59	37	16	9	3.36	18	1
1929	ST. LOUIS	NL	22	132	33	23	9	8	3.89	8	0
1930	PHILADELPHIA	NL	9	22	6	6	0	3	9.14	0	0
	Dallas	Texas	5	24	4	11	1	2	8.28	*	*
MAJOR LEAGUE TOTALS			696	5190	2199	953	373	208	2.56	438	90

TONY LAZZERI

Ironically, Tony Lazzeri, the young star whose name became inextricably linked with Alexander, was also an epileptic, although Tony did a much better job than Alex of dealing with his disability.

Lazzeri accepted his affliction and didn't attempt to hide it. If a new teammate was sitting next to him for a long train ride, Tony would explain his condition to him and carefully describe what would happen and what actions should be taken in the event of a seizure. Mark Koenig, Lazzeri's keystone partner from 1926 to 1929, said that Tony only had seizures in the morning and evening. This was fortunate since night baseball wasn't introduced until the tail-end of Lazzeri's career and most games were played in the afternoon. Tony was the regular Yankees second baseman for 12 years and played another two seasons in the National League without ever having an episode on the field.

Tony Lazzeri was born in San Francisco on December 6, 1903. The 5'11", 170-pound second baseman arrived in the major leagues in 1926 accompanied by much hoopla. Playing for Salt Lake City, he'd slammed

60 homers in the Pacific Coast League in 1925, and the Yankees had paid dearly to acquire his contract. He didn't disappoint them. As a rookie his 18 homers were the third highest total in the American League and his 114 runs batted in tied him for second place in that department. Lazzeri was the first in the Yankees' line of great Italian-American heroes, setting the stage for the likes of Crosetti, DiMaggio, Rizzuto, and Berra.

The 1926 World Series confrontation with Alexander probably made Lazzeri the most ignominious strikeout victim in history, and it might have ruined a less stouthearted young player. But Tony shook it off and went on to enjoy a brilliant career. He gained a reputation for icy calmness on the field and was considered one of the smartest players in the game, hardly characteristics that were attributed to epileptics back then. Though anything but colorful on the field, he earned the flamboyant nickname "Poosh 'Em Up Tony" for his ability to push runners across the plate.

In a major league career that spanned 14 seasons, Lazzeri batted .292 and blasted 178 home runs. He played in six World Series with the Yankees, and the 1926 Classic was the only one they didn't win. After the 1937 season he was shipped to the Cubs to make room for Joe Gordon at second base. The deal was somewhat puzzling in that the Cubs already had a younger future Hall of Famer, Billy Herman, manning second base. Apparently, Lazzeri was acquired to eventually succeed old favorite Gabby Hartnett as manager, but the Cubs' late season drive to the 1938 National League pennant dashed those plans. Tony spent his year in Chicago as a utility infielder and appeared as a pinch hitter in the World Series against his former New York teammates. Tony hung around for part of another year in the National League before drifting down to the minor leagues where he remained an active player until 1943. He was named to the Hall of Fame in 1991 by the Veteran's Committee.

At the age 42 in 1946, only three years removed from his last base hit, Lazzeri died of what was almost certainly an epileptic seizure. While alone at his San Francisco home, Tony fell and struck his head against a banister. He'd been dead for more than a day when he was found by his wife upon returning home from an out-of-town trip.

Although Lazzeri was more than 16 years younger than Alexander and certainly took better care of himself, epilepsy ended his life four years earlier than the old pitcher.

ANTHONY MICHAEL "TONY" LAZZERI
B. December 6, 1903 D. August 6, 1946

YEAR	TEAM	LEAGUE	G	AB	R	H	HR	RBI	AVE	SB	POS
1922	Salt Lake City	Pac Coast	45	78	9	15	1	8	.192	0	1B-3B
1923	Peoria	Three I	135	436	63	108	14	*	.248	9	2B
	Salt Lake City	Pac Coast	39	130	25	46	7	21	.354	4	SS
1924	Lincoln	Western	82	316	65	104	28	*	.329	8	INF
	Salt Lake City	Pac Coast	85	293	51	83	16	61	.283	8	SS-3B
1925	Salt Lake City	Pac Coast	197	710	202	252	60	222	.355	39	2B-SS
1926	NEW YORK	AL	155	589	79	162	18	114	.275	16	2B
1927	NEW YORK	AL	153	570	92	176	18	102	.309	22	2B-SS
1928	NEW YORK	AL	116	404	62	134	10	82	.332	15	2B
1929	NEW YORK	AL	147	545	101	193	18	106	.354	9	2B
1930	NEW YORK	AL	143	571	109	173	9	121	.303	4	2B-3B
1931	NEW YORK	AL	135	484	67	129	8	83	.267	18	2B-3B
1932	NEW YORK	AL	141	510	79	153	15	113	.300	11	2B
1933	NEW YORK	AL	139	523	94	154	18	104	.294	15	2B
1934	NEW YORK	AL	123	438	59	117	14	67	.267	11	2B-3B
1935	NEW YORK	AL	130	477	72	130	13	83	.273	11	2B
1936	NEW YORK	AL	150	537	82	154	14	109	.287	8	2B
1937	NEW YORK	AL	126	446	56	109	14	70	.244	7	2B
1938	CHICAGO	NL	54	120	21	32	5	23	.267	0	SS-3B
1939	BROOK-N.Y.	NL	27	83	13	24	4	14	.289	1	3B-2B
	Toronto	Internat'l	39	97	19	22	1	20	.227	*	INF
1940	Toronto	Internat'l	13	17	0	3	0	0	.176	*	INF
1941	San Francisco	Pac Coast	102	315	40	78	3	39	.247	*	INF
1942	Portsmouth	Piedmont	98	310	32	75	2	40	.242	*	INF
1943	Wilkes-Barrie	Eastern	58	181	25	49	3	21	.271	*	INF
MAJOR LEAGUE TOTALS			1739	6297	986	1840	178	1191	.292	148	

JIMMY PIERSALL

Baseball has always had its share of eccentrics. The history of the game is filled with the adventures of zany, outrageous characters. Many old-timers will even argue it that doesn't hurt a ballplayer to be a little on the crazy side; that it may help drive a player to heights that may not have been achieved if he were encumbered by normal inhibitions. The great Ty Cobb, for instance, was considered by some to be a highly functioning psychotic, whose maniacal obsession to always be first drove him to become a baseball legend.

Chapter 5—Neurological and Psychological Disorders   171

Imagine baseball lore without cherished anecdotes of fabled characters like Rabbit Maranville, Babe Herman, Yogi Berra, Mark "the Bird" Fidrych, Rube Waddell, or Dizzy Dean. In fact, the man considered by many to be the greatest player in the history of the game, Babe Ruth, is revered as much for his herculean off-the-field appetites and larger than life escapades as for his incredible accomplishments at the plate.

The other side of the coin is the self-destructive behavior demonstrated by such men as Cincinnati catcher Willard Hershberger, who committed suicide in 1940 because he thought he'd let his team down; Cleveland first baseman Tony Horton, whose promising carrier ended in 1970 when the 25-year-old slugger was institutionalized after a nervous breakdown during a game; Denny McLain, baseball's last 30-game-winner, who gambled and ate himself out of baseball and into prison when he should have been in his prime; Darryl Strawberry, whose sad story of drug abuse ruined his Hall of Fame talent; Billy Martin, whose brilliance as a manager was overshadowed by his uncontrollable temper; Pete Rose, the all-time major league leader in base hits, whose gambling addiction caused him to be thrown out of baseball; or talented left-hander John Rocker, who recently succeeded in turning the baseball world against him with a series of incredibly insensitive and prejudicial comments.

Outfielder Jimmy Piersall, who entertained baseball fans for 17 years with his brilliant fielding and crowd-pleasing antics, is included in the first bunch of colorful performers, but he could just as easily have slipped into the latter group of legendary losers if not for his courage and determination to fight his affliction.

While playing for the Boston Red Sox in his 1952 rookie season, Piersall suffered a severe mental breakdown. He was institutionalized for six weeks and missed the last half of the season. He became so violent that he was transferred out of the private sanitarium where he was originally admitted and placed in a state mental hospital. At the state institution he received electroconvulsive shock therapy which left him unable to remember anything that had occurred since the beginning of spring training, except the birth of his daughter early in the season. Many thought the 23-year-old Piersall's baseball days were over. One newspaper reported, "[Piersall] will never play baseball again. Now a hopeless mental case, he will spend the rest of his life in an institution."

But the young outfielder made an incredible comeback the next season to capture a regular spot in the Red Sox outfield. He overcame his self-doubts and withstood the tremendous pressure of knowing that one slip could mean the end of his career. He managed to ignore the catcalls and insults of fans and opponents and, despite occasional relapses, went

Jimmy Piersall circles the bases backwards after 100th homer

on to establish himself as a dependable major league performer and one of the finest defensive outfielders of his time.

Jimmy Piersall was born in on November 14, 1929, in a run down section of Waterbury, Connecticut, just after the beginning of the Great Depression. The Piersall household was hardly conducive to sound emotional development. Jimmy's parents, who were already middle-aged when he was born, had one other child — a son about 20 years older than Jimmy,

Chapter 5—Neurological and Psychological Disorders   173

who died when Jimmy was a tot. John Piersall, the patriarch of the family, was a house painter who had difficulty finding steady work during the depression. Jimmy's mother, meanwhile, was in and out of mental institutions throughout the boy's childhood. The family was on public assistance for a time and Jimmy remembers sometimes being so hungry that he cried.

Piersall wrote of his ordeal in *Fear Strikes Out*, an autobiography he coauthored with Al Hirshberg, that was released in 1955. *Fear Strikes Out* was subsequently made into a 1957 hit movie with the same title starring Anthony Perkins as Piersall. Jimmy hated the film. Aside from the fact that (in Jimmy's words) Perkins threw like a girl, the movie inaccurately depicted the circumstances of his breakdown and subsequent institutionalization. The movie version shows a deranged Piersall being forcibly hauled away after going berserk during a game and frantically climbing the foul screen to get at the hostile fans. In real life he voluntarily admitted himself to a private institution.

In the movie *Fear Strikes Out*, John Piersall is portrayed as an obsessed tyrant who pushes his son too hard. Although Jimmy felt that this was an exaggeration, his father was a domineering personality who wasn't afraid to use the strap. John Piersall's own father had left home and his mother had died while he was still a baby. He grew up in foster homes and had to fight for everything he got. More than anything else he wanted his son to be a major league baseball player for the Boston Red Sox and was determined not to let anything get in the way. For instance, he refused to let Jimmy play football as a youth for fear of injury that might destroy his baseball ambitions.

Jimmy was allowed to play basketball, however. In high school, he was a tremendous talent who drew the interest of the Boston Celtics. But his passion was baseball, where he also developed a reputation as one of the top players in the area.

Even as a youth, Piersall was hyperactive and a chronic worrier. When he was 15 years old, he began experiencing tension headaches and suffered from them almost constantly. He fretted incessantly about his mother's situation. When she was institutionalized, he worried about whether she'd come back, and when she was home he worried about how long she'd stay. During Jimmy's senior year in high school, his father suffered a heart attack, which added financial concerns to the 17-year-old youngster's burden. His greatest problem, however, was the fear of failure—the fear of letting his family down.

Jimmy had planned to attend Duke University after high school, but the family finances wouldn't allow it. The Boston Braves offered a $20,000 bonus for Jimmy's name on a contract, but his father insisted that he turn it down. Under the rules of organized baseball at that time, bonus players had to stay with the parent club and Jimmy's father didn't want him sitting on the bench in the major leagues while his skills deteriorated. Instead, Jimmy signed with the Red Sox and spent the 1948 season leading the Eastern League in doubles and runs batted in for Scranton.

Young Piersall was with Boston's Louisville farm club in the American Association the next two years and got a late season audition with the Sox at the end of the 1950 campaign. The next season, he made the club out of spring training at the age of 21 but bristled at sitting on the bench. Already showing warning signs of the emotional tempest brewing inside of him, he demanded to be sent back to the minors where he could get some playing time. The Red Sox accommodated by shipping him back to Louisville, but he ran into problems there and was sent to Birmingham in the Double A Southern Association where he hit a sensational .346 and became a huge fan favorite.

Jimmy expected to compete for a spot in the Boston outfield in 1952, but Sox management planned to try the kid at shortstop — a position he'd never played before. The move made a lot of sense. The Red Sox roster was loaded with aging, former All-Star shortstops, none of whom could still do justice to the position on defense. Slugging Vern Stephens had been an All-Star since his acquisition for the St. Louis Browns in 1948. He'd averaged 147 runs batted in from 1948 to 1950 while playing short but was bothered by injuries in 1951 and had been shifted to third base. Johnny Pesky, an All-Star shortstop in his own right in 1946, who'd moved to third to make room for Stephens, went back to shortstop for the 1951 season, but the 32-year-old veteran's defense was not up to snuff. Manager Lou Boudreau, formerly a star shortstop with the Cleveland Indians, also gave it a try. The 34-year-old player-manager played 52 games at short in 1951, but it was clear that his legs were gone. If Piersall could make the transition, it would solve the shortstop problem and take advantage of his outstanding defensive ability at the key defensive spot.

Unfortunately, the Red Sox never discussed the move with their top prospect. Instead, Piersall happened to read about it in the newspapers during the off-season and immediately leaped to a bizarre conclusion. In a fit of paranoia, the tormented young man decided that the Sox had dreamed up the position change as a ploy to get rid of him. Jimmy was already feeling a little desperate because he hadn't been able to land an off-season job and family financial pressures were weighing heavily on him. While playing for Scranton, he'd met Mary Teevan and they were married in October 1949. Their first of nine children had been born in March 1951

Chapter 5—Neurological and Psychological Disorders 175

and another was already on the way. In addition, he also had the financial support of his parents to worry about.

Jimmy's mental condition became so unstable as the opening of the Red Sox spring training camp approached that he secretly began to spend all of his time hiding at the movies rather than working out. His thinking became so erratic that he intentionally left his glove at home when he reported to camp, figuring that if he didn't have a glove they couldn't make him play shortstop. Despite the turmoil swirling in his head, Piersall looked good in the infield during the spring session and started the 1952 season as the club's regular shortstop. Throughout the first month of the season his defensive play was adequate and his bat was a pleasant surprise, but his manic behavior was another matter. He was a wild man, arguing excessively with the umpires and fighting opposing players. Eventually the Red Sox returned him to the outfield in the hopes that playing a familiar position would calm him down.

But the situation didn't improve. Jimmy's moods swung wildly — when his temper wasn't out of control, he acted like a clown. While playing right field, he mimicked the mannerisms and distinctive gait of veteran center fielder Dom DiMaggio, one of the most respected men in the game. On the bases, he rattled the venerable Satchel Paige by mocking the St. Louis Browns hurler's pitching motion. He was constantly bowing and waving to the crowd and hamming it up with pantomime and slapstick routines. The fans loved an impromptu hula dance that he performed in the outfield in Chicago. When he wasn't in the lineup, Piersall turned pregame infield practice into his personal comedy show.

Piersall's behavior was also becoming increasingly violent. Before a contest with the Yankees, he got into an altercation with New York second baseman Billy Martin and they fought under the stands. Sent to the clubhouse after the Martin episode, he immediately got into another skirmish with teammate Mickey McDermott in the Red Sox locker room. The last straw was when he was accused of spanking Vern Stephens' young son in the Boston clubhouse. Citing Piersall's attitude as detrimental to the club, Boudreau dispatched him back to Birmingham in late June, but the problems continued in Birmingham, where he was ejected half-a-dozen times in only 18 games. Among his pranks was squirting the plate umpire with a water pistol. Finally, at Birmingham's request, Piersall was recalled to Boston, and at the urging of the Red Sox club he agreed to enter a private sanitarium in July. But Piersall became violent and was transferred to Danvers State Hospital and then to Westborough State Hospital in Massachusetts, where he was subjected to electroshock therapy.

Piersall's memory of this turbulent eight-month period is virtually a blank. He remembered checking into the Sarasota Terrace Hotel on January 15 for the beginning of spring training. The next thing he knew he was waking up in the "Violent Room" of Westborough — with no headache for the first time since he was 15 years old. He'd been at Westborough for two weeks before "coming to." After spending six weeks at Westborough, Piersall was released on September 9, 1952. At the suggestion of his psychiatrist he spent the winter in Sarasota, away from his parents, playing golf and working out in preparation for the 1953 season.

Jimmy overcame anxieties about being accepted by his teammates and captured the Red Sox starting right field job in spring training. He batted a steady .272 for the 1953 campaign and fielded brilliantly. He held a regular spot in the Boston outfield from 1953 through 1958 and developed into a star. During the 1954 season, he shifted to center field, where his extraordinary range and ball-hawking skills could be more fully utilized. That season he made the American League All-Star Team and was named the Red Sox Most Valuable Player, honors that he would repeat in 1956. In 1954 he also engaged in an ill-advised exhibition game throwing contest against the New York Giants Willie Mays and permanently damaged his arm in the competition. Prior to that time, Piersall had a rifle for an arm, but it would never be quite as strong after the injury.

After an injury-marred 1958 season, Piersall was swapped to the Cleveland Indians, where he endured another disappointing year in 1959. The Indians finished in second place, but Jimmy lost the regular center field job to hot-hitting Tito Francona and batted only .246 in part-time duty.

In 1960 Francona was moved to left field and Jimmy regained his starting position, but it was a disturbing year. Although his behavior on the field had generally been acceptable since 1952, it hadn't exactly been conventional. He'd continued to clown around on occasion and had never been one to back down from a confrontation. But his behavior began to grow increasingly outlandish and it looked like he was headed for another breakdown. He threw a ball at Bill Veeck's exploding scoreboard in Chicago, brawled with Detroit Tigers hurler and future U.S. Senator Jim Bunning, had several run-ins with umpires, and fought with fans and the press. During a pitching change, he seated himself in the shade of the monuments at Yankee Stadium, which used to be inside the center field fence, and claimed to commune with the spirit of Babe Ruth. Finally, on orders from the Indians, Jimmy saw a psychiatrist. He took a week off from baseball, which seemed to get him straightened out. He finished the 1960 season with a .282 batting average, his highest mark in four years, and slugged 18 homers.

Chapter 5—Neurological and Psychological Disorders

In 1961 Piersall posted a career high .322 batting average for the Indians, but at the end of the season he was traded to the Washington Senators. This, of course, was the second edition of the Senators—an expansion team created in 1961. Jimmy endured an uninspiring 1962 campaign for the last place team and early the next season he was traded to the New York Mets for Gil Hodges, who was immediately named manager of the Senators.

In New York, Piersall joined a team that was actually worse than the Senators. The Mets had dropped a record 120 games in 1962, their initial season, and were on their way to 111 losses in 1963. Jimmy hit only .194 in 40 games for the Mets but managed to make headlines with his only National League home run. The Mets were managed by 72-year-old legend Casey Stengel at the time and they included former Brooklyn Dodger great Duke Snider in their collection of over-the-hill, former stars. When Snider slammed his 400th career homer for the Mets, the feat barely got a mention in the papers. Piersall, who had been dallying at a total of 99 career homers for some time, confided to the Duke that he wouldn't let that happened to him when he finally blasted his 100th circuit shot.

Sure enough, a few weeks later Jimmy finally belted his long-awaited number 100, an opposite-field chip shot off Philadelphia's Dallas Green that barely cleared the short right field fence at the old Polo Grounds. Piersall made sure the landmark event was noted by circling the bases running backwards. He got coast to coast coverage for the stunt and also drew his unconditional release from the Mets shortly thereafter. It seems that "The Old Professor" Stengel insisted on being the only clown in a Mets uniform and resented the competition.

Soon after the Mets cut him loose, Piersall caught on with the Los Angeles Angels and played out his career in Anaheim as a respected elder statesman. His greatest accomplishment with the Angels was winning the Associated Press Comeback Player of the Year award in 1964 with a .314 batting average in part-time duty. He finally hung up his spikes at the age of 37 early in the 1967 season.

For his career, the 6-foot tall, 175-pound right-handed hitter compiled a respectable .272 batting average in 1,734 major league games and finished with 104 home runs. It was in the field, however, that Piersall's star really shown. His lifetime fielding average as an outfielder was an outstanding .997 and he won two Gold Gloves (he probably would have garnered a few more, but the award was not instituted until 1957). Jimmy was an aggressive defender who played an extremely shallow center field. He didn't have tremendous speed, but got a terrific jump on the ball. Former Hall of Fame manager, Bill McKechnie, who was a Red Sox coach in the

1950s, once said, "That kid Piersall gets balls Tris Speaker wouldn't have reached."

After his career as an active player ended, Piersall worked as the general manager for a minor league football team in Roanoke and also managed a hotel in the area. He spent a few years working for Charley Finley in Oakland, managed in the Cardinals' minor league system, and for a time coached for the Texas Rangers under his old foe-turned-friend, Billy Martin. He was selling plastic pipe when he was invited to do a guest spot broadcast with announcer Harry Caray in Chicago and did so well he was hired by the White Sox network.

Piersall became an extremely popular and controversial sports broadcaster and color commentator, whose predilection for speaking his mind kept him in hot water much of the time. A memorable accomplishment was keeping his job after referring to White Sox owner Bill Veeck's wife as a colossal bore on the air when she criticized him for being too hard on the players. When his broadcasting stint with the White Sox ended, Piersall caught on with the Chicago Cubs' organization, scouting and coaching the outfielders. He underwent open heart surgery in 1976 but still remains very active.

The Jimmy Piersall story is one of baseball's most compelling sagas. The movie *Fear Strikes Out* still appears on television from time to time and the book was reprinted in 1999 with a new "Afterword" by Piersall.

In his 1964 book, *The Quality of Courage*, Mickey Mantle referred to Piersall as one of the most courageous players he ever saw. The Mick wrote, "When Jimmy was young he was strangled by fear, but he ended up defeating fear, by striking it out of his life."

OTHER PSYCHOLOGICALLY FRAGILE PLAYERS

Although Jimmy Piersall's mental breakdown and subsequent recovery is the most dramatic and well known, there are other players who've managed to come back from nervous breakdowns or mental disorders.

Chicago Cubs second baseman Johnny Evers' situation was probably the most similar to Piersall's. The 30-year-old Evers, middleman of the famed Tinker-to-Evers-to-Chance double play combination, suffered a nervous breakdown at the height of his career and missed most of the 1911 season.

Like Piersall, Evers was a bundle of nervous energy. The slightly built 5'9", left-handed, singles hitter from Troy, New York, tipped the scales at a mere 125 pounds. He was known as "The Crab" for his less than sunny disposition as well as the manner in which he scuttled after ground balls. He was wound so tight that he often feuded with teammates, including keystone partner Tinker. Reportedly, the two didn't speak to each other off the field for several years. Evers' problems came to a head when he was the driver in a car accident that killed a close friend and then a short time later lost his life savings to his business partner's bad investments. His problems were compounded by with a subsequent bout of pneumonia and the death of his young daughter later that year.

But Evers came back from the breakdown to post a career high .341 batting mark for the Cubs in 1912. In 1914 he was traded to the Boston Braves and won the National League Most Valuable Player Award while leading them to the World Championship.

For his career, Evers batted .270 in 1,783 games. Injuries kept him from being more than a part-timer after his MVP season at the age of 33 and he retired after the 1917 season. He'd replaced Frank Chance and led the Cubs to a third place finish in 1913 as a player-manager. He returned to the Cubs for another managerial assignment in 1921 but was dismissed before the year was out. Johnny then became a coach for the crosstown White Sox and even appeared in a game at second base to the delight of the fans. He handled six chances flawlessly in the field and, naturally, turned a double play. He had a brief stint as White Sox manager in 1924 and then went into the sporting goods business. He returned to baseball in 1929 as assistant manager for the Boston Braves and later scouted and managed in the minor leagues. He later became a minor league executive.

Evers suffered a debilitating stroke in 1942 but recovered enough to celebrate his induction into the Hall of Fame along with double-play mates Tinker and Chance in 1946. Tinker and Evers finally buried the hatchet, and the induction ceremony was a nostalgic reunion for the two old-timers (Chance had died in 1924). Johnny Evers died in 1947, with Joe Tinker following him to the grave a little more than a year later.

In 1927 Johnny "Bananas" Mostil, star center fielder for the Chicago White Sox, slashed his neck and wrists in a bungled attempt to kill himself during spring training. Mostil, a local boy from Chicago, was only 30 years old and at the peak of his career at the time. A premier defensive outfielder, he'd led the American League in walks, stolen bases and runs scored in 1925 and hit a career high .328 and again led the league in steals in 1926.

Mostil's suicide attempt was initially attributed to a painful case of neuritis affecting his jaw, but rumors circulated that Johnny had been having an affair with the wife of teammate Red Faber, who threatened to kill him after he found out about it. Apparently these rumors stemmed from a meeting between Faber and Mostil shortly before the suicide attempt. Another titillating explanation was offered by teammate Bucky Crouse in an interview in *Baseball Players and Their Times*. Crouse's understanding was that Mostil was upset because his girlfriend had fallen in love with roommate and fellow outfielder Jimmy Barrett, who she later married.

Johnny's self-inflicted injuries caused him to miss most of the 1927 campaign, but he returned to play 133 games in 1928 and bat .270, the lowest full-season average of his big league career. He was still rehabilitating his damaged wrists by squeezing a small rubber ball to regain his strength and looking forward to a full comeback in 1929, but he shattered his leg early in the season to end his 10-year major league career at the age of 32.

Mostil finished his career with a tidy .301 lifetime batting mark and stole 176 bases in 972 big league games. Johnny, who captured the regular center field job thanks to the expulsion of outfielder Happy Felsch for his role in throwing the 1919 World Series, was a good leadoff hitter and a brilliant defensive outfielder. He's unofficially credited with once running down a flyball from his center field post and catching in foul territory after the left fielder thought it was going out of play.

After the 1929 season, Johnny went down to play in the minors for several years. His mental health stabilized enough that he became a minor league manager in the White Sox system and coached for the Sox at the major league level for several years. Eventually he became a scout for the Sox until retiring due to ill health a year before his death in 1970.

Almost 20 years after Jimmy Piersall's infamous breakdown, major league baseball was finally forced to recognize that mental problems were just as real and could be just as debilitating as physical ones and needed to be dealt with accordingly. The player who initiated this change was Alex Johnson, a talented and troubled outfielder for eight major league teams from 1964 through 1976.

Alex, whose brother Ron was a professional football star, was a devastating right-handed hitter who combined speed and power. The sensitive young black man began his career with the Philadelphia Phillies, a franchise that was not noted in that era for an understanding attitude toward Negro players. Johnson witnessed the hostility toward fellow rookie Richie Allen in Philadelphia firsthand, and like Allen before him, he was sentenced to a grueling apprenticeship with Arkansas before joining the Phillies during the 1964 season. After averages of .303 and .294 in two years as a part-timer with the Phillies, Alex was the key player in a trade with the St. Louis Cardinals for established stars Bill White and Dick Groat. Under intense pressure with the Cardinals, he flopped miserably but rebounded to record .312 and .315 averages with the Cincinnati Reds in 1968 and 1969. In an era when pitching was king, these averages were good for fourth and sixth place respectively in the National League batting races. But despite great speed and a strong throwing arm, Johnson was a terrible defensive outfielder, leading National League outfielders in errors both years.

Traded again in 1970, this time to the California Angels, Johnson responded with a .329 average to edge Boston favorite Carl Yastrzemski for the American League batting title by a fraction of a point. He banged out 202 hits, stole 17 bases, drove in 86 runs, and scored 85 times as the only offensive threat in the Angels lineup besides shortstop Jim Fregosi. He also proved as adept at leading American League fly chasers in errors as he had in his former circuit.

When Johnson was originally acquired by California he complained, "I'd rather play in hell than for the Angels." In 1971 he showed how much he meant it. During the season Alex, who once admitted that he never gave 100% and didn't hustle, was benched four times and had 29 fines levied against him. In late June, he was suspended for failure to give his best efforts toward winning games. The Players Association filed a grievance on his behalf, arguing that Alex was suffering from emotional stress. Johnson and the Players Association prevailed when an arbitrator ruled in the player's favor and restored approximately $29,000 in back pay.

Although he didn't suffer from any known physical ailments, the defending batting champion played only 65 games for the Angels in 1971 and batted an unremarkable .260. Not surprisingly, he was traded after the season, beginning a journey that would find him with four different teams over the next five years. He dropped out of sight at the age of 33 after the 1976 campaign with a .288 lifetime batting average.

However, the landmark decision in his favor, one of the first major victories for the player's union, established the precedent that emotional impairment is akin to physical injury—even in the world of major league baseball.

JAMES ANTHONY PIERSALL
B. November 14, 1929

YEAR	TEAM	LEAGUE	G	AB	R	H	HR	RBI	AVE	SB	POS
1948	Scranton	Eastern	141	527	74	148	12	92	.280	14	OF
1949	Louisville	Am Ass'n	125	446	58	121	3	58	.271	6	OF

YEAR	TEAM	LEAGUE	G	AB	R	H	HR	RBI	AVE	SB	POS
1950	*Louisville*	*Am Ass'n*	*131*	*487*	*97*	*124*	*3*	*60*	*.255*	*14*	*OF*
	BOSTON	AL	6	7	4	2	0	0	.286	0	OF
1951	*Louisville*	*Am Ass'n*	*17*	*42*	*8*	*13*	*0*	*2*	*.310*	*0*	*OF*
	Birmingham	*Southern*	*121*	*437*	*100*	*151*	*15*	*83*	*.346*	*12*	*OF*
1952	BOSTON	AL	56	161	28	43	1	16	.267	3	SS-OF
	Birmingham	*Southern*	*18*	*56*	*10*	*19*	*1*	*10*	*.339*	*2*	*OF*
1953	BOSTON	AL	151	585	76	159	3	52	.272	11	OF
1954	BOSTON	AL	133	474	77	135	8	38	.285	5	OF
1955	BOSTON	AL	149	515	68	146	13	62	.283	6	OF
1956	BOSTON	AL	155	601	91	176	14	87	.293	7	OF
1957	BOSTON	AL	151	609	103	159	19	63	.261	14	OF
1958	BOSTON	AL	130	417	55	99	8	48	.237	12	OF
1959	CLEVELAND	AL	100	317	42	78	4	30	.246	6	OF
1960	CLEVELAND	AL	138	486	70	137	18	66	.282	18	OF
1961	CLEVELAND	AL	121	484	81	156	6	40	.322	8	OF
1962	WASHINGTON	AL	135	471	38	115	4	31	.244	12	OF
1963	WASH-LA	AL	29	94	9	23	1	5	.245	4	OF
	NEW YORK	NL	40	124	13	24	1	10	.194	1	OF
	LOS ANGELES	AL	20	52	4	16	0	4	.308	0	OF
1964	LOS ANGELES	AL	87	255	28	80	2	13	.314	5	OF
1965	CALIFORNIA	AL	53	112	10	30	2	12	.268	2	OF
1966	CALIFORNIA	AL	75	123	14	26	0	14	.211	1	OF
1967	CALIFORNIA	AL	5	3	0	0	0	0	.000	0	PH-OF
MAJOR LEAGUE TOTALS			1734	5890	811	1604	104	591	.272	115	

JOHN JOSEPH EVERS
B. July 21, 1881 D. March 28, 1947

YEAR	TEAM	LEAGUE	G	AB	R	H	HR	RBI	AVE	SB	POS
1902	*Troy*	*NY State*	*	*	*	*	*	*	*.285*	*	*INF*
	CHICAGO	NL	26	89	7	20	0	2	.225	1	2B-SS
1903	CHICAGO	NL	124	464	70	136	0	52	.293	25	2B-SS
1904	CHICAGO	NL	152	532	49	141	0	47	.265	26	2B
1905	CHICAGO	NL	99	340	44	94	1	37	.276	19	2B
1906	CHICAGO	NL	154	533	65	136	1	51	.255	49	2B
1907	CHICAGO	NL	151	508	66	127	2	51	.250	46	2B
1908	CHICAGO	NL	126	416	83	125	0	37	.300	36	2B
1909	CHICAGO	NL	127	463	88	122	1	24	.263	28	2B
1910	CHICAGO	NL	125	433	87	114	0	28	.263	28	2B
1911	CHICAGO	NL	46	155	29	35	0	7	.226	6	2B-3B
1912	CHICAGO	NL	143	478	73	163	1	63	.341	16	2B
1913	CHICAGO	NL	135	444	81	126	3	49	.284	11	2B
1914	BOSTON	NL	139	491	81	137	1	40	.279	12	2B
1915	BOSTON	NL	83	278	38	73	1	22	.263	7	2B
1916	BOSTON	NL	71	241	33	52	0	15	.216	5	2B
1917	BOS-PHIL	NL	80	266	25	57	1	12	.214	9	2B-3B

Chapter 5—Neurological and Psychological Disorders

YEAR	TEAM	LEAGUE	G	AB	R	H	HR	RBI	AVE	SB	POS
1922	CHICAGO	AL	1	3	0	0	0	1	.000	0	2B
1929	BOSTON	NL	1	0	0	0	0	0	.000	0	2B
MAJOR LEAGUE TOTALS			1783	6134	919	1658	12	538	.270	324	

JOHN ANTHONY MOSTIL
B. June 1, 1896 D. December 10, 1970

YEAR	TEAM	LEAGUE	G	AB	R	H	HR	RBI	AVE	SB	POS
1918	CHICAGO	AL	10	33	4	9	0	4	.273	1	2B
1919	Milwaukee	Am Ass'n	132	500	70	134	2	*	.268	12	OF
1920	Milwaukee	Am Ass'n	155	597	125	190	4	49	.318	27	OF
1921	CHICAGO	AL	100	326	43	98	3	42	.301	10	OF
1922	CHICAGO	AL	132	458	74	139	7	70	.303	14	OF
1923	CHICAGO	AL	153	546	91	159	3	64	.291	41	OF-3B
1924	CHICAGO	AL	118	385	75	125	4	49	.324	7	OF
1925	CHICAGO	AL	153	605	135	181	2	50	.299	43	OF
1926	CHICAGO	AL	148	600	120	197	4	42	.328	35	OF
1927	CHICAGO	AL	13	16	3	2	0	1	.125	1	OF
1928	CHICAGO	AL	133	503	69	136	0	51	.270	23	OF
1929	CHICAGO	AL	12	35	4	8	0	3	.229	1	OF
1930	Toledo	Am Ass'n	91	287	61	96	2	35	.334	11	OF
1931-32		(Did Not Play Organized Baseball)									
1933	Eau Claire	Northern	43	150	*	55	6	*	.367	6	OF
1934	Eau Claire	Northern	83	311	*	100	5	*	.322	3	OF
1935	Eau Claire	Northern	60	159	*	48	2	26	.302	3	OF
1936	Eau Claire	Northern	36	78	16	24	1	17	.308	1	OF
1937	Eau Claire	Northern	17	41	5	10	0	6	.244	0	OF
1938		(Did Not Play Organized Baseball)									
1939	Grand Forks	Northern	19	19	2	6	0	3	.316	0	OF
MAJOR LEAGUE TOTALS			972	3507	618	1054	23	376	.301	176	

ALEXANDER JOHNSON
B. December 7, 1942

YEAR	TEAM	LEAGUE	G	AB	R	H	HR	RBI	AVE	E	POS
1962	Miami	Fla State	113	431	60	135	5	60	.313	7	OF
1963	Magic Valley	Pioneer	120	471	108	155	35	128	.329	12	OF
1964	Arkansas	Pac Coast	90	351	64	111	21	71	.316	11	OF
	PHILADELPHIA	NL	43	109	18	33	4	18	.303	1	OF
1965	PHILADELPHIA	NL	97	262	27	77	8	28	.294	4	OF
1966	ST. LOUIS	NL	25	86	7	16	2	6	.186	1	OF

YEAR	TEAM	LEAGUE	G	AB	R	H	HR	RBI	AVE	E	POS
	Tulsa	Pac Coast	80	293	56	104	14	56	.355	10	OF
1967	ST. LOUIS	NL	81	175	20	39	1	12	.223	3	OF
1968	CINCINNATI	NL	149	603	79	188	2	58	.312	14	OF
1969	CINCINNATI	NL	139	523	86	165	17	88	.315	18	OF
1970	CALIFORNIA	AL	156	614	85	202	14	86	.329	12	OF
1971	CALIFORNIA	AL	65	242	19	63	2	21	.260	7	OF
1972	CLEVELAND	AL	108	356	31	85	8	37	.239	7	OF
1973	TEXAS	AL	158	624	62	179	8	68	.287	1	DH-OF
1974	TEX-NY	AL	124	481	60	138	5	43	.287	8	OF-DH
1975	NEW YORK	AL	52	119	15	31	1	15	.261	0	DH-OF
1976	DETROIT	AL	125	429	41	115	6	45	.268	8	OF-DH
MAJOR LEAGUE TOTALS			1322	4623	550	1331	78	525	.288	84	

JIM EISENREICH

In 1982, 23-year-old rookie outfielder Jim Eisenreich made the big jump from Class A ball to the Minnesota Twins opening day lineup. The youngster was fast and possessed a strong accurate arm, a good batting eye, and a smooth compact swing. In short, he seemed too good to be true.

Unfortunately a serious problem soon popped up. Eisenreich began suffering from what appeared to be a severe nervous disorder that made it impossible for him to take the field. His promising rookie season ended after 34 games and he was able to make only 14 appearances over the next two years because of the condition, before finally being forced to retire from baseball at 25 years of age.

Eisenreich's problems were often compared to those of Jimmy Piersall, another high-strung, young outfielder, whose freshman season ended when he was institutionalized by a nervous breakdown 30 years earlier. Piersall fought back against his disorder to become a first rate major leaguer. Jim Eisenreich, however, seemed to have lost his battle.

But eventually Eisenreich did come back. After sitting out the entire 1985 and 1986 seasons, he resumed his professional baseball career in the Kansas City Royals farm system at the age of 27 and eventually became established as a solid major league outfielder. He played another dozen years in the big leagues, until he was almost 40 years old, before retiring with an excellent .290 lifetime batting average and a World Championship ring.

For Jim Eisenreich, the key to successfully overcoming his disability after years of frustration was correctly identifying his condition. Unlike

Piersall, Jim was suffering from a physiological problem rather than a psychological disorder. Eisenreich is afflicted with Tourette's syndrome, a neurochemical imbalance. Somewhere in his brain an abnormal release of chemicals occurs which triggers unusual behavioral symptoms if not properly treated. It took Jim years to just get his condition correctly diagnosed and have an effective medication program developed.

Tourette's, named for Gilles de la Tourette who first identified the ailment in 1885, is difficult to diagnose and still isn't completely understood more than a century after its discovery. The condition appears to be genetic and the symptoms can be violent and include tics, muscle contractions, shortness of breath, and involuntary guttural sounds like grunting, snorting, or barking. In extreme case victims sometimes uncontrollably shout obscenities.

Jim Eisenreich — overcame Tourette Syndrome to resume his career

James Michael Eisenreich was born on April 18, 1959, in St. Cloud, Minnesota, the third of five children. His father was a schoolteacher and his mother took care of the home front. Jim began showing the first signs of the disorder at the age of six when he developed tics or spasmatic muscle movements where he would wave his arms, jerk his neck, and contort his face. He was psychiatrically evaluated but never diagnosed with a psychological problem. His physicians thought it was just a nervous condition that would eventually disappear, and since it didn't seem to affect his speech, schoolwork, or athletics, there didn't appear to be a compelling need to address it further.

According to Jim, he endured "torture" in grade school, although people eventually seemed to accept his tics and attribute his actions to hyperactivity. Of course, the fact that he was an outstanding athlete in both baseball and hockey made it much easier for him to gain acceptance, and the condition never caused him to leave a game or interfered with his performance. From little league through college, Jim would hum in the dugout to try to suppress the twitching. When he heard taunts from opposing players or fans, he answered with his bat and glove.

Eisenreich attended St. Cloud State College and played baseball there for three years. His coach, Dennis Lorsung, later commented, "Jim was always making some sort of weird noise or movement out there in the field. At first, the other outfielders noticed, but after awhile they realized it was just Jim."

In the 16th round of the 1980 amateur draft, Jim was drafted by the Twins and left college to pursue a career in professional baseball. He rose quickly through the Minnesota farm system. In his first season with Elizabethon in the Appalachian League he was named the circuit's Co-Player of the Year. He followed that with a superb 1981 campaign for Wisconsin Rapids in the Class A Midwestern League, leading the circuit in hits and slamming 23 homers.

Eisenreich was invited to the Twins 1982 training camp and made the team with a spectacular spring performance. Batting leadoff and playing center field, he continued his outstanding play when the regular season opened. The tics and jerks were still there, but it was assumed to merely be a nervous condition. Jim was still playing well in the field and hitting a sensational .344 in mid April when the Twins left Minneapolis for a ten game road trip, but teammates noticed that the tics and involuntary movements were growing worse. During the trip his batting average began to drop and his problems seemed to be reaching a crisis point.

After the Twins returned home, Eisenreich began to behave strangely in center field during the sixth inning of a routine game against the Milwaukee Brewers on April 30. Twins manager Billy Gardner noticed that "Jim seemed to be taking quick, short, stiff-legged steps between each pitch. He would step first to his left and then to his right. Also, between pitches Jim was turning his back to the infield. His movements seemed machine-like. When he bent to anticipate the pitch, his body was rigid. It seemed to hinge 90 degrees from the waist."

Within a few minutes, Eisenreich began to twitch and shake almost convulsively. His breathing became shallower and faster and he began gasping for air. Suddenly he called time and rushed into the dugout tearing at his jersey. The Minnesota trainer told him to take a drink of water and return to field, but Jim couldn't do it. From that point on his problems became worse. When the same symptoms appeared in the Twins' next two games in Boston, he was jeered unmercifully by the Red Sox fans and had to leave both games before the fifth inning.

The Twins traveled to Milwaukee next, where Eisenreich didn't even make it out of the locker room. He scratched himself from the starting lineup shortly before the first game, and the trainer subsequently found him nervously pacing around the clubhouse frantically gulping air. He was rushed to the Mount Sinai Medical Center, where an injection of sedatives finally calmed him down. He spent the next two days huddled in his hotel room while the Twins finished the Milwaukee series.

Eisenreich was placed on the disabled list and admitted to St. Mary's Hospital for psychiatric evaluation when the Twins returned to Minneapolis. After a battery of psychological and mental competency tests, doctors still couldn't agree on a diagnosis, although they'd narrowed it down to three possible conditions. The first was a form of performance anxiety or stage fright caused by fear of failure. The second was "agoraphobia"—the fear of being in open public places. The third condition was Tourette's syndrome, which was espoused by Dr. Frank Abuzzahab, the Tourette's expert at St. Mary's.

Although other medical experts agreed with the Tourette's diagnosis, the Twins team physicians totally disregarded the idea. They preferred either the performance anxiety or agoraphobia findings and decided Eisenreich should be treated for a psychological disorder. He was put on medication and returned to the lineup, but the medicine had a tranquilizing effect and made him groggy. The Twins were worried about his safety and in mid-June they placed him back on the disabled list for the rest of the season. His abbreviated rookie season ended with a fine .303 batting average in the record books.

From the beginning, Jim was convinced that his condition was organic or physical, rather than mental. The differences in opinion between Eisenreich and the Twins management and medical staff soon coalesced into a full-fledged adversarial relationship. Jim refused to follow the medication prescribed by the team's medical experts and sought treatment for Tourette's on his own. The Twins eventually made Eisenreich a virtual outcast, accusing him of hypochondria, sleeping through team meetings, and even stealing baseball bats from other players.

The problems that ruined Eisenreich's 1982 season returned the next two years. He enjoyed impressive spring performances both years, but washed out after only two regular season games in 1983 and twelve in 1984. The situation came to a head during his 1984 troubles when the Twins found that Eisenreich had been taking a combination of drugs for Tourette's syndrome prescribed by his family physician. They demanded that he accept their course of treatment or return to the minor leagues. When Jim found neither option acceptable, the Twins bribed him to quietly retire in exchange for a year's salary.

In "retirement," Jim began playing for the St. Cloud Saints, a local semipro team. He continued taking the medication for Tourette's and working with his own doctors to find the proper combination that would take care of his symptoms without slowing his reflexes. With the help of the medication, he gradually learned how to live with the disorder and control the tics and breathing problems. When he asked the Twins about trying to come back in 1986, they refused to consider it.

After the 1986 season, Jim contacted Bob Hegman, a former St. Cloud State teammate who worked in player development for the Kansas City Royals. The Royals risked the grand sum of $1.00 to acquire the rights to the 27-year-old Eisenreich from the Twins and assigned him to their Southern League Memphis farm team for the 1987 season. Playing strictly as a designated hitter, Eisenreich hit a hefty .382 in 70 games for Memphis and graduated to the Royals later in the year for 44 games. He began the next season with the Royals and on April 6, 1988, he played his first professional game in the field since 1984. A slow start with the bat resulted in a demotion to Omaha in the American Association, but he was recalled later in the year and ended up playing 82 games for the Royals—64 of them in the outfield.

In his first two years with Kansas City, Jim batted only .238 and .218, but in 1989 he finally shook off the rust and began to hit like the Jim Eisenreich of old. For the season he batted a team-high .293 and stole a team-leading 27 bases in 134 games for the second-place Royals. At year end he was named the Royals' Player of the Year over established stars such as George Brett, Bo Jackson, Danny Tartabull, Frank White and Brett Saberhagen.

Eisenreich spent another three years as a valuable member of the Royals' outfield corps. He became so comfortable in the outfield that he led the league with a .996 fielding average in 1990 while hitting .280. In addition, he got married that year, which undoubtedly contributed to his peace of mind. In 1991 he reached the .300 plateau, finishing at .301 for the season. His average dropped to .269 in 1992, but he was the top pinch hitter in the American League. After the season, he filed for free agency and signed a multi-year contract with the National League Philadelphia Phillies.

In Philadelphia, Eisenreich would be playing in a new league in a new city in front of fans who were renown for their harsh treatment of their own players. The fact that he was willing to make the move was a sign of Jim's confidence that he had his affliction fully under control. In his first year with the Phillies, they captured the National League pennant. In the World Series, performing under the glare of the brightest spotlight in sports, Jim started all six games and drove in seven runs. The Phillies, however, lost to the American League's Toronto Blue Jays.

Jim really hit his stride in Philadelphia. The dark-haired, 5'10", 175-pound veteran fit in well with a rowdy, colorful group of characters known as the "Wild Bunch" who affectionately called him "Jeffery Dahmer." He batted over .300 for four straight years as a lefty hitting platoon outfielder, culminating with a lofty .361 average in 1996. He actually topped Tony Gwynn's National League leading .353 mark for San Diego, as well as Alex Rodriguez's Major League high of .358 that year but didn't have enough plate appearances to qualify for the batting title.

The Florida Marlins signed Jim as a free agent before the 1997 season, and he contributed a solid .280 batting average as a part-time outfielder and first baseman. From a wildcard berth in the National League Championship Series the Cinderella squad from Miami fought their way past the heavily favored Atlanta Braves to get to the World Series and then beat the powerful Cleveland Indians in seven games to capture an improbable World Championship. Once again Eisenreich stepped up under the intense pressure of the World Series. He batted .500 and reached base five straight times at one point. In the pivotal third game, he blasted a two run homer to key the Marlins' comeback victory.

The 1998 campaign was Jim's last as an active player. After the World Series, the Marlins set about dismantling their championship squad and Eisenreich was included in the memorable trade that sent stars Gary Sheffield and Bobby Bonilla to the Los Angeles Dodgers in exchange for slugging catcher Mike Piazza. A career-low .215 average for the season convinced the 39-year-old veteran that it was time to hang up his spikes.

In a career that included 10 full seasons and parts of 5 others in the major leagues, Jim appeared in 1,422 games. Other than an excellent .290 lifetime batting mark, his career numbers are relatively modest. Playing mostly right field, he led the league's outfielders in fielding percentage twice and appeared in the American League's top 10 in stolen bases and triples in 1989 and in triples again in 1990. Although he totaled only 52 homers during the regular season play, he blasted two critical shots in the postseason. He was considered a fine pinch hitter throughout his career and gained a reputation as a dependable clutch performer. Quite an accomplishment for a man who was almost abandoned by organized baseball because it was felt that he couldn't handle stress.

Eisenreich parlayed the attention he gained from his accomplishments on the baseball field into a national forum for Tourette's Syndrome. He became a spokesman, as well as an inspiration, for Tourette's sufferers all over the world. In 1995 *USA Today* identified him as baseball's most caring athlete, and in 1996 he was honored with the Tony Conigliaro Award, which is presented annually to the player who best overcomes obstacles and continues to thrive through adversity. In January 1997 he was selected for the Bart Giamatti Award for his efforts in helping others. Today he continues to contribute his time to helping Tourette's victims through the Jim Eisenreich Foundation for Children with Tourette's Syndrome, which he established in 1996 with his wife Leann.

It was truly unfortunate for both Eisenreich and the Minnesota Twins franchise that the two parties weren't able to combine forces to overcome his affliction. In 1982 Eisenreich was part of the first wave of young prospects that would take the Twins from the doldrums of the American League Western Division to a World Championship in five years. Owner Calvin Griffith called him the best young player to ever come up through the team's farm system. First baseman Kent Hrbek, third sacker Gary Gaetti, lefty hurler Frank Viola, catcher Tim Laudner, and outfielders Tom Brunansky and Randy Bush were Minnesota rookies along with Eisenreich in 1982. Second baseman Tim Teufel came up the next year, future Hall of Fame outfielder Kirby Puckett joined the club in 1984, and slick-fielding Greg Gagne took over the shortstop job in 1985. With the exception of Eisenreich, all of these young stars played key roles in the Twins stunning 1987 World Series victory over the St. Louis Cardinals. The weakest link in the lineup was Dan Gladden, who batted a mere .249 as the left fielder and leadoff man, two jobs for which Eisenreich was eminently qualified.

But instead of becoming an ally, the Twins became a major obstacle in Eisenreich's battle against his disability. He not only had to fight to control Tourette's syndrome, but he had to combat the damaging effects of his own team's stubborn misdiagnosis. It cost him at least five prime seasons from his career.

Columnist Jim Murray elegantly summed up Jim's career when he wrote, "Jim Eisenreich joins the hearty company of big leaguers who make playing merely 'hurt' seem sissy. These are men who defy impairments that would institutionalize less doughty mortals." One of his coaches, Jay Johnstone, put it a little more succinctly when he said, "He went through more hell in a couple of years than anyone should have to go through in a lifetime."

JAMES MICHAEL EISENREICH
B. April 18, 1959

YEAR	TEAM	LEAGUE	G	AB	R	H	HR	RBI	AVE	SB	POS
1980	Elizabethon	Appalach	67	258	47	77	3	41	.298	12	OF
	Wisc. Rapids	Midwest	5	16	4	7	0	5	.438	1	OF

Chapter 5—Neurological and Psychological Disorders

YEAR	TEAM	LEAGUE	G	AB	R	H	HR	RBI	AVE	SB	POS
1981	Wisc. Rapids	Midwest	134	489	101	152	23	99	.311	9	OF
1982	MINNESOTA	AL	34	99	10	30	2	9	.303	0	OF
1983	MINNESOTA	AL	2	7	1	2	0	0	.286	0	OF
1984	MINNESOTA	AL	12	32	1	7	0	3	.219	2	DH-OF
1985-86	MINNESOTA	AL	(Did Not Play — On Voluntarily Retired List)								
1987	Memphis	Southern	70	275	60	105	11	57	.382	13	DH
	KANSAS CITY	AL	44	105	10	25	4	21	.238	1	DH
1988	Omaha	Am Ass'n	36	142	28	41	4	14	.289	9	OF
	KANSAS CITY	AL	82	202	26	44	1	19	.218	9	OF-DH
1989	KANSAS CITY	AL	134	475	64	139	9	59	.293	27	OF
1990	KANSAS CITY	AL	142	496	61	139	5	51	.280	12	OF
1991	KANSAS CITY	AL	135	375	47	113	2	47	.301	5	OF
1992	KANSAS CITY	AL	113	353	31	95	2	28	.269	11	OF
1993	PHILADELPHIA	NL	153	362	51	115	7	54	.318	5	OF
1994	PHILADELPHIA	NL	104	290	42	87	4	43	.300	6	OF
1995	PHILADELPHIA	NL	129	377	46	119	10	55	.316	10	OF
1996	PHILADELPHIA	NL	113	338	45	122	3	41	.361	11	OF
1997	FLORIDA	NL	120	293	36	82	2	34	.280	0	OF-1B
1998	FLA-LA	NL	105	191	21	41	1	13	.215	6	OF-1B
MAJOR LEAGUE TOTALS			1422	3995	492	1160	52	477	.290	105	

Six

Other Disabilities

Many other players, besides those featured in the preceding chapters, fought to overcome disabilities. Several are mentioned in this chapter, but there are probably just as many who struggled with afflictions in secret or else never acknowledged that their conditions were disabling. Generally, the following players suffered from disabilities that were either not permanent or not considered as limiting or unusual as the conditions of the featured performers. In addition, a few players are mentioned who made valiant efforts, but weren't quite able to overcome their afflictions.

CONVERTED SOUTHPAWS

Former left-handed pitcher Bud Daley is often remembered as a player who overcame a severe disability to become a major leaguer. Supposedly, Daley suffered from a withered or deformed right arm — a condition that has been compared to that of Jim Abbott in some publications. The popular story is that Daley was a natural righthander who learned to throw from the left side after suffering either a childhood injury or bout with polio that stunted the growth of his right arm — leaving it permanently weakened and significantly shorter than his left one.

The truth, according to Bud Daley himself, is that his right shoulder and arm were damaged by the doctor's forceps during childbirth. The instrument pinched a nerve in his shoulder and his right arm was paralyzed at first. But his mother massaged the injured arm and shoulder, and forced him to use it until it developed into a healthy limb. Bud doesn't know how the severity of his condition became exaggerated.

So much for the legend that he was a converted lefty, unless Bud was throwing from the right side while still in the womb! In fact, the former knuckleballer never considered himself disadvantaged because he could do everything other pitchers could do—and he considered himself a dangerous hitter to boot.

After some prompting, however, Bud finally admitted that his right arm was "a little" shorter and didn't bend quite the way it should, so he usually had to catch the ball kind of backhanded. And at bat, he couldn't twist his arm enough to pull the ball well. But it was no big deal.

Despite those "minor inconveniences," Bud Daley won 16 games in both 1959 and 1960 for the Kansas City Athletics, one of the worst teams in baseball at the time. He was a two-time All-Star for the Athletics and later pitched eight innings in two World Series classics for the New York Yankees without giving up a run. When Bud retired after the 1964 season it was because his left arm gave out, not the right one.

Incidentally, subsequent research uncovered a 1960 *Sports Illustrated* article in which Daley gave exactly the same account of his arm condition. The author, Roy Terrell, described the appearance of Bud's arm as follows: "Although, the right shoulder is carried forward slightly and the elbow is twisted so that it points awkwardly out, the arm itself is a perfectly good-looking one, well developed and strong." Furthermore, the article indicates that Bud won at least five games with his bat the previous year, so he wasn't exaggerating about his hitting ability—as pitchers have long been suspected of doing. According to the record books, Daley hit a solid .295 in 1959 and drove in 13 runs in 78 at-bats.

A natural righthander who really did have to learn to throw lefthanded was Ray "Pop" Prim, whose right arm was badly burned as a child. Prim, who at the age of 38 won 13 games for the pennant-winning 1945 Chicago Cubs, failed several major league trials in the mid-1930s before finally getting the hang of the lefty business and becoming one of the top pitchers in Pacific Coast League history. From 1936 through 1942 he won 126 games for the Los Angeles Angels. Prim pitched out of the Cubs bullpen in 1943 and posted an excellent 2.55 earned run average but returned to Los Angeles for the 1944 season and won 22 games. Recalled to Chicago for the 1945 campaign, Ray started 19 games and relieved in 15 others. The converted southpaw's 2.40 earned run average in 165 innings was the second lowest in the National League, and he gave up the fewest hits and fewest walks per game in the circuit while finishing among the leaders in strikeouts per inning. In the 1945 World Series, Prim started and lost the fourth game and relieved in the sixth contest. Ray didn't see much action with the Cubs in the postwar 1946 season and returned to Los Angeles the next year to finish out his career.

WAR INJURIES

Several professional ballplayers besides Bert Shepard, Lou Brissie, and Eddie Kazak overcame war injuries to resume their careers after World War II. Gene Bearden, a minor league hurler in the New York Yankees organization before the war, survived the July 1943 sinking of the U.S.S. Helena in the South Pacific. Bearden, a machinists mate, was injured by the impact of a Japanese torpedo. Although two thirds of the ship's 600-man crew were lost, Gene was miraculously saved when his unconscious body was loaded onto a life raft and he was rescued after drifting for 48 hours. Bearden suffered a deep gouge to his skull and a crushed kneecap. An aluminum cap was screwed into his knee and a metal plate was implanted in his skull.

The doctors gave Bearden no hope of playing baseball again, but after his discharge he proved them wrong by winning 15 games for the Eastern League Binghamton club in 1945. He posted a fine 15–4 won-lost mark for the minor league Oakland Oaks in 1946 and followed up with a 16–7 record for them in 1947. In the meantime he'd become the property of Bill Veeck's Cleveland Indians.

The Indians won the American League pennant and the World Championship in 1948 thanks to the contributions of 28-year-old rookie southpaw Gene Bearden. Bearden won 20 games while losing only 7 and led the league with a 2.43 earned run average. His 20th victory was a complete game effort after only one day of rest, coming over the Boston Red Sox in a sudden death playoff game for the pennant. In the World Series, Bearden shut out the Boston Braves in game three and saved the sixth contest with scoreless relief work. Unfortunately, Bearden's success was fleeting. He was bothered by persistent leg problems and won only 25 games while losing 31 for 5 teams over the next 5 years. Afterward he drifted back to the minor leagues where he pitched with some success until 1957.

Washington Senators infielder Cecil Travis suffered frost bitten feet in the Battle of the Bulge but returned to play two more seasons after the war. In 1941, his last year before going into the service, Travis' .359 batting average was better than Joe DiMaggio's .357 even though Joe hit in 56 straight games that year. In addition, Cecil's 218 hits that season were more than Ted Williams amassed with his .406 batting mark. Travis was only 32 years old when he was discharged late in the 1945 season, but he couldn't regain his batting eye. He batted .241 in 15 late season games in 1945, hit only .252 in 1946 and retired after hitting .216 for the 1947 season, 98 points below his final career mark of .314. Cecil, however, refused to blame the premature disintegration of his career on his war injuries. "I just didn't have it anymore," he insisted.

Travis wasn't the only soldier-ballplayer to suffer at the Battle of the Bulge. Future Hall-of-Famer Hoyt Wilhelm, a minor league hurler before the war, was wounded in the fighting and received the Purple Heart. Eventually Hoyt recovered to throw his knuckleball for 21 seasons in the major leagues before turning in his toe plate at the age of 49.

Bob Savage and Johnny Grodzicki, a couple of other young hurlers were also shot during the war but returned to pitch in the major leagues. Savage pitched for the Philadelphia Athletics from 1946 through 1948 and spent four more seasons in the minor leagues. Before the war, Grodzicki was one of the brightest young prospects in the vast St. Louis Cardinals' farm system. After winning 19 games for Columbus in 1941, the 24-year-old fireballer advanced to St. Louis, where he posted a glittering 1.35 earned run average in five games down the stretch. But in 1945 he was wounded in the right buttock during the Allied drive on Berlin and suffered extensive muscle and nerve damage. In fact, the sciatic nerve was cut in two and amputation was even considered. The leg was saved, but Grodzicki was only able to regain limited use of his foot. He was fitted for a brace and fought to resume his career but was never able to regain his effectiveness. He did appear in a few games for the Cardinals in 1946 and 1947 and pitched in the minor leagues through 1952.

Phil Marchildon, the Philadelphia Athletics' ace hurler in 1942, suffered from a different kind of wartime affliction. A tailgunner in the Royal Canadian Air Force, Phil's plane was shot down in the summer of 1944 and he was sent to a prisoner of war camp in Poland. After enduring squalid living conditions and forced marches, the emaciated Marchildon was evacuated to an English hospital when the camp was liberated by the British in May 1945. When he got back to the States a few months later, Athletics owner-manager Connie Mack implored him to return to the mound immediately despite his fragile physical condition. Phil reluctantly consented and promptly tore a muscle in his groin. In addition to his physical weakness, Phil suffered from a severe case of nerves and found it difficult to focus on baseball. He couldn't help thinking about his five mates who'd perished when their plane crashed. The 33-year-old righthander managed to get his nerves under control enough to win 13 games in 1946, but not before acquiring the nickname "Fidgety Phil." He posted a 19–9 won-lost mark in 1947 but ran into arm trouble the next year and retired in 1950. In 1983 he was one of the first five inductees into the new Canadian Baseball Hall of Fame.

Another near casualty due to nerves was Washington Senators pitcher

Walter Masterson who took more than a year to regain his form after seeing heavy action at Guam and Midway during World War II. He recovered to finish a solid 14-year career in 1956, winning 78 games and losing 100 decisions pitching for losing teams.

A few major leaguers also suffered disabling injuries from World War I combat. Grover Cleveland Alexander, of course, suffered for the rest of his life from headaches and loss of hearing due to his service in an artillery unit during World War I, and his epileptic condition was probably worsened considerably by combat duty. Another young pitcher, Hal Carlson, was gassed in combat during the first world war and never completely recovered, although he resumed his big league career. Carlson, who had completed a mediocre 1917 rookie season with the Pittsburgh Pirates before the war, returned to the Pirates in 1919 and posted a 2.23 earned run average. He went on to win more than 100 games over the next dozen years, despite lingering abdominal problems. At the age of 37 in 1929 Carlson posted the best winning percentage of his career, with 11 wins against 5 losses for the pennant-winning Chicago Cubs, and appeared in his first World Series. He began the 1930 season in the Cubs rotation but became ill and died two months into the campaign from stomach ailments caused by the poisonous gas.

OSTEOMYELITIS

One of the greatest and most popular players of all time, Mickey Mantle, suffered from osteomyelitis, the same bone disease that infected Lou Brissie and Whitey Kurowski. The condition was discovered after a high school football injury and for a time amputation was a possibility. The incurable condition was brought under control, but it no doubt contributed greatly to an assortment of injuries and ailments that hampered the slugging outfielder throughout his magnificent career with the New York Yankees. Nevertheless, Mickey won the triple-crown in 1956, leading the American League in batting average (.353), homers (52), and runs batted in (130). He blasted 54 homers in 1961 and won the American League Most Valuable Player Award in 1956, 1957, and 1962. Despite his ailments, Mantle played in the big leagues for 18 years, finishing with 536 career home runs and a .298 lifetime batting average. He also established numerous World Series records and was elected to the Hall of Fame in his first year of eligibility.

Maimed or Disfigured Extremities

Although he was no "Three Finger Brown," Dave Keefe pitched in the major leagues despite the absence of the middle finger on his pitching hand as the result of a childhood accident. His best of five big league seasons resulted in a fine 2.97 earned run average and a 6–7 won-lost mark for the Philadelphia Athletics in 1920. He's credited with inventing the forkball, which was a natural given his disfigurement. Keefe stayed in baseball as a coach and batting practice pitcher after his playing days and eventually became the Athletics' traveling secretary.

Near the end of the 1988 season, 31-year-old lefty Bobby Ojeda of the New York Mets severed the middle finger of his pitching hand with a hedge trimmer. The finger was sewn back on, but knowing that it would never be fully functional, the surgeons deliberately reattached it at a crooked angle designed to help him grip his curveball. Ojeda's 18–5 won-lost record in 1986 had been the best in the National League, but a complicated elbow operation ruined his 1987 season. When the injury to his hand occurred, he was finishing up an excellent comeback campaign, with 10 victories and a 2.88 earned run average. After the finger mishap, Bobby bounced back again in 1989 to win 13 games for the Mets, but additional misfortune still lay in store for him. He suffered recurring arm problems and during spring training with the Cleveland Indians before the 1993 season, he was injured in a boating accident that claimed the lives of teammates Steve Olin and Tim Crews. Ojeda survived with a deep scalp laceration and other traumatic injuries and returned to the mound later that year after orthoscopic surgery to repair damage to his left shoulder, but his career lasted only 11 more games.

Roger Metzger, a slick fielding National League shortstop for 10 years, wasn't able to successfully continue his career after losing parts of four fingers on his glove hand in a power saw accident after the 1979 season. He returned to play 28 games in 1980, but he couldn't grip the bat well and was released with a woeful .074 batting mark.

Curt Simmons and Pat Zachary are a couple of pitchers who severed toes with lawn mowers but returned with minimal disruption to their careers. Hall of Famer Jim "Catfish" Hunter also lost part of a foot in a hunting accident before beginning his career but managed to win 224 major league games.

Right-handed pitchers Claude Passeau and Joe Black enjoyed major league careers despite defective fingers. Passeau had to use the tiniest glove in the league because the third and little finger of his glove hand were bent and useless, but it didn't keep him from winning 162 games in 12 seasons and going three straight years without an error from 1943 through 1945 with the Chicago Cubs. Black was unable to lift the middle and index fingers on his pitching hand, a condition he'd been born with. But it didn't stop him from winning the National League Rookie of the Year Award in 1952 as a 28-year-old freshman with the Brooklyn Dodgers or becoming the first black pitcher to win a World Series game that fall. The next year he experimented with his grip in an attempt to add another pitch and lost his touch. His spectacular 15–4 rookie year won-lost mark dropped to 6 and 3 in 1953 and his earned run average more than doubled. Joe never regained his first-year effectiveness. He spent most of the 1954 season in the minors and was out of baseball in 1957 after a few mediocre campaigns with the Cincinnati Reds and Washington Senators.

Impaired Vision

There have been several major leaguers who were blind in one eye and, of course, most of them were pitchers. Bill Irwin, who pitched a few games for Cincinnati in 1886 was probably the first. Then there was Hi Jasper, who didn't get his first shot at the big time until he was 34 years old and won a grand total of 10 games in parts of four seasons. Another one-eyed hurler was Charles "Whammy" Douglas, who won 27 games in the minor leagues in 1954 and 3 in the majors in 1957. Crusty veteran reliever Art Fowler continued pitching for another two years in the major leagues after losing the sight in his left eye when hit by a batting practice line drive in 1962. Fowler, who was 40 years old at the time of the injury, was still pitching in the minors eight years later, posting a 9–5 won-lost record and a 1.59 earned run average for Denver in the American Association. Left-hander Tom Sunkel lost his sight in one eye to a cataract, but won 9 games and lost 15 in a big league career that spanned 8 years. In 1944 he began his final major league campaign with the Brooklyn Dodgers but was sent down early in the year to make room for "One Eyed Jack" Franklin, who lasted only one game. Ironically, both of these one-eyed hurlers hailed from Paris, Illinois.

The only non-pitcher who was thought to be blind in one eye was Paul O'Dea, a wartime outfielder with the Cleveland Indians. O'Dea batted an excellent .318 in 76 games for the Indians in 1944 but slumped to .235 the next season. He returned to the minors after the war, where he batted well over .300 for the next five years before leaving the game. Veteran Chicago White Sox second baseman Jackie Hayes attempted to continue playing after losing the sight in his right eye in 1939 but had to quit after playing 18 games and hitting .195 in 1940. Three years later he was totally blind.

Some hitters managed to get by fairly well with poor, uncorrected vision. Hall of Fame first baseman George Sisler's eyesight was ruined by a sinus condition that forced him to sit out the entire 1923 season after he'd batted an incredible .420 with 246 hits the previous year for the St. Louis Browns. Although his vision remained blurry, the 31-year-old star returned in 1924 and played in the majors until 1930. He had some good seasons despite his impaired eyesight, batting .345 with 224 hits in 1925, .327 with 201 hits in 1927, and .326 with 205 hits in 1929 after moving to the Boston Braves. In fact, he always kept his average above .290 for the rest of his career, although he was never the hitter he'd been before encountering sinus problems.

Boston Red Sox outfielder Tony Conigliaro was only 22 years old when he was hit in the eye by a wild pitch during the 1967 season. Conigliaro, who'd become the youngest player to reach 100 career homers a few days earlier, missed the rest of the year and all of the next season. His vision never fully recovered, although he returned to slam 20 homers in 1969. In 1970 he improved to 36 home runs while batting in 116 runs, but he had become virtually a one-eyed hitter. He retired at the age of 26 in the middle of the 1971 season when his eyesight and batting average continued to deteriorate.

Years later, Houston Astros shortstop Dickie Thon suffered a similar fate. The 25-year-old All-Star, who'd batted .286 with 20 homers and 34 stolen bases in 1983, was beaned in the first week of the 1984 season and missed the rest of the year. Although he returned to play in the big leagues through 1993, he battled vision problems for the rest of his career and never attained the heights of stardom originally projected for him.

Heart Problems

Hal Newhouser, who won consecutive Most Valuable Player Awards in 1944 and 1945, tried to enlist in the service several times during the war but was rejected because of a bad heart. In fact, Newhouser's own physician advised him that pitching might be too much of a strain on his heart, but Hal was determined to keep going. He developed a regimen where he ate six or seven small meals every day, averaged about eleven hours of sleep each night, and took iron pills six times a day. Apparently it worked. From 1944 through 1950 Hal averaged more than 21 victories a season. He lived to be 77 years of age, long enough to enjoy a belated induction into the Hall of Fame in 1992.

St. Louis Cardinals regular catcher Hal Smith was forced to retire at the age of 30 during the 1961 season because of a heart condition. Four years later, his health had improved enough for him to move from the coach's box to fill in behind the plate for the Pittsburgh Pirates.

Cancer

In June 1997, 35-year-old Baltimore Orioles outfielder Eric Davis underwent surgery for the removal of a malignant tumor the size of a baseball in his abdomen. Since his arrival in the major leagues with the Cincinnati Reds in 1984, Davis' blend of speed and power had made him the heir apparent to Willie Mays. In 1986 he stole 80 bases and slammed 27 homers and in 1987 he narrowly missed becoming the first player with 40 homers and 40 steals in the same season. But injuries, caused by his aggressive style of play, dogged his career, and by 1995 his battered body had forced him into retirement. The layoff helped and Davis returned to action for the Reds in 1996 to win the Comeback Player of the Year Award with 26 homers, 23 stolen bases, and a .287 batting average. He signed with the Baltimore Orioles as a free agent for the 1997 season and was off to a sensational start when the tumor was discovered.

The determined outfielder defied all odds and managed to return to the Orioles lineup in the latter stages of the 1997 campaign while still undergoing chemotherapy treatment. Eric made the postseason roster by going 4 for 4 in the season finale and then blasted a key homer in the League Championship Series. For the 1997 season, he hit .304 in 42 games. Davis finished up his chemotherapy treatments in the spring of 1998 and went on to enjoy one of the best seasons of his career, hitting a career high .327, slamming 28 homers in 131 games, and once again capturing the Comeback Player of the Year Award.

While Davis was putting together his spectacular 1998 campaign, his childhood buddy from the Los Angeles ghetto area, Darryl Strawberry was in the midst of a stirring comeback of his own. Strawberry, a superstar with the New York Mets in the late 1980s, had been kicked out of organized baseball for drug use in the mid-1990s. He was eventually reinstated and signed by the New York Yankees but missed most of the 1997 season with a knee injury. Darryl came back in 1998 to blast 24 homers in only 295 at-bats, but just before the beginning of postseason play he was felled by colon cancer. A 16-inch portion of his large intestine was removed in October 1998. Darryl hoped to return as the Yankees designated hitter in 1999, but those plans were delayed due to another drug relapse and he didn't return to duty until late in the season. Strawberry batted .327 in 24 games down the stretch and helped the Yankees to the World Championship with a .333 average and a pair of homers in the postseason. Unfortunately, more drug problems ended his career before the 2000 campaign got under way.

In May 1996 Los Angeles Dodgers center fielder and leadoff man Brett Butler had a malignant tumor the size of a plum removed from his throat. Over the next two months he underwent radiation treatments and was placed on a liquid diet. Despite the fact that he could barely walk, he was determined to play again that year. Sure enough, he took the field again on September 6 and scored the winning run in the game. Four days later, however, he broke his hand attempting to lay down a bunt and was through for the year. He returned the next season for one last productive year at the age of 40 before retiring with a .290 lifetime batting average.

Ironically, Eric Davis, Darryl Strawberry, and Brett Butler comprised the regular outfield for the Los Angeles Dodgers in 1992. Butler, however, was the only one of the trio to finish out the year in the lineup as the others succumbed to injury.

Thanks to modern medicine it's not unusual for cancer victims to resume productive baseball careers after treatment, although Eric Davis is the only player known to keep playing while undergoing treatment.

At the beginning of the 1994 season, 26-year-old Chicago White Sox reliever Scott Radinsky was diagnosed with Hodgkin's disease, a serious type of lymphoma or cancer of the lymphatic system. Radinsky, who'd led the American League with eight relief wins in 1993, missed the entire 1994 season while undergoing radiation and chemotherapy treatment. He returned to the mound in 1995 but didn't regain his effectiveness until he signed with the Los Angeles Dodgers as a free agent a year later. From 1996 through 1998 with the Dodgers he averaged 65 appearances and kept his earned run average under 3.00 each year. His performance deteriorated after that and he drifted to the minor leagues. Radinsky, undoubtedly the only Jewish, punk rocker, left-handed relief specialist to ever play in the majors, was released by the Florida Marlins organization early in the 2002 season and resumed his successful musical career with Pulley, a well-known punk rock band.

Cleveland Indians reliever Jerry DiPoto was diagnosed with thyroid cancer at the age of 26 after a fine 1993 rookie season. After missing most of the 1994 campaign, he returned to pitch in 58 games for the New York Mets in 1995. DiPoto posted a 7–2 won-lost record the next year with the Mets and saved 19 games in 1998 for the Colorado Rockies.

Lefty Danny Jackson, a 23-game winner in 1988, had his thyroid removed after a successful 1994 season when he won 14 games for the

Philadelphia Phillies. The 31-year-old veteran received a big free agent contract from the St. Louis Cardinals for the 1995 season and may have rushed his return from surgery. He pitched three more years in the big leagues but never regained his effectiveness.

Veteran first baseman Andres Galarraga began experiencing back problems during a sensational 1998 season in which he blasted 44 homers and drove in 121 runs for the Atlanta Braves. Examinations revealed a tumor in his back and he sat out the entire 1999 season undergoing treatment. While with the Colorado Rockies, Galarraga had led the National League in batting with a .370 mark in 1993, in homers with 47 in 1996, and in runs batted in with 150 in 1996 and 140 in 1997. He made a remarkable comeback to slam 28 homers and drive in 100 runs in 2000 for the Braves at the age of 39 and was still active and productive during the 2002 campaign.

Eli Marrero, a 26-year-old St. Louis Cardinals catcher, underwent surgery for thyroid cancer after hitting only .192 in a difficult 1999 sophomore season. He played sparingly in 2000 while regaining his strength but hit a solid .266 as the Cardinals' backup catcher in 2001. In 2002 Marrero became an invaluable supersub and helped the team capture the division crown. In 131 games he batted .262 with 18 home runs and 66 runs batted in. He caught 44 times, played some first base, and made more than 30 appearances at each of the three outfield spots.

Several players have made complete recoveries from testicular cancer to resume baseball careers. As a 22-year-old minor leaguer in the Oakland A's system back in 1983, Mike Gallego was diagnosed and underwent surgery and radiation treatment. The scrappy little second baseman became a regular for several fine Oakland A's and New York Yankees teams before finally winding up a 13-year major league career in 1997.

John Kruk, a husky, colorful first baseman for the Philadelphia Phillies was operated on for testicular cancer prior to the 1994 season. The 33-year-old Kruk had just batted .316 with 85 runs batted in for the Wild Bunch, the 1993 pennant-winning edition of the Phillies. He made a complete recovery from the cancer, but aching knees forced him to retire two years later with a lifetime batting average of .300 for 10 major league seasons.

In 1999 testicular cancer was discovered in Mike Lowell, a 25-year-old rookie third baseman whom the Florida Marlins had just obtained from the Yankees. Lowell recovered from surgery to have a decent, though abbreviated, rookie season with 12 home runs in 97 games. From 2000 through 2002 he averaged 21 homers and 94 runs batted in and is considered one of the finest third sackers in the game.

Epilepsy

There have been a few other major leaguers known to suffer from epilepsy besides Grover Cleveland Alexander and Tony Lazzeri. In fact, during Alex's rookie year with the Philadelphia Phillies, teammate Sherry Magee was thought to have experienced a violent epileptic attack that was brought on by an umpire's call.

One unusually hot day midway through the 1911 season, plate umpire Bill Finnerman made a questionable call on a pitch with Magee at the plate. Sherry went wild and began frothing at the mouth. When Finnerman made the mistake of removing his mask, Magee slugged him in the face, knocking him down. The outfielder was initially suspended for the remainder of the season, but the sentence was later reduced to 30 days because his suspension placed the Phillies in such dire straits.

At the time, Magee was one of the top players in the game. Playing in the National League from 1904 to 1919, he led the circuit National League in runs batted in four times, led in slugging percentage twice, and captured the batting championship in 1910. Magee began his career with the Phillies and starred for them for 11 years. He and Alex were teammates on the Phillies from 1911 through 1914, before Sherry was traded to the Boston Braves. After seeing action for the Cincinnati Reds in the 1919 World Series against the ill-fated Black Sox, Magee returned to the minor leagues to finish out his career.

After his retirement as a player, Magee became — of all things — an umpire. He called games for one season in the major leagues before becoming ill and dying of pneumonia at the age of 44. He has been under consideration for induction into the Hall of Fame by a special committee charged with nominating turn-of-the-century old-timers.

In 1965 Hal Lanier, a promising young infielder with the San Francisco Giants developed epilepsy after a severe beaning. Lanier had batted .276 as a 1964 rookie, but in nine subsequent seasons he never hit higher than a .233 average. Lanier later went on to be a successful major league manager. Third baseman Buddy Bell revealed that he was an epileptic after his 18-year major league career came to a close in 1989. Bell, who was a five-time All-Star, is the middleman in a three-generation lineup. His father, Gus, was an outstanding National League outfielder in the 1950s and his son, David, is currently a solid major league third sacker. Like Lanier, Buddy also went on to become a big league manager.

Kidney Ailments

Like cancer and epilepsy, many ailments that ended careers and even lives in baseball's earlier years can now often be effectively controlled or cured. Kidney disorders are an example.

In 1925 New York Giants outfielder Ross "Pep" Youngs' batting average tumbled to a mediocre .264 from a lofty .356 level the previous year. Youngs was only 28 years old and prior to the 1925 season his career batting average was .332. It was obvious that something was wrong, and in the spring of 1926 tests revealed that the young star was suffering from a serious kidney ailment. The diagnosis was Bright's disease, which at that time covered a host of kidney disorders that have since been more distinctly categorized. In those days, there weren't many good options available for the treatment of kidney problems. Rest, dietary restrictions, and blood transfusions were widely prescribed treatments.

Youngs, however, was determined to continue his career. A male nurse, who Ross laughingly referred to as "my keeper," was hired to accompany him wherever the Giants went. Amazingly, the reluctant patient seemed to be putting together an excellent comeback season. At the beginning of August 1926 he'd played in 84 of the teams first 100 games and was hitting .316. But within a week he was out of action and running a high temperature. By the middle of the month, his illness forced him to abandon the team with a .306 batting average in 95 games. Youngs was hospitalized in San Antonio, Texas, and remained bedridden for much of the next 14 months. Persistent rumors of his return to the active ranks turned out to be nothing more than a valiant attempt on the part of the ballplayer to will himself back to health. He died in October 1927 at 30 years of age.

Ross Youngs was one of Giants manager John McGraw's favorite players. Photos of Youngs and Christy Mathewson were said to be the only pictures of players to adorn McGraw's Polo Grounds office. Although Youngs was a full-time player for less than nine years, he compiled a .322 lifetime batting mark in 1,211 games, all with the Giants. He was an aggressive baserunner and a brilliant defensive right fielder, who schooled his teenage successor, Mel Ott, in the intricacies of outfield play during his final season. Mel would go on to hold down the Giants right field job for almost two decades and blast 511 homers, a National League record at the time. Ott entered the Hall of Fame in 1951 and his mentor, Ross Youngs, followed in 1972 when he was selected for induction by the Veterans Committee.

Several years later, St. Louis Browns infielder Oscar Melillo's career and life were also threatened by Bright's disease, but Melillo religiously stuck to a prescribed diet of nothing but spinach and was eventually cured.

After three seasons of part-time work, he was the Browns regular second baseman from 1929 through 1934 and put in a few more years with the Boston Red Sox before beginning a lengthy coaching career.

Fortunately, great advancements in the treatment of kidney disorders had occurred by the time star pitcher Ewell Blackwell began experiencing problems. Pitching for the Cincinnati Reds, Blackwell won 22 games and led the National League in strikeouts and complete games in a spectacular 1947 campaign. But after he dropped to a mere seven wins the following season, it was determined that his right kidney was not functioning and it was removed before the 1949 campaign. After a year of rehabilitation pitching out of the bullpen, Blackwell returned to form. He won 17 games in 1950 and 16 in 1951, pitching more than 200 innings each season and registering good earned run marks for second division Cincinnati squads.

In 1966 a kidney ailment impacted the career of another promising young player, Rick Reichardt. The California Angels' signing of Reichardt in 1964 for the biggest bonus in baseball history at the time led to the implementation of the amateur draft by organized baseball. Describing young Reichardt, baseball wit Joe Garagiola once said, "The first time I saw him I thought he fell off a Wheaties Box." The young outfielder, who was also a football star at the University of Wisconsin, was wooed by 18 teams before inking a reported $200,000 pact with the Angels. Although he was rushed to the majors before he was ready, he was showing signs of developing into a star when he was struck down. In 1966 he was batting .288 with 16 homers in only 89 games when his kidney had to be removed in August. Reichardt was able to return to regular duty the next year, but he never lived up to expectations. He did, however, develop into a useful major league outfielder with good power. He moved to the Chicago White Sox and then to the Kansas City Royals over the next seven seasons, but was barely 31 years old when he was released by the Royals after a single appearance in 1974.

A couple of lesser lights who enjoyed success in the major leagues despite losing a kidney were Estel Crabtree and Norm Larker. Crabtree, who had to have a damaged kidney removed after an outfield collision, was a regular outfielder for the Cincinnati Reds in 1931 and 1932 before moving to the St. Louis Cardinals in a trade for Jim Bottomley and getting buried in the Cardinals' expansive farm system. But in 1941, at the age of 37, he returned to the big leagues to bat .341 in part-time duty with the Cards. He was back in the minors in 1942, but with a 4F draft rating due to the missing kidney, he became a valuable commodity again when the war depleted major league rosters. He returned to Cincinnati and spent the 1943 and 1944 seasons with the Reds as a reserve outfielder and dangerous pinch hitter.

Norm Larker also lost a kidney due to an on-field accident which occurred in his first year in the minor leagues. The young first baseman returned to action the next year but spent nine seasons in the Brooklyn Dodgers minor league system while Gil Hodges monopolized first base at the major league level. Despite a lack of speed, Larker eventually learned to play the outfield and finally made it to the big leagues in 1958, the year the Dodgers moved to Los Angeles. He was an extra outfielder and backed up Hodges at first for two years and contributed a .289 batting mark as a valuable reserve on the 1959 World Championship squad. In 1960 he supplanted Hodges at first base and finished second in the National League batting race with a .323 average. He platooned with Hodges in 1961 and was the regular first baseman for the new Houston Colts expansion team in 1962, but his batting average never approached its 1960 level again. He exited the big leagues after the 1963 campaign with a .275 lifetime batting average.

Tuberculosis

Tuberculosis or TB is another disease for which there were tremendous advances in treatment during the 20th century. Veteran second baseman Red Schoendienst was a key to the Milwaukee Braves' back-to-back pennants in 1957 and 1958. Somehow the 35-year-old former Cardinal star managed to get through the latter campaign while suffering from tuberculosis. He was institutionalized soon after batting .300 in the Braves' seven-game World Series loss to the New York Yankees and missed all but a few token contests in 1959. Red's absence that year undoubtedly cost the Braves a third straight pennant. The team never found an adequate replacement and lost to the Los Angeles Dodgers in a three-game pennant playoff after the regular season ended in a first place tie. Although Schoendienst returned to reclaim his regular keystone spot in the spring of 1960, he was still too weak to play full time and was benched for most of the second half of the campaign. He was released by the Braves and returned to the Cardinals in 1961, where he spent two years as a "pinch hitter deluxe" and backup second baseman. For the 1961 and 1962 seasons combined he hit .317 in the pinch (.300 overall) and led the National League in pinch-hit appearances and pinch hits. The redhead retired early in the 1963 campaign to become a coach for the Cardinals and managed the club for 12 seasons from 1965 to 1976, a tenure that included two pennants and a

World Championship. He spent some time as a coach with Oakland after his term as St. Louis manager but eventually returned to the Cardinals organization and even filled in twice as interim manager.

Less than a decade after Schoendienst's bout with TB, another Brave's player came down with the disease. The club knew something was seriously wrong when slugging outfielder Rico Carty's batting average dropped from .326 in 1966 to .255 in 1967. After being diagnosed with tuberculosis, the 28-year-old Carty had to sit out the 1968 campaign undergoing treatment and regaining his strength. Thanks to his youth and medical advances, Rico came back to hit .342 in an injury-marred 1969 season. He then led the league in batting in 1970 with a .366 average, the highest mark by a right-handed hitter since Joe DiMaggio's day. Although Carty recovered from tuberculosis, he continued to experience dismal luck. A badly broken leg suffered in a Dominican Republic Winter League game forced him to the sidelines for the 1971 season. Rico returned to action in 1972 and played through 1979, but the injury slowed him down considerably and he was relegated almost exclusively to designated hitter duties for the last five years of his career. He finished with a .299 lifetime batting average.

Schoendienst and Carty were extremely lucky compared to Bill DeLancey, who came down with tuberculosis in 1935 before many of the modern techniques and medication for treating the disease were developed. At the tender age of 22 DeLancey came up to the St. Louis Cardinals to stay in 1934 after a sensational season with Columbus in the American Association. During the regular season, the young left-handed power hitter shared the catching job with veteran Virgil Davis and hit a robust .316 with 13 homers in 93 games. In the 1934 World Series, the rookie caught every inning as the "Gas House Gang" downed the Detroit Tigers in seven games. In 1935 Bill won the regular backstop job and seemed to be on the verge of greatness, but in the last half of the season he slumped badly. He lost his pep and his appetite, had trouble sleeping, and began to feel woozy much of the time. DeLancey managed to struggle through the campaign, finishing with a .279 batting average for 103 games, but in the off-season he collapsed while participating in a local sandlot game. He was sent to a sanitarium in Phoenix and spent the next eight months confined to bed. After his release from the hospital, Bill remained in the Phoenix area for health reasons. The dry air was better for his damaged lungs, which would have to be tapped and drained every other day for the next four years.

From 1937 through 1939 DeLancey managed Albuquerque in the Arizona-Texas League despite his weakened condition and the invasive draining procedure. He ran a temperature the whole first year, but by the end of his second season as manager he started feeling a little better. He began to do some pinch-hitting and occasionally took the mound in runaway games to please the crowd. In the spring of 1940 Bill returned to the Cardinals and made the roster as a bullpen catcher and pinch hitter. Still weakened by the disease, DeLancey didn't have much stamina, but he played in 15 major league games that season. The 29-year-old catcher was still harboring hopes of eventually returning to regular duty and went to the minor leagues for the 1941 season, but his health didn't hold up and he was forced to retire. The man whom Branch Rickey once named as the catcher on his all-time team, despite the fact that he appeared in only 219 major league games, died on Thanksgiving Day of 1946 — his 35th birthday.

Meningitis

Meningitis is a viral or bacterial infection of the membranes surrounding the brain. It's another former killer than has been tamed by modern medicine, although the effects can linger indefinitely. In baseball, the disease seems to have a strange affinity for Cleveland players. In 1911 it claimed the life of Cleveland's ace hurler Addie Joss two days after his 31st birthday.

The first victim of the disease to recover enough to play at the major league level was also a Cleveland player. Bruce Campbell, a regular American League outfielder from 1932 to 1942, was originally the property of the Chicago White Sox but was traded to the St. Louis Browns early in the 1932 season. He averaged almost 90 runs batted in per year in three promising seasons with the downtrodden Browns and was rewarded with a trade to the contending Cleveland Indians after the 1934 campaign. The move seemed to ignite the 25-year-old left-handed hitter's bat. In early August, Bruce was hitting at a .325 clip when he was struck down by cerebral spinal fever. Initially, Campbell was only given a 50/50 chance for survival, but he managed to pull through and was back in uniform the next spring. Though not fully recovered, he hit a robust .372 in part-time duty. He experienced a frightening relapse in May but again managed to overcome the illness. After the season, Philadelphia sportswriters honored Campbell as the most courageous athlete of the year. Although Bruce went on to play another six years as a regular outfielder for three different teams, he never achieved the stardom he seemed to be approaching before his illness.

Almost 30 years later, still another promising young Cleveland player was struck down by meningitis. Max Alvis slammed 22 homers and hit .274 in 158 games as a rookie third baseman for the Indians in 1963. The next season, the 26-year-old infielder was sidelined in midseason with a career-threatening case of spinal meningitis. Alvis recovered to return to active duty later in the year and played regularly for four more years. Although he made the American League All-Star Team in 1965 and 1967, he seemed to fade in the latter stages of the season and was never able to fulfill the rich promise he displayed as a rookie. Max was through as a full-timer at 30 and out of baseball at 32 years of age.

CONGENITAL BACK PROBLEMS

Bad backs generally could be considered an occupational hazard in the world of professional sports. There have been scores of players who were able to continue their careers after debilitating back injuries. A few others managed to reach the major leagues despite congenital back problems that plagued them from an early age.

George McQuinn, a smooth fielding first baseman for the St. Louis Browns, Philadelphia Athletics, and New York Yankees, played with an awkward back brace throughout his career but still managed to be named to the American League All-Star Team six times and hit .438 in the 1944 World Series. McQuinn was stuck in the Yankees farm system for years behind Lou Gehrig before being drafted by the Browns and hitting .324 in his first full season in the big leagues. The publicity he attracted because of his 1944 Series performance led to demands that he be inducted into the military despite his back problem, but the armed forces continued to reject him. He was released by the Athletics after a dismal 1946 season but caught on with the Yankees and hit .304 with 80 runs batted in for the 1947 world champions at the age of 37.

New York Yankees outfielder Charlie Keller was a five-time All-Star in the 1940s but was through as a regular at the age of 30 because of hereditary back problems. Regrettably, his son also inherited the condition. Charlie Jr., a bright prospect in the Yankees system, had to give up the game a year after leading the Eastern League in batting with a .349 average in 1961.

Earl Averill enjoyed a Hall of Fame career with the Cleveland Indians and Detroit Tigers despite suffering from a congenital spinal malformation. The condition became so bad that it caused a temporary paralysis in his legs in 1937, a year after he'd batted .378 with 28 homers and a league-leading 232 hits for Cleveland. Forced to revamp his batting style and sacrifice power, Earl's average plummeted to .299 in 1937, but he rebounded to hit .330 in 1938, his last good year. He retired after spending most of the 1941 season in the minor leagues.

Arthritis

The magnificent career of all-time great Sandy Koufax was curtailed at the age of 31 because of an arthritic condition in his pitching arm that he could no longer endure. But despite pitching in constant pain, the lefty fireballer reached performance levels that have rarely been matched. Koufax was a bonus baby who had to be kept on the Brooklyn Dodgers' roster for the 1955 and 1956 seasons under the rules of the time. Although his development was delayed, by 1962 he was regarded as the most dominating pitcher in the game. But in July of that year, he came down with a rare disease called Raynaud's phenomenon (usually misspelled "Reynaud's" in baseball literature). The circulatory problem prematurely ended his first really outstanding campaign and forced him to drop a devastating sidearm curve from his pitching repertoire. After coming back to win 25 games in 1963, Sandy developed traumatic arthritis in his left elbow which shut him down during the 1964 season after 19 victories. Thereafter, Koufax followed a regimen of cortisone shots, oral medications, and hot and cold treatments before and after every game in order to keep pitching. He had to abandon his slider and was often unable to use his outstanding overhand curveball. Yet he won 26 games in 1965 and 27 in 1966 before retiring. "When I'm forty years old, I'd still like to be able to comb my hair," Sandy explained upon his decision to hang it up while still at his peak. In his abbreviated career, Koufax led the major leagues in victories three times and in strikeouts four times. In three different seasons he won 25 or more games, recorded an earned run average of less than 2.00, and struck out more than 300 men. Sandy also led the National League in shutouts three times and in earned run average in each of his last five seasons. He was elected to the Hall of Fame in his first year of eligibility.

Migraine Headaches

Another top player who struggled mightily with a painful, debilitating condition that eventually forced him out of the game early was Hal Trosky, a slugging first baseman for the Cleveland Indians and Chicago White Sox. From his 1934 rookie year through the 1940 campaign, Trosky batted .314 and averaged 29 homers and 121 runs batted in. But he was tormented by severe migraine headaches that seemed to be getting worse all the time. The condition limited him to 89 games and a .294 batting average in 1941, and he retired after the season at the age of 28. Three years later he came back to play a full 1944 season with the Chicago White Sox, but the chronic headaches again forced him back to the sidelines after he hit only .241 in 135 games. Hal valiantly made one last comeback attempt in 1946 at the age of 33 but wasn't productive in 88 games and retired for good after the season.

STOMACH AILMENTS

Shortstop Charlie Hollocher was another star performer who was able to overcome a disabling condition for a time but eventually saw his career end prematurely due to the condition. In fact, Hollocher, ruined his career and his life attempting to play with a serious abdominal ailment. As a 22-year-old rookie phenom with the Chicago Cubs in 1918 Charlie led the National League in games played, hits, and total bases. He also finished among the league leaders in batting average, slugging average, on-base percentage, runs scored, stolen bases, doubles, walks, and sacrifice hits. In 1922 he led National League shortstops in fielding and hit a sensational .340 in 152 games, the highest average for a shortstop since Honus Wagner batted .354 in 1908.

Despite these heroics, Hollocher was not a well man. At the age of 27 he had already missed significant playing time due to illness in his short career, when he was stricken with a mysterious stomach disorder in the spring of 1923. A specialist he was referred to told him that he would destroy his health if he played that year, but the Cubs desperately needed Charlie in the lineup and persuaded him to ignore the medical diagnosis and rejoin the team. He played only 66 games during the 1923 season but hit a sensational .342. Hollocher still hadn't recovered in 1924 yet played in 76 games before being forced to the sidelines for good. He lived the rest of his life in poor health and finally killed himself with a newly purchased shotgun at the age of 44.

Another player who managed to forge a major league career despite recurring stomach maladies was outfielder Gary Geiger, one of the most consistently unhealthy players in baseball history. Geiger is listed in the *Baseball Encyclopedia* as standing an even 6 feet tall and weighing a gaunt 168 pounds—but that must have been with his winter coat on. A weight of 155 pounds was more like it for most of his career. Gary started his career in professional baseball as a pitcher in the St. Louis Cardinals chain and at the age of 18 he posted a 20–7 won-lost record and sparkling 1.98 earned run average in the Pony League. Apparently there was a shortage of light hitting outfielders in the Cardinals organization at the time, so Geiger turned in his toeplate in 1957 and proceeded to hit a meager .223 for the Rochester Red Wings. This caught the attention of the Cleveland Indians, who drafted him before the 1958 season and kept him for a year before swapping him to the Boston Red Sox for Jimmy Piersall.

After a mediocre 1959 campaign, the promising 23-year-old was hitting .302 in late July of 1960 when he was drilled in the back by an Early Wynn fastball. Gary suffered a collapsed left lung and was through for the year. He returned to regular center field duty in 1961 and 1962 but was hospitalized following the latter season with stomach ulcers and an intestinal obstruction. Four transfusions ensued and he was on diet of milk and poached eggs for several weeks. Somehow Geiger returned to the lineup to hit .263 with 16 homers in 1963, but the ulcers flared up again and he underwent surgery to remove them and also repair the intestinal obstruction. Gary tried to play in 1964, but at 133 pounds he was simply too weak and voluntarily retired after only five games. He attempted to come back in 1965 but promptly broke his hand in three places trying to make a diving catch. A metal pin was necessary to hold the bone in place. With his dreams of stardom shattered, Geiger was waived to the National League and quietly spent the last four years of a disappointing career as a reserve outfielder.

Asthma

Asthma is a chronic respiratory disease marked by recurrent attacks of wheezing or shortness of breath. It's caused by acute bronchial sensitivity and is usually associated with an allergy to materials like dust, pollen, fungi, or animal fur, although symptoms can also be brought on by chest infection, emotional distress, or exercise. In milder cases, asthma is easily controlled and even cured, but more serious conditions can be incapacitating and occasionally life threatening.

Pitcher Bob Gibson suffered from asthma as a youth but recovered to play college basketball at Creighton and tour with the Harlem Globetrotters before embarking on a Hall of Fame baseball career with the St. Louis Cardinals.

Another hurler, Jack Kramer was discharged from the Navy during World War II because he was asthmatic. Kramer had bounced up and down between the St. Louis Browns and the minors before the war but became a Brownie stalwart after his discharge. Despite his asthma, his 17 victories and 2.49 earned run average made him the ace of the Browns 1944 pennant-winning staff and he posted a league-leading 18–5 won-lost record after being traded to the Boston Red Sox in 1948. He lasted in the majors until 1951, winning 95 games.

Pitcher Dave "Boo" Ferriss of the Boston Red Sox also received a discharge during World War II when he developed a severe asthmatic condition. Ferris, who began his professional career in the Red Sox organization before the outbreak of the war, developed into an outstanding hurler for the U.S. Army Air Corps. But asthma attacks disabled him for days at a time and he was released from military duty after 26 months of service. Doctors advised Ferriss to move to a warm, dry climate like Arizona and pursue another profession. Instead he decided to spend his time pitching for the Red Sox in damp, chilly New England.

Ferriss began the 1945 American League season with eight straight victories, four of them shutouts. But as the season wore on and the humidity intensified, frequent asthma attacks became a problem and he won only three of his last 10 decisions. For the year, he won 21 games against 10 losses and posted a 2.96 earned run average. A good hitter, he also made 20 appearances as a pinch hitter.

Despite his rookie success, there were serious doubts about young Dave Ferriss' future prior to the 1946 campaign. Doctors continued to advise him to give up baseball because of his condition. In addition, there was the suspicion that veteran stars returning from the war wouldn't find his deliveries as baffling as the wartime talent had. But after a slow start, he reeled off 10 straight victories and won 25 games while losing only 6 for the pennant-winning Sox. In the 1946 Series, he shut out the St. Louis Cardinals in game three, but was chased in the fifth inning of the final game — the game in which Enos Slaughter gained lasting fame in the eighth inning with his mad dash to score the winning run from first base on a Harry Walker hit to center field.

During the 1947 season, Ferriss' performance was only ordinary and he injured his arm in midseason. After winning 26 games in his first two seasons, a total that has only been exceeded by Grover Cleveland Alexander, he posted an ordinary 12–11 record for his third year. The 1948 campaign was even worse. Dave's arm continued to bother him and his asthma made it difficult to get in shape. He started only nine games for the Red Sox and finished with seven wins and an unsightly 5.23 earned run average. The arm went completely dead in 1949 and Ferriss pitched only a few innings. He was sent to the minors leagues the next year and spent the remainder of his career at that level before retiring in 1953.

Exotic Diseases

Several players have made seemingly complete recoveries from exotic and sometimes serious ailments, making it virtually impossible to tell if or how much of a toll was taken on their careers.

The great Christy Mathewson came down with a case of diphtheria in 1906 which "limited" him to 22 wins and drove his earned run average up to a mortal 2.97. Apparently Matty's health was fully restored, as he won a career high 37 games two years later and he pitched for another 10 years.

John McGraw, Mathewson's legendary manager with the New York Giants reportedly contracted a case of malaria while a player with the old Baltimore Orioles in the 1890s. McGraw recovered and was an active player through 1902 before turning to managing full time. His lifetime batting average as a player was an impressive .333.

As a struggling young player with the Pittsburgh Pirates, Roberto Clemente also suffered through an episode of malaria. Clemente regained his strength and went on to win four National League batting crowns, a Most Valuable Player Award, and 12 All-Star Game selections. He batted .317 for his career and lashed out hit number 3,000 on the last day of the 1972 campaign. On December 31, 1972, he died when a plane he had hired to deliver emergency supplies to Nicaraguan earthquake victims crashed. Shortly thereafter he was elected to the Hall of Fame in a special balloting.

First baseman Vic Wertz of the Cleveland Indians was diagnosed with polio in 1955 and missed half the season. He came back in 1956 to blast a career high 32 homers and drove in more than 100 runs three more times before retiring after the 1963 campaign.

Dave Nilsson, the first Australian to star in the big leagues, was felled by an unusual case of Ross River fever in 1995. He recovered to bat .331 in 1996, the sixth highest mark in the league. Originally a catcher, Nilsson spent most of his time in the outfield and at first base after his illness but moved back behind the plate in 1999. That year, the 29-year-old veteran made the American League All-Star Team for the first time. He batted .309 and slammed a career high 21 homers in 115 games before leaving American baseball after the season to concentrate on the Australian 2000 Olympic baseball team. In the spring of 2003 Nilsson, who spent his entire major league career with the Milwaukee Brewers, briefly pursued a comeback with the Boston Red Sox but left camp before exhibition games got underway.

Former star outfielder Tim Raines, one of the top leadoff men and base stealers of all time, developed lupus late in his career and missed the entire 2000 campaign. He returned to the game in 2001 with the Montreal Expos, the team that he'd originally achieved stardom with during the 1980s. Raines enjoyed a successful year, hitting .308 as a part-timer. Late in the season he got a chance to play in the same outfield with his son Tim Jr. when a trade was orchestrated to move him to the Baltimore Orioles. During the 2002 season, Raines was still active as a pinch hitter and extra outfielder with the Florida Marlins at the age of 42. The seven-time All-Star and former National League batting champ officially retired at the end of the 2002 campaign with a .294 lifetime batting average and a total of 808 stolen bases, which ranks as the fifth highest career total of modern times.

A number of players suffered from rickets during childhood but seemed to avoid any lasting effect. Jackie Robinson, Bob Gibson, and Tommie Agee are three notable players who didn't let the ailment keep them from becoming big league stars.

SIZE (STATURE)

Unless it's an extreme case such as dwarfism, smallness of stature is generally not considered a disability, but it can certainly be a barrier to becoming a major league baseball player. Scouts and managers love the big guys, and the old adage, "a good big man is better than a good little man," has always been held as gospel.

Nevertheless, some pretty good little guys managed to hurdle the size obstacle and become outstanding major league players.

Wee Willie Keeler's nickname certainly conjures up an image of a vertically challenged player, and his wee 5'4", 140-pound frame fits the image exactly. All Willie did was compile a .343 batting average in 18 full seasons, good for immediate admittance to the newly established Hall of Fame in 1939.

Phil Rizzuto, who stood 5'6" and weighed 150 pounds, and Rabbit Maranville, who packed 155 pounds on his 5'5" frame, are a pair of diminutive shortstops whose flashy gloves also got them into the Hall of Fame. Rizzuto, who played for the New York Yankees from 1941 through the midway point of the 1956 campaign, was the American League Most Valuable Player in 1950 and was often described as the glue that held the Yankees together through nine pennants. Maranville was probably the smallest cleanup hitter in the history of the game when he manned that spot for the Boston Braves through much of their 1914 World Championship season. Rabbit was considered the "Ozzie Smith" of his era and enjoyed a career that spanned 24 years.

But Joe Morgan, who stood 5'7" and is listed as weighing only 150 pounds, has to be considered the greatest of the little guys. In a career that spanned 22 seasons, "Little Joe" was named to the National League All-Star Team nine times, including eight consecutive nominations from 1972 to 1979. He was the league's Most Valuable Player in 1972 and 1973 and won five straight Gold Gloves at second base from 1973 to 1977. He played for seven Division Champion squads and four Pennant Winners. Morgan was an integral part of the Big Red Machine that dominated the National League during the 1970s and won two World Championships. He stole more than 40 bases a year from 1969 through 1977 and finished with 268 lifetime home runs. Despite his size, he broke the legendary Rogers Hornsby's all-time record for career homers by a second baseman and held it until his numbers were topped by Ryne Sandberg.

Other small guys who made their mark in the major leagues are Sparky Adams (5'5", 151 pounds), who played 13 years in the National League, appeared in two World Series, and was still a regular third baseman at the age of 38; Fred Patek (5'5", 148 pounds), who lasted 14 seasons and was a three-time American League All-Star shortstop with the Kansas City Royals; outfielder Albie Pearson (5'5", 140 pounds), who was the American League Rookie of the Year in 1958 and an All-Star in 1963; pitcher Bobby Shantz (5'6", 139 pounds), who won 24 games and the American League Most Valuable Player Award in 1952; and Roy Face (5'8", 155 pounds), a sensational reliever from 1953 to 1969, who recorded 17 straight wins in relief for the 1959 Pittsburgh Pirates.

Two of the tiniest modern day (post-1950) major leaguers were a couple of pint-sized shortstops who never really got a chance at the big league level. Harry Chappas (5'3", 150 pounds) got into 72 games in three years with the Chicago White Sox from 1978 to 1980, and Pompei Davalillo (5"3", 140 pounds) hit .293 in a 17-game trial for the Washington Senators in 1953. Although both mighty mites performed fairly well in limited big league opportunities, they quickly faded into oblivion.

Today the smallest player in the majors looks to be Anaheim Angels shortstop David Eckstein, although he's officially listed at exactly the same size (5'8", 170 pounds) as second baseman Ray Durham of the San Francisco Giants. Veteran relief pitcher Tom Gordon (5'9", 160 pounds), who saved 46 games for the Boston Red Sox in 1998 and is a featured real life character in a recent Stephen King thriller, is probably the smallest active hurler.

Mental Blocks

A mental block is a behavioral problem that usually doesn't rise to the level of a disability, except in extreme circumstances. In the world of sports, however, uncontrolled mental blocks can ruin a career as surely as a disastrous injury. The career of Los Angeles Dodgers second baseman Steve Sax seemed to be on such a course, only a year after he'd won the 1982 National League Rookie of the Year Award. By the 1983 All-Star Game break, Sax had committed 24 errors, most of them on routine throws to first. Sax was suffering from a serious mental block. He was feeling like a prisoner of his condition and worried endlessly about his grip on the ball and the angle of his arm. Fans behind the first base dugout started wearing batting helmets, and Dodgers manager Tommy Lasorda put a greasy pig's head in his bed, Godfather-style, with a note telling him to throw the ball right — or else. Somehow, Steve endured the mostly good-natured abuse and managed to come out a winner with the support of Lasorda and the entire Dodgers organization. His throwing woes stopped almost as suddenly as they had begun and Sax made only six miscues the rest of the season. Although the problem threatened to re-emerge from time to time throughout his rest of his career, Sax managed to control it and enjoy an excellent major league career. In fact, he led American League second basemen in fielding percentage in 1989 after moving over to the New York Yankees. The four-time All-Star ended his career in 1994 with a .281 lifetime batting average and 444 stolen bases.

Steve Sax's ordeal was eerily duplicated by Chuck Knoblauch in the 1990s. Like Sax, Knoblauch was an All-Star second baseman, a former Rookie of the Year, and one of the game's premier leadoff hitters, who developed a debilitating mental block that made it almost impossible for him to make accurate throws to first base. Even the most routine tosses became an adventure. Chuck had been a Gold Glove winner with the Minnesota Twins before he was acquired by the New York Yankees in 1998 in the midst of a lucrative multi-year contract. Like many before him, Knoblauch never seemed to get comfortable with the Yankees. Throwing problems first surfaced late in his first season in New York when after fielding grounders, he developed a tic or hesitation in the process of throwing the ball.

In contrast to Steve Sax, Knoblauch did not receive the unwavering support of the Yankees organization and didn't succeed in conquering his affliction. In 1999 the problem became so bad that he committed 26 errors, double his total of the previous year. In 2000 he made 15 errors in only 82 games at second base and was frequently used in the designated hitter role. The Yankees finally moved him to the outfield because of his throwing, but by that time his offense had also begun to decline. The Yankees let him go after he hit only .250 as an outfielder in 2001, and he was released by the lowly Kansas City Royals after a poor 2002 campaign. As the 2003 season began, no major league team appeared willing to give him a chance to revive his career.

Mental blocks are not limited to second basemen, however. Catchers also seem to be particularly prone to the disorder. Several have developed a serious problem simply returning the ball back to the pitcher. A notable example is Dale Murphy of the Atlanta Braves, who came up as a promising catcher but was forced to move to the outfield when he developed the condition. Of course, Murphy became a star and won two Most Valuable Player Awards as a fly chaser. Mackey Sasser and Dave Engle are two other receivers who suffered from the condition and found themselves moved to other positions, while Clay Dalrymple overcame a rookie case of the disorder and went on to gain a reputation as an excellent defensive backstop for 12 years in the major leagues.

The most extreme manifestation of the disorder, however, is the puzzling case of former Pittsburgh Pirates pitcher Steve Blass. After being named World Series Most Valuable Player in 1971 and enjoying a career best 19–8 won-lost record in 1972, Blass developed a crippling mental block and simply couldn't get the ball over the plate. His arm was fine and he still threw great on the sidelines, but during the game he just couldn't throw strikes. In 1973 he walked 84 men in 88 innings and posted a horrendous 9.85 earned run average for the Pirates. The next year was even worse as he walked 103 in 61 innings for the Pirates' Charleston farm club. His condition was blamed on everything from a fear of hitting the batter to a reaction to the tragic death of teammate Roberto Clemente. Blass tried psychotherapy, hypnosis, transcendental meditation, and various mechanical experiments without success. He pitched only once in 1974 before leaving baseball for good, still only 31 years old.

ACTIVE PLAYERS

There are several players who are still active in the major leagues who perform or have performed with serious afflictions. Pitcher Jim Mecir is featured in one of the chapters. Cancer survivors Galarraga, Marrero, and Lowell have already been mentioned, as have Tim Raines and Scott Radinsky, whose baseball careers seem to be over.

John Olerud, who underwent an operation for a brain aneurysm before beginning his professional career, is playing in his 15th season at the major league level. The former American League batting champ carried an even .300 batting average into the 2003 season and is still productive as the Seattle Mariners regular first baseman.

Pitchers Roberto Hernandez and David Cone, who both had surgery to remove blood clots in their throwing arms earlier in their careers are continuing their careers, with new teams. Hernandez, a 38-year-old right-hander who had surgery to remove two clots from his right forearm before reaching the majors, is trying his hand as a setup man for the Atlanta Braves. In his previous role of closer for several teams he saved 320 games in 12 seasons through 2002, the ninth highest total of all time and the third highest among active pitchers. Cone was 33 years old when he had a clot removed from his right shoulder in 1996. After the surgery, he recovered well enough to pitch a no-hitter and win 20 games in a season. A 193-game winner going into the 2003 season, Cone is trying to nail down a spot in the New York Mets rotation after sitting out the 2002 campaign.

Jason Johnson, who was also mentioned in an earlier chapter, is an insulin-dependent diabetic who's in his fifth year with the Baltimore Orioles. The 6'6" tall, 29-year-old right-hander was one of the Orioles' top performers in 2001 with a 10–12 won-lost record. But his record slumped to 5–14 in 2002 and his earned run average was a disappointing 4.59, putting his spot in the starting rotation in jeopardy.

A current player who is still struggling mightily to overcome a psychological disorder is St. Louis Cardinals hurler Rick Ankiel, once considered the most promising young hurler in the Cardinals organization — if not the whole league. Ankiel is attempting to conquer "Steve Blass disease," as the psychological disorder has come to be known in baseball circles. Ankiel's problem started during the 2000 National League Division Series against Atlanta when the 21-year-old rookie mysteriously lost control and uncorked five wild pitches in the second inning of his first postseason start. Two more appearances in the League Championship Series were equally disturbing.

Ankiel had posted a 11–7 won-lost record, recorded a fine 3.50 earned run mark, and struck out 194 batters in 175 innings during the regular 2000 campaign, his first full season in the big leagues. Although the Cardinals showed great patience and handled him with kid gloves, his control problems continued in the spring of 2001 and he spent most of the year pitching in the low minors. The youngster sat out the 2002 season with arm problems, but seemed to be making progress heading into the 2003 campaign.

Hopefully Rick Ankiel will not follow the path of Steve Blass but will emulate Steve Sax to overcome the disorder and take his place among the best hurlers in the game.

Bibliography

Books

Alexander, Charles C. *Rogers Hornsby: A Biography*. New York: Henry Holt, 1995.
Allen, Maury. *Baseball's 100: A Personal Ranking of the Best Players in Baseball History*. New York: A&W Publishers, 1981.
Appel, Marty. *Yesterday's Heroes: Revisiting the Old-Time Baseball Stars*. New York: William Morrow, 1988.
____, and Burt Goldblatt. *Baseball's Best: The Hall of Fame Gallery*. New York: McGraw-Hill, 1977.
Bernotas, Bob. *Nothing to Prove: The Jim Abbott Story*. New York: Kodansha International, 1995.
Boswell, Thomas. *The Heart of the Order*. New York: Viking Penguin, 1989.
Broeg, Bob. *The Ol' Ball Game: Chick Hafey's Heartaches*. New York: Barnes & Noble, 1993.
Cavanaugh, Jack. *Damn the Disabilities: Full Speed Ahead*. Waco, TX: WRS Publishing, 1995.
Clark, Steven. *Fight Against Time: Five Athletes — A Legacy of Courage*. New York: Athenaeum, 1979.
Conigliaro, Tony, and Jack Zanger. *Seeing It Through*. New York: Macmillan, 1970.
Conner, Floyd. *Baseball's Most Wanted*. Washington, D.C.: Brassey's, 2000.
Craft, David. *Rookies of the Year: New Kids Who Took the Field*. New York: Friedman/Fairfax, 1995.
____, and Tom Owens. *Redbirds Revisited: Great Memories and Stories from St. Louis Cardinals*. Chicago: Bonus Books, 1990.
Davis, Eric, and Ralph Wiley. *Born to Play: The Eric Davis Story*. New York: Viking Penguin, 1999.
Davis, Mac. *Baseball's All-Time Greats: The Top Fifty Players*. New York: Bantam, 1970.
____. *Baseball's Unforgettables*. New York, 1966.
____. *The Greatest in Baseball*. New York: Scholastic, 1969.
Deane, Bill. *Award Voting*. Cleveland: SABR, 1988.
Dravecky, Dave, and Tim Stafford. *Comeback*. San Francisco: Harper & Row, 1990.
Eskenazi, Gerald. *Bill Veeck: A Baseball Legend*. New York: McGraw-Hill, 1988.
Fitzgerald, Ed. *The American League*. New York: Grossett and Dunlap, 1959.
____. *The National League*. New York: Grossett and Dunlap, 1959.
Gibson, Bob, with Lonnie Wheeler. *Stranger to the Game: The Autobiography of Bob Gibson*. New York: Viking Penguin, 1994.

Gilbert, Bill. *They Also Served: Baseball and the Home Front, 1941–45.* New York: Crown, 1992.

Goldstein, Richard. *Spartan Seasons: How Baseball Survived the Second World War.* New York: Macmillan, 1980.

Golenbock, Peter. *The Spirit of St. Louis: A History of the St. Louis Cardinals and Browns.* New York: HarperCollins, 2000.

Gutman, Bill. *Jim Abbott, Star Pitcher.* New York: Grey Castle Press, 1992.

_____. *Overcoming the Odds.* New York: Raintree, Steck & Vaughn, 1996.

Gutman, Dan. *Baseball Babylon: The Real Stories Behind the Scandals that Rocked the Game.* New York: Penguin, 1992.

Hirshberg, Al. *The Man Who Fought Back: Red Schoendienst.* New York: Julian Messner, 1961.

Hodges, Russ. *Baseball Complete: Dramatic, Unusual Stories from Baseball's Colorful History.* New York: Grossett and Dunlap, 1952.

Honig, Donald. *Baseball America: The Heroes of the Game and the Times of Their Glory.* New York: Barnes & Nobles, 1997.

_____. *Baseball Between the Lines: Baseball in the 1940s and 1950s as told by the Men Who Played It.* Lincoln: University of Nebraska Press (Bison Books), 1976.

_____. *Baseball When the Grass was Real: Baseball from the 20s to the 40s told by the Men Who Played It.* New York: Coward, McCann & Geoghegan, 1975.

_____. *The Greatest Pitchers of All Time.* New York: Crown Publishers, 1988.

_____. *Up from the Minor Leagues: Seven Top Major Leaguers Recall Their Early Days in Baseball.* New York: Cowles, 1970.

Horgan, Tim. *Cult Baseball Players.* New York: Simon & Schuster, 1990.

Hunter, Jim "Catfish," and Armen Keteyian. *"Catfish"—My Life in Baseball.* New York: McGraw-Hill, 1988.

Ivor-Campbell, Fredrick. *Baseball's First Stars.* Cleveland: SABR, 1996.

_____. *Nineteenth Century Stars.* Cleveland: SABR, 1989.

Jackson, Bo, and Dick Schaap. *Bo Knows Bo.* New York: Doubleday, 1990.

Jacobs, Bruce. *Baseball Stars of 1953.* New York: Timely Comics, 1953.

James, Bill. *Historical Baseball Abstract.* New York: Villard Books, 1988.

_____. *The New Bill James Historical Baseball Abstract.* New York: Simon & Schuster, 2001.

_____, and Don Zminda. *The Great American Baseball Stat Book, 1988 Edition.* New York: Villard Books, 1988.

Jordan, David M. *A Tiger in His Time: Hal Newhouser and the Burden of Wartime Ball.* South Bend, IN: Diamond Communications, 1990.

Karst, Gene, and Martin J. Jones, Jr. *Who's Who in Professional Baseball.* New Rochelle, NY: Arlington House, 1973.

Kashatus, William C. *One-Armed Wonder: Pete Gray, Wartime Baseball and the American Dream.* Jefferson, NC: McFarland, 1995.

Kavanagh, Jack. *Grover Cleveland Alexander: Baseball Legends.* New York: Chelsea House, 1990.

Kelley, Brent. *Baseball Stars of the 1950s: Interviews with All-Stars of the Game's Golden Era.* Jefferson, NC: McFarland, 1993.

_____. *The Case for Those Overlooked by the Baseball Hall of Fame.* Jefferson, NC: McFarland, 1992.

_____. *100 Greatest Pitchers.* New York: Crown, 1998.

Kiersh, Edward. *Where Have You Gone, Vince DiMaggio: Where Did They Go When the Cheering Stopped?* New York: Bantam, 1983.

Klapisch, Bob. *High and Tight: The Rise and Fall of Dwight Gooden and Darryl Strawberry.* New York: Random House, 1996.

LaPlante, Eve. *Seized: Temporal Lobe Epilepsy as a Medical, Historical, and Artistic Phenomenon.* New York: Harper Collins, 1993.
Libby, Bill. *Star Pitchers of the Major Leagues.* New York: Random House, 1971.
Lieb, Fred. *Baseball As I Have Known It: Seven Decades of Baseball Lore.* New York: Grossett and Dunlap, 1977.
Light, Jonathan Frazier. *The Cultural Encyclopedia of Baseball.* Jefferson, NC: McFarland, 1997.
Lindberg, Richard. *Who's on 3rd: The Chicago White Sox Story.* South Bend, IN: Icarus Press, 1983.
Linkugel, Wil A., and Edward J. Pappas. *They Tasted Glory: Among the Missing at the Baseball Hall of Fame.* Jefferson, NC: McFarland, 1998.
Mantle, Mickey. *The Quality of Courage: True Stories of Heroism and Bravery.* New York, Toronto, London: Bantam, 1964.
Marazzi, Rich, and Len Fiorito. *Aaron to Zipfel: The New Major League Players of the Sixties.* New York: Avon, 1985.
Mead, William B. *Baseball Goes to War.* New York: Broadcast Interview Source, 1998.
_____. *The 10 Worst Years of Baseball: The Zany, True Story of Baseball in the Forties.* New York: Van Nostrand, Reinhold, 1978.
Meany, Tom. *Baseball's Greatest Players.* New York: Grosset & Dunlap, 1953.
Moffi, Larry. *This Side of Cooperstown: An Oral History of Major League Baseball in the 1950s.* Iowa City: University of Iowa Press, 1996.
Murdock, Eugene. *Baseball Players and Their Times: Oral Histories of the Game, 1920-1940.* Westport, CT: Meckler Publishing, 1991.
Neft, David, and Richard M. Cohen. *The Sports Encyclopedia of Baseball.* New York: St. Martin's Press, 1993.
Nemec, David. *The Great Encyclopedia of 19th Century Major League Baseball.* New York: Don I. Fine Books, 1997.
Okrent, Daniel, and Steve Wulf. *Baseball Anecdotes.* New York: Oxford University Press, 1989.
Panara, Robert, John Panara, and Kevin Mulholland. *Great Deaf Americans.* Silver Spring, MD: T. J. Publishers, 1983.
Peary, Danny. *We Played the Game: 65 Players Remember Baseball's Greatest Era, 1947-1964.* New York: Hyperion, 1994.
Pepe, Phil. *Winners Never Quit.* New York: Prentice Hall, 1968.
Piersall, Jimmy, and Al Hirshberg. *Fear Strikes Out: The Jimmy Piersall Story.* Lincoln: University of Nebraska Press, 1999.
_____, and _____. *The Truth Hurts.* Chicago: Contemporary Books, 1984.
Pietrusza, David, Matthew Silverman and Michael Gershman. *Baseball: The Biographical Encyclopedia.* New York: Total *Sports Illustrated*, 2000.
Rains, Rob. *The St. Louis Cardinals; 100th Anniversary.* New York: St. Martin's Press, 1992.
Ritter, Lawrence S. *The Glory of Their Times: The Story of the Early Days of Baseball Told by the Men Who Played It.* New York: William Morrow, 1984.
Robinson, Ray. *Baseball Stars of 1963.* New York: Pyramid Books, 1963.
_____. *The Greatest Yankees of Them All.* New York: Putnam & Sons, 1969.
Salin, Tony. *Baseball's Forgotten Heroes: One Fan's Search for the Game's Most Interesting Overlooked Players.* Chicago: Masters Press, 1999.
Santa Maria, Michael, and James Costello. *In the Shadows of the Diamond: Hard Times in the National Pastime.* Dubuque, IA: Elysian Fields Press, Brown & Benchmark, 1992.
Santo, Ron with Randy Minkoff. *Ron Santo: For Love of Ivy.* Chicago: Bonus Books, 1993.

Schneider, Russell. *The Boys of the Summer of '48*. Champaign, IL: Sports Publishing, 1998.
Shannon, Mike. *Tales from the Dugout: The Greatest True Baseball Stories Ever Told*. Chicago: Contemporary Books, 1997.
Shatzkin, Mike, and Jim Charlton. *The Ballplayers: Baseball's Ultimate Biographical Reference*. New York: Arbor House, William Morrow, 1990.
Shlain, Bruce. *Baseball Inside Out: Winning the Games within the Games*. New York: Viking Penguin, 1992.
____. *Oddballs: Baseball's Greatest Pranksters, Flakes, Hotdogs, and Hotheads*. New York: Viking Penguin, 1989.
Smith, Ira. *Baseball's Famous Pitchers*. New York: A.S. Barnes, 1954.
Smith, Ken. *Baseball's Hall of Fame*. New York: Grosset & Dunlap, 1962.
Smith, Red. *To Absent Friends from Red Smith*. New York: Athenaeum, 1982.
Smith, Robert. *Baseball in the Afternoon: Tales from a Bygone Era*. New York: Simon & Schuster, 1993.
____. *Heroes of Baseball*. New York: World Publishing, 1952.
Solomon, Burt. *The Baseball Timeline*. New York: DK Publishing, 2001.
Tellis, Richard. *Once Around the Bases: Bittersweet Memories of Only One Game in the Majors*. Chicago: Triumph Books, 1998.
Thorn, John. *The National Pastime: The Best Articles, Essays, Stats, and Lore from America's #1 Historical Baseball Publication*. New York: Warner Books, 1987.
____, and John Holway. *The Pitcher*. New York: Prentice Hall, 1987.
____, and Pete Palmer, Sean Lahman, David Pietrusza, Matthew Silverman, and Michael Gershman. *Total Baseball*. New York: Total Sports, 1999.
Turner, Frederick. *When the Boys Came Back: Baseball and 1946*. New York: Henry Holt, 1996.
Veeck, Bill, with Ed Linn. *Veeck — As In Wreck*. New York: Bantam Books, 1962.
Voight, David Quentin. *American Baseball: From Gentleman's Sport to the Commissioner System*. Norman: University of Oklahoma Press, 1966.
Waldman, Frank. *Famous American Athletes of Today: Eleventh Series*. Boston: L.C. Page, 1949.
Westcott, Richard. *Diamond Greats: Profiles and Interviews with 65 of Baseball's History Makers*. Westport, CT: Meckler Publishing, 1988.
Wilbert, Warren N. *Rookies Rated: Baseball's Finest Freshman Seasons*. Jefferson, NC: McFarland, 2000.
Zoss, Joel, and John Bowman. *Diamonds in the Rough: The Untold History of Baseball*. Chicago: Contemporary Books, 1996.

Articles

Anderson, Dave. "What Bo Didn't Want to Know." *The New York Times*, March 1, 1992.
Beverage, Richard E. "Tony Lazzeri: Baseball's First 60-Homer Man." *The Baseball Research Journal*, 1991.
Buckley, Steve. "Wild Things." *Sport*, September 1993.
Frank, Stanley. "As Good as He Has to Be: The Story of Red Ruffing, Pinch Pitcher. *Saturday Evening Post*, March 16, 1940.
Greenwood, Chuck. "A Battle On and Off the Field." *Sports Collectors Digest*, June 12, 1998.
Hirshberg, Al. "Carlos May: The Man Who Wouldn't Quit." *Sport*, June 1970.

Holway, John B. "Renewed Interest in "One-Arm" Daily." *The Baseball Research Journal*, 1991.
Kaese, Harold. "Can Carlos May Make it Back?" *Baseball Digest*, December 1969.
Kermisch, Al. "Forgotten Facts Fill Researcher's Notebook." *The Baseball Research Journal*, 1985.
Manning, Gordon. "Kazak Spelled Backwards Is Kazak." *Collier's*, September 17, 1949.
Naiman, Joe. "Bert Shepard." *The National Pastime*, 1999.
Nightengale, Bob. "After a Long, Dark Winter, Santo Walks in the Sunshine." *USA Today Baseball Weekly*, March 5, 2002.
Overfield, Joseph. "Dummy Hoy." *Nineteenth Century Stars*, 1989.
_____. "Hugh Ignatius Daily." *Nineteenth Century Stars*, 1989.
Schechter, Arnold. "Sports Rx." *Sports Illustrated*, April 22, 1985.
Shear, Jeff. "When Anxiety Comes to Bat." *New York Times Magazine*, March 8, 1987.
Stockton, Roy. "The Cardinals Forgotten Man." *St. Louis Post Dispatch*, 1935.
Tekulsky, Joseph D. "Russ Christopher: Courageous Athlete." *The National Pastime*, 1995.
Terrell, Roy. "The Pork Chop All-Star." *Sports Illustrated*, July 11, 1960.
Vaccaro, Frank. "One-Arm Daily." *The National Pastime*, 1999.
Weaver, Maurice. "Pain and Glory." *Ebony*, August 1993.
Wendel, Tim. "Return Engagement." *USA Today Baseball Weekly*, September 9, 1998.

Internet

The Associated Press, July 12, 1995, "Bo Knows Life After Baseball." www.sportserver.com/newsroom/feat/archive/071295/mlb17218
The Associated Press, April 4, 1995, "Jackson Retires to Pursue New Sport: Acting." www.nando.net/newsroom/ap/bbo/1995/mlb/mlb/04049553696
Beck, Peggy. "Replacement Joints Not for Elite Athletes." Health and Wellness. www4.xpresssites.com/waf.srv/buffalo/buffalo/hw
CBS Sportsline, March 31, 1997, "Veteran Lefthander Jim Abbott Released by Angels." cbs.sportsline.com/mlb
Marazzi, Rich. "Lou Brissie: A Baseball War Hero." *Connecticut's Best*. www.connecticutbest.com/userpages/Lou_Brissie
Lowe, John. "Abbott Retires at 31: 'It's Time to Admit Reality.'" *Detroit Free Press*, July 27, 1999. www.freep.com/sports/baseball/qabbott27
Puma, Mike. "More Info on Jimmy Piersall." ESPN Classic, March 21, 2001. espn.go.com/classic/s/piersalljimadd000817
Flattner, Ron. "Bo Knows Stardom and Disappointment." ESPN Sports Century, January 3, 2000. espn.go.com/sportscentury/features/00016045
HistoricBaseball.com. "The Amazing Comeback of Lou Brissie." www.historicbaseball.com/sep_brissie_lou
Lollis, Dean. "Baseball's Ultimate Comeback: The Story of Jimmy Piersall. www.historicbaseball.com/TMS_piersall
The Jim Eisenreich Foundation for Children with Tourette Syndrome. "Jim's Story." www.tourettes.org/abtjim
"Former 'M' star, Abbott, bats in first MLB game." *The Michigan Daily Online*, April 9, 1999. www.pub.umich.edu/daily/1999/apr/04-09-99/sports/sports6
Seguine, Joel. *Michigan Today*, Summer 1999.
Seguine, Jim. "Jim Abbott Returns to Baseball." *Michigan Today*, Summer 1999. www.umich.edu/~newsinfo/MT/99/Sum99/mtl0j99

The Official Mordecai "Three Finger" Brown website. "Mordecai Brown Biography." www.cmgww.com/baseball/brown/

Newell, Rob. "Boys of Summer Head to War." The Retired Officer Magazine. www.troa.org/Magazine/October2001/feature3.asp

Sports Stars USA. "Curtis J. Pride." www.sportsstarsusa.com/baseball/pride_curtis

Turner Learning; John Rolfe; September 1994, "Jim Dandy." www.turnerlearning.com/efts/bball/jimdandy

WorkersforJesus.com "I'm Not Afraid of Anything!" www.workersforjesus.com/pride

The Zephr; Lynn McKeown, "Alexander the Great." www.thezephyr.com/alex

Index

Page numbers in **bold** indicate photographs

Aaron, Hank 69, 103
Aaron, Tommie 103
Abbott, Chad 10
Abbott, Dana Douty 15
Abbott, Jim 5, **11**, 19, 23, 24, 32; profile 9–18; record 18
Abbott, Kathy 10
Abbott, Mike 10
abdominal cancer 200
Abuzzahab, Dr. Frank 187
Adams, Sparky 65, 216
Agee, Tommie 215
Aikman, Troy 107
Alexander, Aimee 160, 163, 165–67
Alexander, Grover Cleveland 37, **161**, 168, 169, 196, 203, 213; profile 159–67; record 167–68
Alexander, Ray 160
Alexander the Great 162
Alfonseca, Antonio 4
Allen, Dick (Richie) 101, 137, 145, 180
Allyson, June 35
Alou, Felipe 103
Alou, Matty 103
Altman, George 135
Alvis, Max 209
amputated limbs 19–46
Ankiel, Rick 219
Appling, Luke 35, 37
arthritis 210
Ashburn, Richie 52
asthma 212, 213
Autry, Gene 15
Averill, Earl, Sr. 209, 210

back problems (congenital) 209, 210
Banks, Ernie 14, 135, 136

Barrett, Jimmy 180
Bearden, Gene 52, 194
Beazley, Johnny 57
Beckert, Glenn 136
Bell, Buddy 203
Bell, David 203
Bell, Gus 203
Bell, Lester 126
Belle, Albert 74
Bennett, Doc 90
Berardino, John 143
Berra, Yogi 169, 171
birth defects 9–18, 106–11, 118–20, 123–27, 140–44, 192, 193
Black, Joe 197, 198
Blackwell, Ewell 205
Blass, Steve 218, 219
blindness (partial) 198, 199
blood clots 219
Bluege, Ossie 41, 44
Blyleven, Bert 13, 154
Boggs, Wade 15
Bond, Walt profile 156–57; record 158
Bonilla, Bobby 189
Bonura, Zeke 35, 37
Boras, Scott 15
Borowy, Hank 142
Boswell, Tom 71
Bosworth, Brian 71
Bottomley, Jim 63, 94, 95, 129, 205
Boudreau, Lou 134, 141, 143, 174, 175
Bowerman, Frank 117
Boyer, Clete 103
Boyer, Ken 103, 136
brain aneurism 218, 219
Breadon, Sam 166, 167
Brecheen, Harry 57
Brett, George 74, 188

Bright's disease 204, 205
Brissie, Lou **50**, 194, 196, profile 48–54; record 54
Brock, Lou 135
Brouthers, Dan 20
Brown, Chris 77
Brown, Jimmy 56
Brown, Morecai "Three Finger" **84**, 89, 97, 197; profile 82–88; record 88–89
Brown, Tommy 29
Brubaker, Dr. W.K. 49
Brunansky, Tom 190
Bryan, Chet 152
Bunning, Jim 176
burns 193
Bush, Joe 92
Bush, Randy 190
Butler, Brett 201
Byrne, Tommy 142
Byrnes, James F. 28, 29
Byrnes, Milt 31

Cagney, Jimmy 124
Cameron, Mike 110
Campanella, Roy 140
Campbell, Bill 148
Campbell, Bruce 208
cancer 75–81, 200–2
Canseco, Jose 4
Caray, Harry 178
Cardenas, Leo 152
Carew, Rod 152
Carlson, Hal 196
Carradine, Keith 32
Carty, Rico 207
Case, George 105
Chance, Frank 83–85, 178, 179
Chappas, Harry 216
Chase, Hal 127

227

Index

Christopher, Lloyd 141
Christopher, Lloyd, Jr. 142
Christopher, Russ **141**; profile 140–44; record 144
Clayton, Royce 110
Clemens, Roger 14, 19, 22
Clemente, Roberto 214, 218
club foot 106–11
Coan, Gil profile 104–5; record 105–6
Cobb, Ty 127, 170
Colavito, Rocky 156
Collins, Ripper 63, 66
colon cancer 200, 201
Combs, Earle 164
Cone, Dave 219
Conigliaro, Tony 199
Conigliaro, Tony (Award) 17, 101, 189
Cooper, Mort 57
Cooper, Walker 57
Courtney, Clint 131
Crabtree, Estel 205
Craig, Roger 75, 93
Crews, Tim 197
Criss, Harry (Hugh Daily) 20
Crosetti, Frank 169
Crouse, Bucky 180

Dahmer, Jeffery 189
Daily, Hugh "One Arm" 112; profile 19–24; record 24
Daley, Bud 192, 193
Dalrymple, Clay 218
Damon, Johnny 110
Dark, Al 52
Davalillo, Pompei 216
Davis, Eric 200, 201
Davis, Mark 77
Davis, Russ 108
Davis, Tommy 98
Davis, Virgil 207
Day, Doris 160
deafness 112–20
Dean, Dizzy 38, 63, 66, 171
Dean, Paul 66
DeLancey, Bill 66, 207, 208
de la Tourette, Gilles 185
Derringer, Paul 65
Devlin, Art 86
diabetes 132–40, 219
Dickson, Murry 57
DiMaggio, Dom 103, 131, 175
DiMaggio, Joe 92, 103, 169, 194, 208
DiMaggio, Vince 103

diphtheria 214
DiPoto, Jerry 201
Doanes, Ran 27
Doerr, Bobby 14
Dolan, Tom 23
Douglas, Charles "Whammy" 198
Downey, Mike 15
Dravecky, Dave **76**; profile 75–81; record 81
Dravecky, Janice 76, 78
Dundon, Ed 6; profile 116; record 121
Duren, Ryne 131
Durham, Ray 216
Durocher, Leo 44, 65, 66, 136, 137
Durst, Cedric 92
Dykes, Jimmie 35, 39

early childhood illness or injuries 24–34, 54–59, 82–88, 112–16, 118, 192, 193, 215
Eckstein, David 216
Edmonds, Jim 73
Eisenreich, Jim **185**; profile 184–90; record 190–91
Eisenreich, Leann 190
Elliott, Bob 57
Ellsworth, Dick 135
Engle, Dave 218
epilepsy 159–69, 203
Esiason, Boomer 107
Evans, Darrell 131
Evers, Johnny "Crab" 84, 85; profile 178–79; record 182–83
exotic diseases 214, 215
eyesight problems 123–31, 198, 199

Faber, Red 179, 180
Face, Roy 148, 216
Feller, Bob 45, 52
Felsch, Happy 180
Ferrell, Wes 94
Ferriss, Dave "Boo" 213
Fidrych, Mark 171
Finley, Charley 178
Finley, Chuck 13
Finnerman, Bill 203
Finney, Lou 31, 32
Fisher, Jack 136
Flood, Curt 145
Folkers, Rich 107, 108
foot injuries 89–96, 194, 195
Ford, Whitey 94
Foster, Greg 12

Fowler, Art 198
Foxx, Jimmie 29, 131
Francona, Tito 176
Franklin, "One-Eyed" Jack 198
Fraser, Willie 13
Fregosi, Jim 181
Frick, Ford 56
Frisch, Frank 65, 66, 126
frostbite 194, 195
Fullerton, Hugh 22

Gaetti, Gary 190
Gagne, Greg 190
Galarraga, Andres 202, 218
Gallego, Mike 202
Galvin, Pud 20
Garagiola, Joe 115, 205
Garber, Gene 148
Garciaparra, Nomar 107
Gardner, Billy 186
Gehrig, Lou 132, 164
Geiger, Gary 211, 212
Gelbert, Charley **64**; profile 62–67; record 67–68
Gelbert, Jerri 63
Gentile, Jim 157
Gettel, Al 142
Giambi, Jason 103, 107, 110
Giambi, Jeremy 103
Giametti, Bart (Award) 189
Gibson, Bob 212, 215
Gladden, Dan 190
Glaviano, Tommy 60, 61
Gomez, Lefty 92, 131
Goodman, Billy 52
Gordon, Joe 169
Gordon, Tom 216
Graffanino, Tony 107
Gray, Pete 6, **26**, 46, 89; profile 24–34; record 34
Green, Dallas 177
Greenberg, Hank 30
Griffey, Ken, Jr. 12
Griffith, Calvin 154, 157, 190
Griffith, Clark 43
Grimes, Burleigh 28
Grimm, Charlie 37, 134
Groat, Dick 180
Grodzicki, John 195
Gullickson, Bill 139
gunshot wounds 19–24, 34–39, 62–67, 96, 194, 195
Gutteridge, Don 100
Gwynn, Tony 189

Hafey, Chick profile 128–31; record 132

Index

Haines, Jesse 164, 165
Hamm, Mia 107
Hamner, Granny 29
hand injuries 82–88, 97–105, 197
Hands, Bill 136
Hanssen, Dr. Arlen 74
Harder, Mel 130, 131
Hartnett, Gabby 169
Hayes, Jackie 35, 198, 199
hearing impairment 112–20
heart conditions 140–49, 199, 200
Heaton, Neal 107
Hegman, Bob 188
Herman, Babe 29, 171
Herman, Billy 169
Hernandez, Roberto 219
Hershberger, Willard 171
Hickman, Charlie "Piano Legs" 112
High, Andy 126
Hill, Carmen 123
Hiller, John profile 147–49; record 149–50
hip replacement 68–74
Hirshberg, Al 173
Hitchcock, Sterling 108
Hodges, Gil 177, 206
Hodgkins disease 201
Hoerner, Joe profile 144–46; record 146–47
Hofman, Solly "Circus" 84
Hollocher, Charlie 211
Hooton, Burt 13
Hopp, Johnny 57
Horner, Bob 13
Hornsby, Rogers 65, 93, 125, 126, 130, 164–66, 216
Horton, Tony 171
House of David 163, 166
Houtteman, Art 29
Hoy, Anna Marie 115
Hoy, Carson 115
Hoy, William "Dummy" 6, 114, 117–19; profile 112–16; record 120
Hoyt, Waite 92
Hrbek, Kent 190
Hubbell, Carl 108
Hubbs, Ken 135, 136
Hundley, Randy 136
Hunter, Jim "Catfish" 197
Hutchinson, Fred 155

Irwin, Bill 198
Ishii, Kazuhisa 4
Isringhausen, Jason 109, 110

Jackson, Bo 5, **70**, 188; profile 68–74; record 75
Jackson, Danny 201, 202
Jackson, "Shoeless" Joe 50
Jakucki, Sig 31
James, Bill 15
Jasper, Hi 198
Jay, Joey 133
Jenkins, Ferguson 136
John, Tommy 5
Johnson, Alex profile 180–81; record 183–84
Johnson, Jason 139, 219
Johnson, Ron 180
Johnson, Walter 127, 165
Johnstone, Jay 190
Jones, Sam 92
Jones, Todd 149
Joost, Eddie 53
Joss, Addie 208

Kazak, Eddie 59, 194; profile 60–61; record 61–62
Keefe, Dave 197
Keeler, William "Wee Willie" 112, 215
Keller, Charlie, Jr. 209
Keller, Charlie, Sr. 209
Kennedy, Vern 35, 37
Kessinger, Don 136
Key, Jimmy 15
kidney ailments 204–6
kidney removal 204–6
Killebrew, Harmon 155
Killefer, Bill 163
Kilroy, Matt 19
King, Stephen 216
Kling, Johnny 84, 85
Knoblauch, Chuck 217, 218
Koch, Billy 107, 110
Koenig, Mark 164, 168
Konstanty, Jim 131
Koufax, Sandy 210
Kramer, Jack 212, 213
Kreevich, Mike 31, 35, 36
Kruk, John 202
Kuenn, Harvey 156
Kuhel, Joe 37
Kurowski, Frank 55
Kurowski, Joan 58
Kurowski, Whitey 6, **56**, 60–62, 89, 196; profile 54–59; record 59–60

Laabs, Chet 31
Lacheman, Marcel 16
Landis, Kenesaw Mountain 56
Lanier, Hal 203

Lanier, Max 57
Larker, Norm 205, 206
Larkin, Steve 131
LaRoche, Dave 152
LaSorda, Tommy 217
Laudner, Tim 190
Lavan, Doc 125
Lazzeri, Tony 164, 165, 203; profile 168–69; record 170
Lee, Thornton 37
Lefferts, Craig 77
Lemon, Bob 52, 94
leukemia 150–57
Lieb, Fred 166
Lindell, Johnny 142
Lobert, Hans 160
Loidl, Dr. 45, 46
Lolich, Mickey 147
Long, Dale 4
Long, Howie 69
Lorsung, Dennis 186
Lowell, Mike 202, 218
Lundgren, Carl 84
lupus 214, 215
Lyons, Ted 35, 37

MacFayden, Danny 130, 131
Mack, Connie 27, 30, 42, 51–53, 96, 116, 142, 195
Madlock, Bill 137
Magee, Sherry 203
maimed or disfigured extremities 9–24, 40–46, 82–111, 197, 198
malaria 214
Mantle, Mickey 5, 178, 196
Maranville, Rabbit 63, 126, 164, 171, 215, 216
Marchildon, Phil 195
Marion, Marty 57
Marrero, Eli 202, 218
Marshall, Mike 108
Martin, Babe 31
Martin, Billy 171, 175, 178
Martin, Casey 3
Martin, Jap 162
Martin, Pepper 63, 66
Martinez, Tino 108
Masterson, Walter 196
Mathewson, Christy 86, 87, 108, 117, 165–67, 204, 214
Mattingly, Don 15
Mauch, Gene 154
Maxvill, Dal 146
May, Carlos **99**, 104; profile 97–103; record 104
May, Lee 98, 100, 103
May, Margaret 100
Mays, Carl 92

Index

Mays, Willie 69, 176, 200
McCarthy, Joe 92, 163, 164
McCarver, Tim 145
McCaskill, Kirk 13
McDermott, Mickey 175
McDowell, Jack 12
McGinnis, George "Jumbo" 112
McGinnity, Joe 117
McGraw, John 85, 117, 130, 204, 214
McGwire, Mark 58
McKechnie, Bill 177
McLain, Denny 147, 171
McQuinn, George 209
Meadows, Lee 123, 128
Mecir, Jim **107**, 218; profile 106–11; record 111
Mecir, Pamela 108
Medwick, Joe 63, 65, 66
Melillo, Oscar 204, 205
Melton, Bill 102, 137
meningitis 208, 209
mental blocks 217, 218
Merkle, Fred 85, 124
Metkovich, George 44
Metzger, Roger 197
Meusel, Bob 164
migraine headaches 210, 211
Minoso, Minnie 53
missing digits 82–105
Mitchell, Kevin 77, 78
Moore, Gene 31
Morgan, Joe 216
Mostil, Johnny profile 179–80; record 183
Murphy, Dale 218
Murray, Eddie 103
Murray, Jim 190
Murray, Rich 103
Musial, Stan 45, 56, 57
Mutrie, Jim 20
Myers, Billy 67

Nelson, Jeff 108
nephrectomies 204–6
nervous conditions 195, 196
Newhouser, Hal 52, 199
Nilsson, Dave 214

O'Dea, Paul 198
Ojeda, Bobby 197
Olerud, John 4, 218
Olin, Steve 197
O'Neill, Paul 15
O'Rourke, Jim 20
Orsatti, Ernie 66
osteomyelitis 48–54, 59, 196

Ott, Mel 204
Overall, Orval 84

Paige, Satchel 143, 175
Passeau, Claude 197
Patek, Fred 216
Patterson, Robert 43
Pearson, Albie 216
Peck, Hal profile 96; record 97
Pennock, Herb 92
Perkins, Anthony 173
Pesky, Johnny 174
Pfiester, Jack 84
Piazza, Mike 189
Pierce, Billy 29
Piersall, Jimmy 5, **172**, 180, 212; profile 170–78; record 181–82
Piersall, John 173
Piersall, Mary Teevan 174
Piet, Tony 38
Piniella, Lou 102
polio 214
Pollet, Howie 57
Pride, Curtis profile 118–20; record 122–23
Pride, Sally 119
Prim, Ray 193
psychiatric disorders 170–81, 217–19
Puckett, Kirby 190
Pyle, Ernie 49

Quilici, Frank 154

Radcliff, Rip 35, 37
Radinsky, Scott 201, 218
Raines, Tim 76, 79, 214, 215, 218
Ramsey, Toad 19
Reagan, Ronald 160
Reichardt, Rick 205
Reiser, Pete 101
Reulbach, Ed 84, 86
Reuschel, Rick 79
Rice, Grantland 52
rickets 215
Rickey, Branch 125, 130, 208
Rigney, Johnny 37
Ripken, Cal, Jr. 132
Rizzuto, Phil 169, 215
Robinson, Brooks 136
Robinson, David 12
Robinson, Jackie 6, 14, 139, 140, 215
Rocker, John 171
Rodriguez, Alex 189
Rojas, Cookie 145

Rose, Pete 79, 171
Ross River fever 214
Rothrock, Jack 66
Ruffing, John 89
Ruffing, Pauline Mulholland 95
Ruffing, Red 6, 56, **91**, 96; profile 89–95; record 95
Russell, Lillian 117
Ruth, Babe 65, 92, 164, 165, 171, 176
Ryan, Nolan 14, 24

Saberhagen, Bret 188
Sandberg, Ryne 216
Sanders, Ray 57
Santo, Ron **133**; profile 132–40; record 140
Sasser, Mackey 218
Savage, Bob 195
Sax, Steve 217, 219
Schoendienst, Red 57, 206, 207
Schulte, Frank "Wildfire" 84, 85
Score, Herb 101
Selee, Frank 113
Seminick, Andy 60
Shantz, Bobby 216
Sheckard, Jimmy 84
Sheffield, Gary 189
Shepard, Bert 6, **41**, 48, 51, 54, 194; profile 40–46; record 46–47
Short, Chris 145
sight impairment 123–31, 198, 199
Simmons, Curt 197
Sipek, Dick 119; profile 118; record 121–22
Sisler, George 199
size (stature) 215, 216
Slagle, Jimmy 84
Slaughter, Enos 57, 213
Smalley, Roy, Jr. 154
Smith, Hal R. 200
Smith, Ozzie 216
Smith, Red 143
Snider, Duke 177
Spahn, Warren 14
Speaker, Tris 127, 178
Steinbacher, Hank 37
Steinbrenner, George 16
Steinfeldt, Harry 84, 85
Stengel, Casey 93, 177
Stephens, Vern 174, 175
Stewart, Jimmy 35
stomach ailments 196, 211, 212
Stout, Allyn 65

Stratton, Ethel 35, 37
Stratton, Monty 6, **36**, 101; profile 34–39; record 40
Strawberry, Daryl 171, 200, 201
Street, Gabby 65
Sunkel, Tom 198
Swanson, Billy 125

Talbert, Bill 140
Tartabull, Danny 15, 188
Taylor, Jack "Brakeman" 83, 84
Taylor, Luther profile 117–18; record 121
Terrell, Roy 193
Terry, Bill 65, 129
testicular cancer 202
Teufel, Tim 190
Thevenow, Tommy 126
Thomasson, Dr. A.R. 37, 38
Thompson, Danny **150**, 157; profile 150–56; record 156
Thompson, Jim 151
Thompson, Jo 151, 153
Thompson, Monty 151
Thon, Dickie 199
throat cancer 201
thyroid cancer 201, 202

Tinker, Joe 84, 85, 87, 88, 178, 179
Toporcer, George 6, **123**, 128–31; profile 123–27; record 128
Toporcer, Mabel 127
Toporcer, Rudy 124
Torre, Joe 134
Tourette's syndrome 184–90
Travis, Cecil 194, 195
Trosky, Hal 210, 211
tuberculosis 206–8

Vedor, Bertha 33
Veeck, Bill 96, 142, 143, 176, 178, 194
Ventura, Robin 12
Veryzer, Tom 107
Viola, Frank 190
vision problems 123–31, 198, 199

Waddell, Rube 5, 171
Walker, Dixie 37, 103
Walker, Gee 37
Walker, Harry 57, 103, 213
war related disabilities 40–46, 48–54, 60–61, 194–96
Ward, Pete 98
Wertz, Vic 214

White, Bill 180
White, Ernie 57
White, Frank 188
White, Will 123
Whitney, Jim "Grasshopper" 112
Wilhelm, Hoyt 195
Williams, Bernie 15
Williams, Billy 132, 135, 136
Williams, Rick 110
Williams, Ted 52, 194
Williams, Walt "No Neck" 102
Winfield, Dave 13
Wingard, Ernie 14
Witt, Mike 13
Wood, Kerry 19, 22
Wood, "Smokey" Joe 127
Wynn, Early 212
Wyshner, Peter (Pete Gray) 26

Yamaguchi, Kristi 107
Yastrzemski, Carl 107, 181
Youngs, Ross 204

Zachary, Pat 197
Zernial, Gus 53
Zimmer, Don 134

www.ingramcontent.com/pod-product-compliance
Ingram Content Group UK Ltd.
Pitfield, Milton Keynes, MK11 3LW, UK
UKHW041944140426
5217IPUK00014B/655